Gulf South

Louisiana,
Southern Mississippi, and
the Gulf Coast of Alabama

by Bethany Ewald Bultman,
Malia Boyd, and Stanley Dry

Photography by Syndey Byrd and Brian Gauvin

COMPASS AMERICAN GUIDES
An Imprint of Fodor's Travel Publications

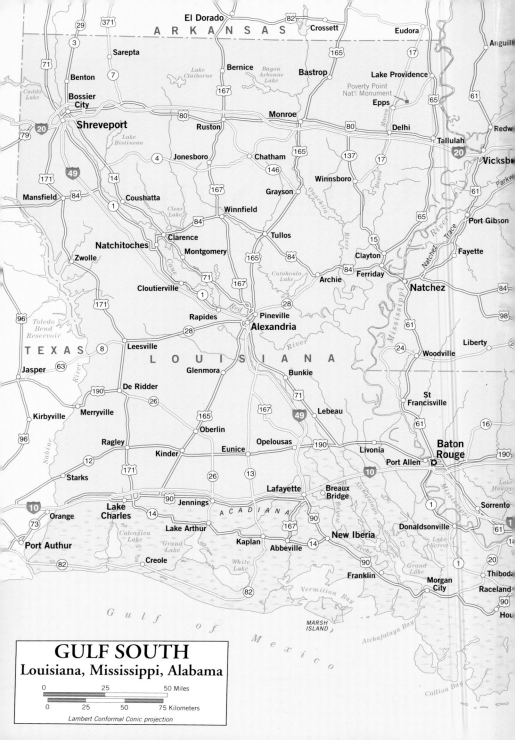

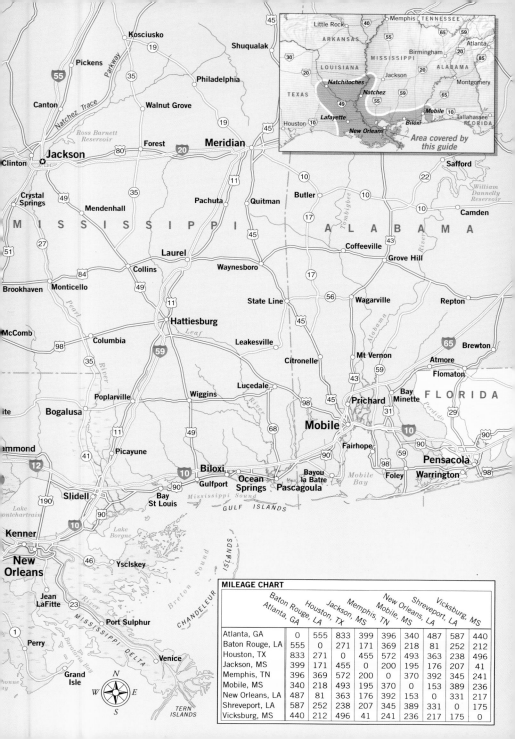

MILEAGE CHART

	Atlanta, GA	Baton Rouge, LA	Houston, TX	Jackson, MS	Memphis, TN	Mobile, MS	New Orleans, LA	Shreveport, LA	Vicksburg, MS
Atlanta, GA	0	555	833	399	396	340	487	587	440
Baton Rouge, LA	555	0	271	171	369	218	81	252	212
Houston, TX	833	271	0	455	572	493	363	238	496
Jackson, MS	399	171	455	0	200	195	176	207	41
Memphis, TN	396	369	572	200	0	370	392	345	241
Mobile, MS	340	218	493	195	370	0	153	389	236
New Orleans, LA	487	81	363	176	392	153	0	331	217
Shreveport, LA	587	252	238	207	345	389	331	0	175
Vicksburg, MS	440	212	496	41	241	236	217	175	0

Gulf South
Louisiana, Mississippi, Alabama
First Edition 2001

Copyright © 2001 Fodor's Travel Publications
Maps copyright © 2001 Fodor's Travel Publications
Compass American Guides and colophon are trademarks of Random House, Inc.
Fodor's is a registered trademark of Random House, Inc.
   Compass American Guides, 5332 College Ave, Suite 201, Oakland, CA 94618, USA
ISBN 0-679-00533-1

Editors: Kit Duane, Nancy Falk, Cheryl Koehler
         Pennfield Jensen, Julia Dillon   Designers: Christopher Burt, Kit Duane
Managing Editor: Kit Duane   Production Editor: Julia Dillon
Photo Editor: Christopher Burt   Map Design: Mark Stroud, Moon Street
Production house: Twin Age Ltd., Hong Kong   Manufactured in China

10 9 8 7 6 5 4 3 2 1

COMPASS AMERICAN GUIDES ACKNOWLEDGES the following institutions and individuals for the use of their photographs and/or illustrations:
   Bethany Bultman (courtesy of) p. 212; The Briars, Newton Wild and Bob Cannon p. 199; Bobby DeBlieux p. 23; Dinkins Collection p. 119; Kit Duane p. 179; Historic New Orleans Collection pp. 14, 19, 25, 30-31, 37; Collection of Thomas H. Gandy and Joan W. Gandy pp. 200, 203, 215; Library of Congress pp. 72 (both), 117, 269; Louisiana Hayride, Country Music Museum (Rebel State Comm. Area) p. 182; Louisiana State Univ. Art Museum p. 195; Louisiana State Univ. Press, reprinted by permission from Folklife in Louisiana Photography: Images of Tradition, by Frank de Caro, copyright 1991 by Louisiana State Univ. Press. p. 130; Mississippi Dept. of Archives and History p. 253; New Orleans Museum of Art p. 18; Northwestern State Univ. of Louisiana, Watson Memorial Library, Cammie G. Henry Research Center p. 169; Ogden Museum of Southern Art/Univ. of New Orleans p. 248; Roger Houston Ogden Collection, New Orleans pp. 60-61; St. Augustine Catholic Church, Natchitoches p. 177; Wadsworth Atheneum, Hartford. Gift of Citizens of Hartford by Subscription p. 304.
   Susan Horton at the USGS National Wetlands Research Center in Lafayette, LA; Linda York, curator at the Poverty Point Indian sites in northeast Louisiana. We would especially like to thank Julia W. Sanders for her photographs and text on the flora of the region which appear on pp. 90, 97, 129, 181, 218, and 257. We also thank expert reader Bobby DeBlieux, indexer Jolanka Fisher, and proofreader Nancy Falk.

To my parents and all of our ancestors who have made Mississippi, Louisiana, and Alabama their homes for the past five generations. Thanks from the bottom of my heart; you couldn't have planted our roots in a more magnificent place.
—Bethany Ewald Bultman

C O N T E N T S

Topical Essays & Sidebars

Maps

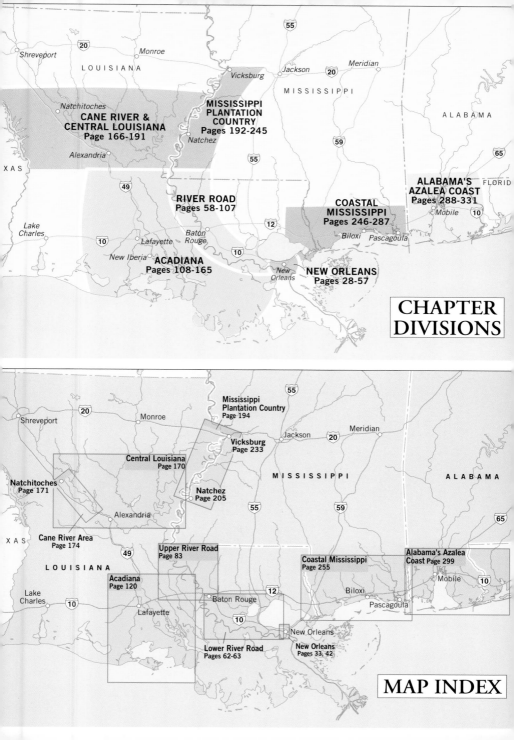

CHAPTER DIVISIONS

Shreveport
Monroe
LOUISIANA
Vicksburg
Jackson
Meridian
MISSISSIPPI
Natchitoches
CANE RIVER & CENTRAL LOUISIANA Page 166-191
MISSISSIPPI PLANTATION COUNTRY Pages 192-245
ALABAMA
Natchez
Alexandria
XAS
ALABAMA'S AZALEA COAST Pages 288-331
FLORID
RIVER ROAD Pages 58-107
COASTAL MISSISSIPPI Pages 246-287
Mobile
Lake Charles
Baton Rouge
Lafayette
Biloxi
Pascagoula
New Iberia
ACADIANA Pages 108-165
New Orleans
NEW ORLEANS Pages 28-57

MAP INDEX

Shreveport
Monroe
Mississippi Plantation Country Page 194
Jackson
Meridian
Vicksburg Page 233
Central Louisiana Page 170
MISSISSIPPI
ALABAMA
Natchitoches Page 171
Natchez Page 205
Alexandria
Cane River Area Page 174
Upper River Road Page 83
XAS
LOUISIANA
Coastal Mississippi Page 255
Alabama's Azalea Coast Page 299
Mobile
Acadiana Page 120
Lake Charles
Baton Rouge
Biloxi
Pascagoula
Lafayette
New Orleans
Lower River Road Pages 62-63
New Orleans Pages 33, 42

O V E R V I E W

WELCOME TO THE GULF KINGDOM
of moss-draped live oaks and deep
piney woods, a region defined by
its relationship to the Gulf of Mexico, the Mississippi River, and a
labyrinth of wetlands. Here life's
stew was boiled down to a potent
roux so rich it needed plenty of
strong drink and luscious food to
wash it down. And in the back-

ground there is always a rollicking soundtrack of indigenous zydeco, Cajun,
gospel, rockabilly, and jazz to tap your feet to.

NEW ORLEANS *pages 28-57*

The name invariably conjures up the syncopation
of jazz, the ramble of the street car along the live-
oak-lined avenues, and the juxtaposition of images
of tawdry Bourbon Street and old-world charm of
the historic French Quarter. Fine cuisine, music,
and fun.

LOUISIANA MUSIC

Listen to jazz and blues in New Orleans,
by sampling the music venues or attending Jazz Fest. In rural areas night-life
abounds in country bars where the locals come to dance the night away to zydeco
and Cajun music. *(photos by Syndey Byrd)*

(opposite) The Bayou at Chicot State Park. (Syndey Byrd)

RIVER ROAD RAMBLES *pages 58-107*

The River Road runs from New Orleans to Baton Rouge passing one extraordinary antebellum plantation home after another. Come to visit or spend the night, as many are now inns. Enormous live oaks shade small benches, old cemeteries tell long-lost stories of their own, and history is everywhere. Above Baton Rouge visit the lovely town of St. Francisville as naturalist painter John James Audubon once did.

ACADIANA *pages 108-165*

Laissez Les Bon Temps Rouler (Let the Good Times Roll) is the theme song for the lifestyle the hearty Cajuns created in the lush wetland region of Louisiana. Visit the beautiful gardens and Tabasco sauce factory on Avery Island, visit the magnificent Atchafalaya wetlands to fish or take a boat tour, and spend a few nights in historic small towns such as New Iberia or Breaux Bridge.

CANE RIVER RAMBLES *pages 166-191*

French colonial planters settled the rich farmlands of the Cane River in the 1700s creating a unique culture that still endures. Visit Melrose Plantation, home to the prosperous Free People of Color, the Metoyers; see author Kate Chopin's home, where she wrote *Bayou Folk;* and visit the charming, old-world town of Natchitoches.

MISSISSIPPI PLANTATION COUNTRY

pages 192-245

Natchez is the belle of this old, Deep South landscape; her magnificent homes open during the famous Spring Pilgrimage run by one of the most prestigious garden clubs in the United States. Come to be tantalized by the gracious lifestyle of a lost cotton kingdom. North on the park-like Natchez Trace lie historic Washington, Church Hill, and Vicksburg, where one of the decisive battles of the Civil War was fought.

COASTAL MISSISSIPPI *pages 246-287*

The 88 miles of Mississippi Gulf coastline serves as a sugar-soft welcome mat to the playground of the Gulf South. Discover its rich history while languishing under the ancient live oaks of Bay St. Louis, pit your skills against the world's largest variety of fish in the Gulf of Mexico, and enjoy the nightlife of the Biloxi casinos.

ALABAMA'S AZALEA TRAIL

pages 288-331

Mobile Bay beckons with its lacy fringe of hot-pink azaleas and its evocative past. From the polo matches at Point Clear and the utopian grace of Fairhope to a mullet toss at the Flora-Bama Lounge on the Redneck Riviera, coastal Alabama speaks with its own unique cadence.

HISTORY

GULF SOUTH HISTORY
COLONIAL & ANTEBELLUM
by Bethany Ewald Bultman

WELCOME TO THE GULF SOUTH, WHERE HISTORY STRETCHES back across the centuries and where we don't eat to live, we live to eat. As one born and raised here, I can say there is no place like it on earth. All of the regions we cover in this book share the same remarkable 18th-century colonial progenitorship. And to be honest, a sorrier lot of ancestors you will not encounter anywhere else in United States history. These folk were of varied races, social classes, and traditions, and were molded by chaos, violence, fear, growling bellies, and tyrannical local leaders. Most held the fanciful notion that if they survived, they would become very rich. Some endured, some even became New World princelings, leaving behind the country's finest repository of 18th- and 19th-century antebellum architecture.

The first settlers encountered clouds of fever-bearing mosquitoes that attacked them with the force of a battalion of airborne syringes. And if that wasn't bad enough, there were venomous reptiles, the blood-lusty deer flies, varmint-infested palmetto thickets, and capricious floods and hurricanes. Yet, the Gulf Coast proved to be a wonderland of nature, boasting countless flora and fauna, including more than 450 species of indigenous and migratory fowl.

For all their misfortunes, our ancestors must have done something right for they created the Fertile Crescent of American music—being the parents of Cajun and zydeco music and jazz tradition, and kinfolk to R&B and rockabilly. And the Gulf South's contributions to cuisine—among them Creole and Cajun cooking—are known to every American chef worth his salt.

■ GEOGRAPHY

The Mississippi River defines Natchez, Vicksburg, Baton Rouge, New Orleans, and St. Francisville, just as the Gulf of Mexico defines the Mississippi Gulf Coast, and Mobile Bay the Alabama coastline.

After the 12,000-mile-long Mississippi River crosses the border dividing Louisiana and Mississippi, it sets its own course, snaking its way toward the Gulf of Mexico, seemingly free from any obstacle that might divert its path. It's muddy, ornery, and a vital life force for the farmlands and industrial complexes it serves and dominates. While geographers reserve the term "delta" for lands along the Mississippi below New Orleans, Mississippians and Louisianans refer to all 30,000 square miles of fertile alluvial carpet from just below the Mason-Dixon line to the Gulf of Mexico as The Delta.

This 1720 map draws upon the geographical knowledge provided by French explorer Sieur de La Salle, who floated the length of the Mississippi River in 1682 from French possessions in the north. It demonstrates the importance of the river as a trade route for North American colonies.

■ GULF LAND GRABBERS

Before we take you traveling, it may be helpful to acquaint you with the area's egregiously inglorious colonial origins.

The New World land rush began in 1492 when Christopher Columbus made landfall on Salvador Island in the Caribbean. Thinking he'd landed in Indo-China, he claimed that region for the king of Spain. Not long afterward, bloodthirsty, gold-mad Spanish conquistadors, fresh from their victories in Mexico and Peru, began whacking their way through the thickets of the North American wilderness. Hernando de Soto arrived on the western coast of Florida in 1539. From there he traipsed back and forth across what would become Alabama, Mississippi, and Louisiana, going as far north as Arkansas in a disappointing quest for gold and silver. He was followed by more godfearing Spanish colonists who attempted to settle along the coast, but most were driven off by hostile Indians and howling hurricanes.

In 1682, the French explorer René-Robert Cavalier Sieur de la Salle floated down the Mississippi River from the far north and arrived at a site about 90 miles below New Orleans. He proclaimed the area drained by the river a possession of the Sun King, Louis XIV. La Salle was followed by two French Quebec–born brothers, Sieur d'Iberville (Pierre le Moyne) and Sieur de Bienville (Jean Baptiste le Moyne), who cruised into the Caribbean and landed at what is now Ocean Springs, Mississippi. On March 2, 1699, they sailed to the mouth of the Mississippi and landed at a point near a tiny bayou. They named it Pointe du Mardi Gras, as the Catholic holiday ("Fat Tuesday") was to fall on March 3 that year.

In 1682, explorer La Salle claims the Louisiana Territory for the French crown after sailing down the Mississippi River. (Historic New Orleans Collection)

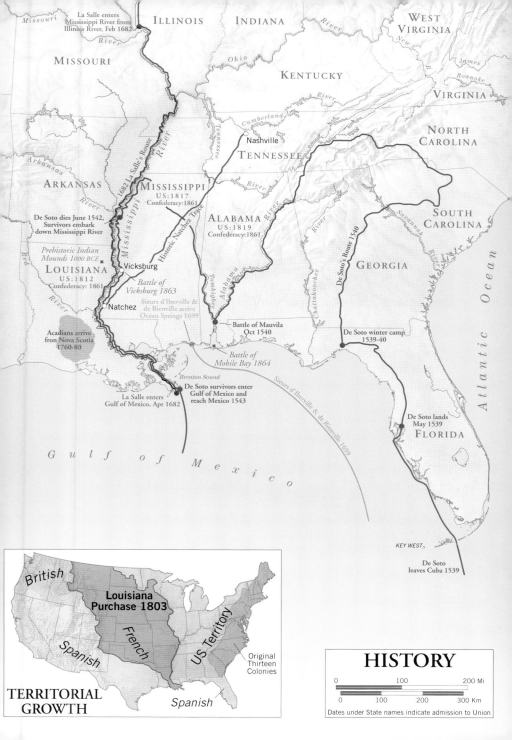

La Salle enters Mississippi River from Illinois River, Feb 1682

ILLINOIS

INDIANA

WEST VIRGINIA

Missouri

MISSOURI

River

Ohio

KENTUCKY

VIRGINIA

James

New R.

Roanoke

Cumberland

Tennessee

Nashville

NORTH CAROLINA

TENNESSEE

Arkansas

ARKANSAS

1682 La Salle's Route

MISSISSIPPI
US:1817
Confederacy:1861

River

River

ALABAMA
US:1819
Confederacy:1861

SOUTH CAROLINA

Savannah River

De Soto dies June 1542, Survivors embark down Mississippi River

Historic Natchez Trace

River

De Soto's Route 1540

GEORGIA

Prehistoric Indian Mounds 1000 BCE

Vicksburg

LOUISIANA
US:1812
Confederacy: 1861

Red River

Battle of Vicksburg 1863

Natchez

Sieurs d'Iberville & de Bienville arrive Ocean Springs 1699

Tombigbee River

Alabama

Chattahoochee

Battle of Mauvila Oct 1540

De Soto winter camp 1539-40

Mississippi River

Acadians arrive from Nova Scotia 1760-80

Brenton Sound

Battle of Mobile Bay 1864

Atlantic Ocean

La Salle enters Gulf of Mexico, Apr 1682

De Soto survivors enter Gulf of Mexico and reach Mexico 1543

Sieurs d'Iberville & de Bienville 1699

De Soto lands May 1539

FLORIDA

G u l f   o f   M e x i c o

KEY WEST

De Soto leaves Cuba 1539

British

Louisiana Purchase 1803

French

US Territory

Spanish

Original Thirteen Colonies

TERRITORIAL GROWTH

Spanish

HISTORY

0	100	200 Mi

0	100	200	300 Km

Dates under State names indicate admission to Union

Louisiana Indians Walking Along a Bayou *by Alfred L. Boisseu, 1847.*
(New Orleans Museum of Art)

Once the French government faced the fact that the new territory was not a fount of gold, silver, pearls, or eternal youth, they decided its value would be in the indigo, sugar, and cotton that could be wrestled from its fertile soil. But who would willingly move to an area described on maps as being inhabited by "savage man-eaters"? Voila! Soon military deserters, the defiant, the insane, thieves, and debtors were chained into rat-infested ships in France for transportation to the Louisiana colony. By 1719, banishment to the "new colony" became the treatment of choice for those desirous of parting with mooching in-laws, incorrigible siblings, and chronically ill relatives. A special French police force was rewarded with a "head tax" for each "colonist" they could haul off to Louisiana. Between 1717 and 1720, 43 ships carried shackled colonists from France to Louisiana. But riots in Paris by prisoners awaiting "colonization" grew so fierce that in 1720, King Louis XV forbade further deportations to the Louisiana colony.

By 1731, the population of the French coastal colony had risen from 1,000 to nearly 8,000, the majority of whom were slaves. Diron d'Artaguette wrote from Mobile in 1733, "our planters and merchants are dying of hunger, and those at Nouvelle Orleans are in no better situation. Some are clamoring to return to France; others secretly run away to the Spaniards in Pensacola." The 1740 census confirms that the white population of the colony was less than 1,200. Word was out: the French gulf coastal region was as close to hell as a man could get. Its reputation for blood-slowing humidity and monstrous alligators preceded it.

◆ NATIVE PEOPLE

It is estimated that 15–20,000 Indians lived in the French coastal colony from Mobile in the southeast to Natchitoches in the northwest at the time Louis XIV claimed the land for his own. Today fewer than 5,000 Indians remain in the present-day areas of Mississippi, Louisiana, and Alabama. Europeans not only brought disease, but disrupted age-old migration and hunting patterns, appropriated cropland, and encouraged intertribal warfare to such an extent that some of the smaller tribes ceased to exist.

◆ ENSLAVED SENEGAMBIANS

Into a chaotic colony of desperate Indians and French shirkers was brought the African. More than two thirds of the slaves who came to the Louisiana territory were from the Senegambia region of West Africa, exported from the present-day port of Dakar. Although just 7–10 percent of all Africans transported to the New World came from that region, it was the only source of slaves available to the French, and later the Spanish, who ruled Louisiana. A glance at the Lafayette, Louisiana, telephone directory hints at the West African origins of many residents —just look under the last name "Senegal."

African slaves had a life of their own, meeting in Congo Square and dancing on rare days off.
From these days of music and dancing evolved America's great musical form, jazz.
(Historic New Orleans Collection)

The "peculiar institution" of slavery was one of the principal forces that shaped the Louisiana Territory, the Mississippi Territory, and the New World. The economy in the agrarian Gulf South was based, until very recently, on the stoop labor of blacks who hacked through razor sharp palmetto to clear the land, planted and harvested the crops, made the bricks, cut the wood and milled it, built the master's palatial homes and houses of worship, cooked the master's meals and reared his children, and, in some cases, bore his babies.

In 1719, the first two slave ships landed on the beach in Biloxi, the territorial capital. The starving Africans had been shackled below decks at sea for six months, before being taken by shallow-draft boats across Lake Borgne and Lake Pontchartrain to Bayou St. John to be sold in New Orleans. The passage from Africa was a one-way trip. All they brought with them were their ancient skills, their memories, and a few barrels of Oryza *glaberrima*—a species of wet rice, cultivated for centuries in middle Niger. Their knowledge of herbal medicine proved more valuable for treating fevers and scurvy than did French medicinal practices, which consisted mainly of bleeding and surgery. The Senegambians also brought the technology for the construction of earthen dams and patties and techniques for refining rice. They also became the army of laborers to wage war on the mighty Mississippi River, building and re-building levees, digging canals, constructing docks, and dredging the sandbars that often prevented ships from docking anywhere near New Orleans or Natchez.

Between 1726 and 1731, almost all of the slave trade voyages organized by the Company of the Indies went to the French Gulf coastal area. During that time, 13 slave ships from Senegambia docked at Nouvelle Orleans. The 1731-1732 French census reports that Africans outnumbered whites in lower Louisiana by more than two to one. As the number of slaves rose, the white settlers' ranks were depleted by high rates of infant mortality, plague and pestilence, and out-migration.

The importation of African slaves to the United States was banned in 1808 by Congress, and slavery itself ended with the Civil War.

■ CAJUNS (FRENCH ACADIANS)

Just west of New Orleans is the land of the Acadians where the original byways were a labyrinth of bayous. The traditional Cajun culture has survived by dint of dogged chauvinism. The Cajuns you meet may give the impression that they are a people for whom nothing has ever been complicated. Nothing could be farther

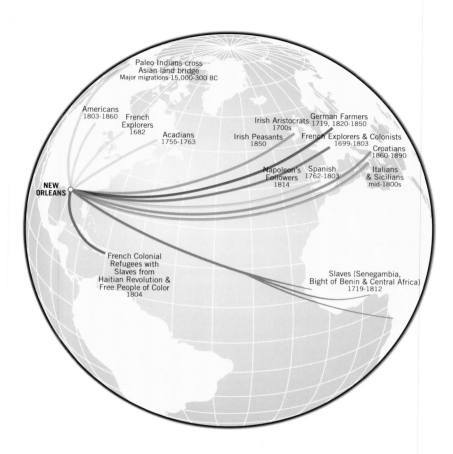

Paleo Indians cross
Asian land bridge
Major migrations 15,000-300 BC

Americans
1803-1860 French
Explorers
1682
Acadians
1755-1763

Irish Aristocrats
1700s
Irish Peasants
1850

German Farmers
1719, 1820-1850

French Explorers & Colonists
1699-1803
Croatians
1860-1890

Napoleon's Spanish
Followers 1762-1803
1814

Italians
& Sicilians
mid-1800s

NEW
ORLEANS

French Colonial
Refugees with
Slaves from
Haitian Revolution &
Free People of Color
1804

Slaves (Senegambia,
Bight of Benin & Central Africa)
1719-1812

from the truth. Their ancestors—Acadian farmers, codfishers, and whalers—had crossed the perilous North Atlantic from France in 1604 to make their homes along the Baie Française in Acadie, in present-day Nova Scotia. They were joined in 1632 by 300 settlers from Poitou, who were fleeing religious persecution in France. Here the Acadians lived in relative isolation for a hundred years until the French and Indian Wars made the English their landlords.

Condemned for treason by the British, the Acadians were forcibly banished, then invited by the Spanish to Louisiana. By 1763, the first Acadians had begun to burrow deep into the southern Louisiana swamps, adapting quickly to both the

CREOLE CUISINE: A MELTING POT

Indigenous people, Africans, Cajuns, and Creoles have had a profound influence on the way the region eats. Indians introduced the first French colonists to breads and mushy cereals made from corn; various kinds of squash, including the chayote (or "mirliton") and cashaw, which are still popular in Louisiana today; and dried beans and hot tamales. The French sweet tooth was satisfied with syrups made from persimmons, and piqued with chokecherries which were used to flavor smoked meats. Stews were thickened with powdered sassafras, today called filé powder. Grits (ground corn) are served for breakfast and seasoned like mashed potatoes with lots of butter and salt and pepper, not like porridge. Sometimes they have garlic and cheese, other times just enough bacon fat to take you "straight to Jesus," whether that is where you want to go or not.

Despite the abundance of Indian foods, the colonists were still Frenchmen to the core and yearned for the flavors they had known at home. In France during this period thousands of new recipes were created and volumes written on the subject of food, and it was fashionable for every nobleman to have not only his own accomplished chef, but also a sauce named for him. Of course, settlers who classified as noblemen were few and far between. Most settlers were peasants unaccustomed to a particularly luscious diet. Before coming to Louisiana, they had been eating boiled, grainy, weevil-laden flour mush mixed with animal blood, roots, and even topsoil. Bread was literally the highlight of their diet, and in Louisiana that was what was missing. Unfortunately, the area around New Orleans was too soggy to grow wheat.

It was the Ursuline Sisters, the daughters of French aristocratic and middle-class families, who brought to Louisiana the knowledge of the latest French culinary skills. The Ursulines taught settlers the benefits of using bay leaf in stews and soups to prevent souring and in flour to prevent weevils; dill for soothing sleep; oregano to reduce swelling; and sage "to put fever to flight."

While the Ursulines were teaching the rudiments of French cuisine, the African slaves were on the culinary frontlines. Black cooks took the French peasant's thickener, the roux (from the French *roux beurre,* literally "reddish brown butter") and transformed it into a dark, redolent base for many local specialties such as etouffée, gumbo, Creole sauce, grillades, and turtle soup. To the roux, a cook would add tough old pork or fowl, a few herbs, and lots of onions and garlic, and cook it all day in a cast-iron pot into a rich, flavorful stew. Germans added an array of tasty sausages and vegetables.

Creole cuisine might have remained a slightly countrified reproduction of 18th-century French cuisine had not the Spanish come to the Gulf. The Spaniards began the practice of adding green pepper to sauces and meat dishes in part to slow spoiling. The tomato, when coupled with a roux, became an integral component in Shrimp Creole;

This French cook-book was brought to the Cane River by French settlers in the 18th-century. Today it belongs to a descendant of the original owners, who still uses its recipes at Tante Huppé Inn in Natchitoches. (courtesy Robert DeBlieux)

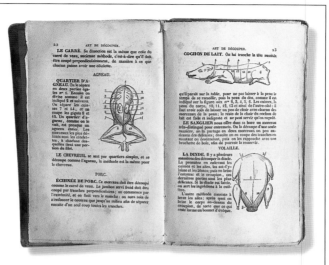

the rich gravy for grillades; and the base for court bouillon (pronounced "coo-bo-yon"), a thick seafood stew similar to bouillabaisse. The Spanish paella, a rice and shellfish dish, became the zesty Creole dish jambalaya when jambon, or ham, was added to it.

In the mid-19th century, Sicilians added their talent for concocting rich red gravies and using plenty of garlic and bread crumbs: dishes such as stuffed artichokes inspired the Louisiana classic, stuffed Indian mirliton, also known as a vegetable pear.

Note: The term "Creole," as used in Louisiana, is extremely confusing because it has taken on many shades of meanings over the years. All we know for certain is that a creole tomato is born and raised in Louisiana. Originally, the term Creole was used by Portuguese slave traders to distinguish those slaves born in Africa from those born in the New World. By the mid-18th century, colonists of European parentage born in the New World began calling themselves Creole to distinguish themselves from the pure Yankees. Soon mixed-race blacks with one European-born parent were being referred to as "Creoles of Color" to distinguish themselves from slaves. And if *that* isn't confusing enough, in Cajun country "Creole" is used by blacks of full or partial African ancestry to indicate that their ancestors were French-speaking Catholics, born in Louisiana before the Civil War. In this area people will carefully say whether a person is "white Creole" or "black Creole." The term has sometimes been used to denote people of mixed race, and some old white Louisiana families, particularly in New Orleans, have attempted to claim the term as theirs exclusively. Creoles of Color described those who were born of mixed-race parentage; often they were freed slaves.

open prairies and the bayous—a land of alligators, poisonous snakes, and bountiful fresh foods. It was a place of primordial beauty, and the Cajuns dug in like crawfish. They learned to build canoe-like cypress *pirogues* that were light enough to skim on dew. Their raised cottages were built along lazy, meandering bayous tangled with palmettos and moss-draped cypress, where "Dutch nightingales" (frogs) croaked an antiphonal opera, and water moccasins and alligators slithered from one spot of dry land to the other. Cajuns were isolated from the urban French in New Orleans, and their language retained much of the 17th-century French of their ancestors.

■ THE YANKEES

At the conclusion of the American Revolutionary War, the United States consisted of 13 fledgling states struggling to forge a democracy on a continent they shared with European powers. The English commanded Canada and many profitable islands in the Caribbean; Napoleon owned the vast fan-shaped tract of land west of the Mississippi River; and the Spanish controlled Florida, coastal Alabama and Mississippi, and all the land west of Napoleon's Louisiana territory. To make things more confusing, Napoleon may have held the deed to the 600 million or so acres, but he was letting the Spanish continue to govern it as he was busy trying to conquer the world.

So while the Americans were the new kids in the North American neighborhood, they had the home-team advantage, since by the late 18th century most of the prosperous settlers in areas controlled by Spain around Natchez, Mobile, and St. Francisville considered themselves to be American.

The Treaty of Paris (1783), ending the American Revolution, fixed the boundaries of the United States from the Atlantic Ocean in the east, to the Mississippi River in the west, and from English Canada to Spanish Florida, at the 31st parallel. Just 17 years later, at a dinner party in Paris on April 12, 1803, given to welcome the American emissary James Monroe, a French official announced that Napoleon wanted to sell a fan-shaped tract of land extending from the Mississippi River to the Rocky Mountains, and from the Gulf Coast and Canada. After two weeks of negotiations, the U.S. President, Thomas Jefferson, had finessed the greatest real estate deal in history, acquiring over 900,000 square miles—600 million acres—for a total, with interest, of about $27 million. And then the tight Yankees squawked at the cost.

By mid-August word reached the colony that it would soon pass out of the jewel-encrusted fingers of the Catholic European powers into those mud-under-the-fingernails hands of the Protestant rabble-rousing Americans. The Ursuline Sisters in New Orleans were so frightened that they temporarily fled to Cuba.

■ ANTEBELLUM ROMANCE

It took Eli Whitney's invention of the cotton gin in 1793 and thousands of slaves to turn the lush primordial forest land north of the moist coast into puffs of white gold, and the cotton factors, or brokers, of Mobile and New Orleans into millionaires. The advent of the first steamboat in 1811 enabled planters to get their crops to the factories in England and the Continent, by shipping them down the Mississippi to the port of New Orleans. By the Golden Age of the American steamboat in the 1850s, these vessels were both luxurious and tough workhorses, able to tote up to 10,000 bales of cotton. Between 1789, when 1,000 pounds of cotton were

The Henry Frank *at the New Orleans levee. Steamboat captains boasted about the number of cotton bales their ships carried. This vessel is dangerously overloaded. (Historic New Orleans Collection)*

shipped from the United States to England, and 1861, when 4.5 million bales were sold there, great fortunes were made in the South.

Cotton and, in Louisiana, sugarcane, allowed big-time planters and their brokers to live like princelings. And it's this small number of aristocrats, with their galas, brawling, horse racing, and dueling that have come to represent the South in the popular imagination. Wealthy planters of the Gulf South bought their wines in Le Havre and their frills in New Orleans, Philadelphia, New York, and London; educated their sons at Harvard and Yale; and enjoyed grand tours of Europe— while their slaves did the heavy lifting. Their daughters were "belles," harnessed into elaborate flounces and crinolines. (One myth is that they had 18-inch waists —about the same circumference of a roll of paper towels. In fact, the corsets into which they were laced were not meant to meet in the back, but allow for inches of flesh to be exposed. Nevertheless, you think the panty hose of today are uncomfortable? Their undergarments were so tight that they could hardly breathe.) Once married, a belle was expected to offer Southern hospitality in her pillared plantation homes. She also functioned as doctor, fire marshall, florist, and curator.

Currier and Ives capture the romantic ideal of Southern antebellum life in their lithograph, a A Home on the Mississippi.

The refinement and purity expected of Southern women made odd purchase with the fact that their menfolk had children by their female slaves. Often, one slave half-sister fluffed the down pillows on a marriage bed for a white half-sister; and the slave child pulling the cord on the Punkah that fanned their dining tables was related to the family at the table.

■ CIVIL WAR AND RECONSTRUCTION

When white folks in the Gulf South refer to "The War" it's a good bet their talking about the Civil War. Actually, many such Southerners prefer the name The War Between the States, while others will call it The War to Suppress Yankee Arrogance, The Lost Cause, The Late Unpleasantness, or simply Round One. Residents of Vicksburg and Mobile fought valiantly to war's end, while New Orleans and Natchez were occupied early and bloodlessly. Many white Southern men may forget their own wedding anniversaries, but they can still tell you the date of every Civil War battle. In the meantime, black Southerners struggle to get the Confederate flag taken off public buildings.

The secession of the Southern states from the United States was precipitated by the election of Abraham Lincoln to the Presidency in the fall of 1860. As the candidate of the Republican party (known for its abolitionist sentiment) Lincoln became anathema to Southerners, many of whom urged the formation of a new nation in which slavery and their planter economy would be protected. The Rebels met in Montgomery, Alabama, to create the Confederate States of America, with Jefferson Davis of Mississippi as President.

In Washington, D.C., the U.S. Congress declared war on any state that left the Union, and the agrarian South was no match for the powerful and industrial North. By April of 1865, the Confederacy's commanding general, Robert E. Lee, had surrendered to the Union at Appomattox. Soon after, 20,000 federal troops occupied the South, making this the only (non-Indian) area in the country to suffer the humiliation of the domination of a conquering force.

For a hundred years after the Civil War the spirit of the people and their diverse cultures were preserved by an isolation bred from the doldrums of Reconstruction, the invasion of the cotton-eating boll weevil, and the poverty of the Depression. But in the Gulf South, for the planter class, even life in the slow lane was a pleasure for most.

N E W   O R L E A N S

by Bethany Ewald Bultman

NEW ORLEANS

■ HIGHLIGHTS   *page*

Lodgings, page 49; restaurants, page 53
Maps, pages 33, 42, 48

■ TRAVEL OVERVIEW

New Orleans, though geographically "Southern" (Rhett brought Scarlett here for their honeymoon, remember) is not a garden-variety Southern city in the sense of Natchez, St. Francisville, Vicksburg, or Mobile. It is more of a Caribbean port city, anchored in the continental United States by geographical accident. The name New Orleans invariably conjures up the succulent aroma of sweet olive, the syncopation of jazz and ceiling fans, and the vision of black-haired, magnolia-fleshed damsels fanning themselves as they sit in white wicker chairs on lacy wrought-iron verandas.

New Orleans is fueled by diversity, and its neighborhoods are a crayola box of bright, intense, ethnic influences. The ambiance and magic of New Orleans are impossible to appreciate at a fast clip. It is a city that gladly relinquishes its secrets to those who take the time to wander. For those who have only a short time between meetings, parades, concerts, or meals, the best thing to do would be to see one area thoroughly, preferably on foot.

Climate: In New Orleans climate is a reliable conversation opener. December through February temperatures hover between highs in the low 60s and lows in the 40s. Springtime and late fall are most comfortable: 70s down to the 50s at night. By May average temperatures are in the mid-80s, and from June through September it's the 90s, with lows in the 70s. Light clothing is advisable most of the year; comfortable shoes will be needed if you wander the French Quarter, which really is best seen on foot. Bring an umbrella, as rain is frequent in July and August. New Orleans is the rainiest city in the United States.

Restaurants: To eat a meal in New Orleans today is to dive head first into tradition, flavor, and cholesterol. It is a city where food is fried to perfection in lard, where French-fried potato po'boys still appear on some menus, and where sugar, liquor, and coffee—the region's three favorite indulgences—can be obtained in one glorious after dinner concoction: café brulot. About the only nod to healthy eating comes when a local cleanses his palate with iceberg lettuce swimming in rémoulade sauce or runs a lap or two around Audubon Park between a double order of Café du Monde beignets and a slab of Camellia Grill pecan pie.

The local culinary traditions of Creole cooking, the sophisticated urban cuisine containing such jewels as trout meunière and oysters Rockefeller; and Cajun cooking, its country cousin known for its stew-like etouffées and gumbos, did not evolve directly from French cooking. In each bowl of gumbo served in Louisiana today, there is French roux, African okra, American Indian filé, Spanish peppers, Cajun sausage, and oysters supplied by Yugoslav fishermen, served over Chinese-cultivated Louisiana rice.

Try a meal at Antoine's, the oldest restaurant in America; sandwiches at Uglesich, one of the oldest neighborhood po'boy places; and drinks at the Napoleon House and Lafitte's Blacksmith Shop. **See page 53 for restaurant listings.**

Nightlife: New Orleans is known for it. See page 48.

Lodging: The best way to establish a relationship with old New Orleans is to stay in one of the small hotels or guest houses operated in one of the older neighborhoods— places such as the Soniat House and the Maison de Ville in the French Quarter; the Columns or the Josephine near St. Charles. **See page 49 for lodging listings; see page 333 for price designations and toll-free numbers for chain accommodations.**

NEW ORLEANS

■ NEW ORLEANS HISTORY

Sprawling, sultry, seductive, and ageless, the original neighborhood that was New Orleans still exists as the French Quarter just where Sieur de Bienville, its French founder, left it when his 30 convicted salt smugglers first hacked down razor-sharp palmetto thickets to clear a spot for a few ramshackle houses. An area about three-quarters of a mile long and a quarter-mile wide, the Quarter remains both the heartland of old New Orleans and its most progressive neighborhood.

In 1721, shortly after a major flood, a French engineer named Adrien de Pauger, with the help of 10 men, cleared a large swath close to the river and laid out a grid pattern of streets. Soon after, a hurricane blew down almost every one of the original, ramshackle buildings, but the basic plan of the city was established, and the settlers rebuilt their quarters in the same pattern time and again.

By the time New Orleans (as part of the Louisiana Territory) was sold to the fledgling United States, it was a flourishing small city, its citizens a mixture of

At first no more than a few shacks on the site of a cleared palmetto thicket, by 1800 New Orleans had become one of the most important and vibrant of the New World's colonial cities. Situated at a strategic site along the Mississippi River near the Gulf, it became a center of commerce and home to a diverse population of cotton traders, African slaves, Free People of Color, artisans, riverboat captains, and Creole aristocrats.

This birds-eye view depicts the city's busy harbor during the 1850s, a period known as its Golden Age. The harbor is filled with river craft and ocean-sailing vessels, its waterfront lined with impressive architecture. (Historic New Orleans Collection)

French and Spanish-speaking Creoles, Anglo-Americans, slaves, and Free People of Color. By 1810, New Orleans had established itself as the largest city in the South and the fifth largest city in the United States. The city had become home to a flood of Protestant Americans who came to enjoy their new, French-speaking port city. Sophisticated opportunists and hard-working middle-class people arrived in droves, as did the "Kaintocks," buckskin-clad hill people who came pouring downriver from the frontier. Arriving on their flat boats and bringing with them brown crockery jugs of Monongahela whiskey and rough ways, these "hillbillies" thoroughly offended the sensibilities of the Creole families of the Vieux Carré (French Quarter), who slammed shut their wrought-iron gates. After the Louisiana Purchase, altercations between the Catholic Creoles and the Protestant Americans became so frequent that a strip of land between the French Quarter and the American sector was designated as a "neutral ground" by Congress on March 3, 1807. It later became known as Canal Street.

■ VISITING THE OLD CITY

As the decades pass, **Jackson Square**—the old town square that faces the river—continues to be vitally alive with new generations of neighborhood children playing ball, street musicians, pigeons looking for handouts, and itinerant artists sketching the passersby. The neighborhood remains part residential and part commercial. Bourbon Street clubs still serve as a finishing school for local musicians, and both strip joints and gay dance clubs co-exist with T-shirt shops on pedestrian walkways. Not far from all this ebullience and sleaze, expensive antiques are sold from posh shops on Royal and Chartres Streets. Also within the borders of the old city are a thriving public elementary school, an A&P (small by American standards), numerous bakeries, and praline and perfume shops. Above all this exuberance, contradiction, and energy looms the new city of New Orleans—20 or so office and hotel towers that poke up in the uneven pattern of a child's toothy smile. On one side are the twin bridges that span the Mississippi River. The other side of the skyline is dominated by a gigantic aluminum soufflé, the 128,000-cubic-yard Louisiana Superdome.

Next to taking a professionally guided tour, a fine way to get the feel of the architecture of the French Quarter is to take a carriage ride—that is if you can stand

being seen in a carriage displaying advertisements for the Wax Museum and pulled by a mule sporting diapers and a straw hat festooned with plastic flowers. The point is to sit back and enjoy studying the buildings of the French Quarter from the second floor on up. To absorb the rich complex roux of the Quarter, wander about on foot and stop by the sights recommended *(following)*. You'll hear riffs of jazz from the clubs, see locals drinking juleps on their wrought-iron balconies, and inhale the intoxicating odors of French and Creole cooking.

St. Louis Cathedral faces historic Jackson Square and an equestrian statue of Andrew Jackson. (Brian Gauvin)

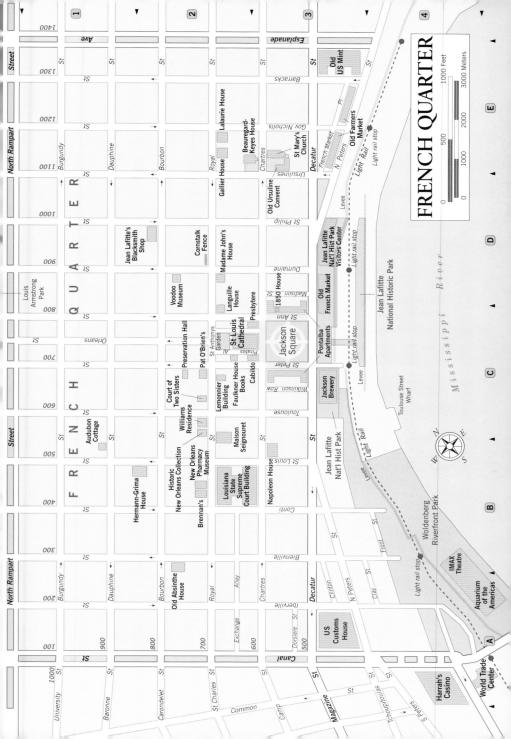

FRENCH QUARTER

1000 Feet

3000 Meters

N
W E
S

Mississippi River

Jean Lafitte National Historic Park

Toulouse Street Wharf

Woldenberg Riverfront Park

Jean Lafitte Nat'l Hist Park

IMAX Theatre

Aquarium of the Americas

World Trade Center

Harrah's Casino

Louis Armstrong Park

North Rampart

F R E N C H   Q U A R T E R

Street

Old US Mint

Old Farmers Market

Old French Market

French Market

St Mary's Church

Beauregard-Keyes House

Lalaurie House

Gallier House

Old Ursuline Convent

Madame John's House

Comstalk Fence

Jean Lafitte's Blacksmith Shop

Voodoo Museum

Languille House

1850 House

Presbytere

St Louis Cathedral

Jackson Square

Pontalba Apartments

Jackson Brewery

Cabildo

Pat O'Brien's

Preservation Hall

St Anthonys Garden

Faulkner House Books

Lemonnier Building

Court of Two Sisters

Williams Residence

Audubon Cottage

Maison Seignouret

Historic New Orleans Collection

New Orleans Pharmacy Museum

Brennan's

Louisiana State Supreme Court Building

Napoleon House

Hermann-Grima House

Old Absinthe House

US Customs House

Jean Lafitte Nat'l Hist Park Visitors Center

Wilkinson Row

Pirates Al

Light Rail

Light rail stop

Levee

Esplanade

Barracks

Gov Nicholls

Ursulines

St Philip

Dumaine

St Ann

St Peter

Toulouse

St Louis

Conti

Bienville

Iberville

Canal

Decatur

N Peters

Clinton

Clay

Front

Exchange

Dorsiere

Chartres

Alley

Royal

Bourbon

Dauphine

Burgundy

Orleans

University

Baronne

Carondelet

St Charles

Camp

Magazine

Tchoupitoulas

S Peters

Common

1400   1300   1200   1100   1000   900   800   700   600   500   400   300   200   100

Ave

Street

Street

◆ JACKSON SQUARE AREA
map page 33
Jackson Square   *map C-3*
The heart of the French Quarter remains its central plaza, Jackson Square, originally constructed in 1721 as a drill field called the **Place d'Armes**, and renamed in 1848 to honor Andrew Jackson, the hero of the 1815 Battle of New Orleans. In 1851, the Baroness Pontalba installed the fences and gardens landscaped in the sun pattern made popular in France during the reign of Louis XIV, the Sun King.

The inscription on the equestrian statue of Jackson, which reads, "The Union must and shall be preserved," was added in the 1860s by the occupying Union army during the War Between the States.

The square itself remains an active plaza serving as a backdrop for tarot card readers, Lucky Dog and ice cream vendors, and mimes.

St. Louis Cathedral   *map C-2/3*
Jackson Square is dominated on Chartres Street by St. Louis Cathedral, the oldest continually active cathedral in the United States, and the third church to be built on this site. (The first, constructed in 1722, was lost to fire, as was the second.) The present cathedral dates in part from 1794, but was largely remodeled in 1845-1851. Its interior contains magnificent stained glass, murals, frescoes, and the graves of many early New Orleans dignitaries.

Pirate's Alley   *map C-2/3*
Père Antoine's Alley runs from Chartres to Royal along the northeastern side of the

cathedral and garden; bounding the opposite side of these sites, Pirate's Alley sounds like its evil twin. Note the flagstone paving and central gutters. In 1925, William Faulkner lived in a humble garret while writing *Soldier's Pay*, his first novel. Today **Faulkner House Books** occupies this space. *624 Pirate's Alley.*

Cabildo and Presbytère   *map C-3*
St. Louis Cathedral is flanked by original late 18th-century Spanish Colonial government buildings, the Cabildo (to the left of the cathedral) and the Presbytère. The Presbytère stands on the site of an early French monastery.

The Cabildo was once a Spanish government building, the *Casa Capitular* where the "Very Illustrious Cabildo," or city council, met. France's Louisiana territory was turned over to the United States in the left-side room on the second floor of the Cabildo on December 20, 1803. Today both buildings are part of the Louisiana State Museum system. *Tues-Sun 9-5; 751 Chartres St.; 800-568-6968.*

Pontalba Apartments   *map C-3*
Flanking Jackson Square on either side of the park are the Pontalba Apartments, which some call the first urban renewal project in the New World, begun in 1849 by the Baroness Micaela Pontalba, the daughter of Don Almonester y Rojas. The infamous 15-year-old Baroness married her French cousin, the Baron Celestin de Pontalba; had a near-fatal altercation with her father-in-law; and fled to Louisiana to escape the scandal. The Pontalba buildings

originally included commercial space on the ground floor, and palatial living quarters and slave quarters above.

In the middle of the state's building, is a beautiful pre-Civil War restoration called the **1850 House**. *Tues-Sun, 9-5; 523 St. Ann St.; 504-524-9118.*

◆ LOWER FRENCH QUARTER
map page 33

The Quarter is conventionally divided into sections, with Jackson Square marking the midpoint between the Lower Quarter (the northeastern half) and the Upper (the southwestern half). The following tour of the Lower Quarter begins at the northern corner of Jackson Square, loops through the northeastern half of the Quarter, takes a quick detour along the Mississippi, then returns to Jackson Square along the river. From the square, head northwest on St. Ann Street to Royal and turn right.

Madame John's Legacy   *map D-2*

A rare remnant of the West Indian/Colonial
–style architecture of the early French Quarter, this house was built in 1726. The house was partially destroyed by the Good Friday fire of 1788, was rebuilt a few years later, and survived the fire of 1794. Some argue that it is one of the oldest buildings in the Mississippi Valley, predating the Ursuline Convent. *632 Dumaine St.*

Don't miss the **Cornstalk Fence** with its 1850s cast-iron motif of ears of corn and morning glories. The story goes that a doctor commissioned the fence from Philadelphia as a present for his wife, who missed the cornfields of her native Midwest. *915 Royal St.*

Lafitte's Blacksmith Shop   *map D-1*

Another structure evocative of the Colonial Period is Lafitte's Blacksmith Shop. Dating from 1782, it was built with the timber and soft-brick construction used by the first colonists. Jean Lafitte and his fellow pirates are said to have sold their booty out of the back door of a blacksmith shop at this address, and it was here that illegally imported slaves were traded after the importation of slaves was outlawed in 1807. In fact, no one really knows where Lafitte's shop was. No matter, the building now houses one of the city's most colorful bars. *941 Bourbon St.*

Lalaurie House   *map E-2*

It is also called the **Haunted House,** doubtless because of its macabre history. Louis McCarty had built the house and presented it to his daughter, Marie Delphine McCarty Lalaurie, in 1831. Unfortunately, the thrice-married Madame Lalaurie found pleasure in torturing her slaves and enough of them "committed suicide" that the neighbors started to talk. When her neighbor called the volunteer fire brigade to her house to put out a fire on April 10, 1834, they discovered seven shackled, starving slaves. An angry mob besieged the house and looted it. *1140 Royal St. at the corner of Governor Nicholls, formerly Hospital St.*

Gallier House   *map E-2*

This lovely townhouse, a National Historic Landmark, is located three blocks from the Mississippi River in the former orchard of the Ursuline convent.

Begun in 1857 by Anglo-Irish architect James Gallier, Jr., the house reflects the

architectural innovations of its time, including an operable etched-glass skylight above the upstairs landing, ventilators in the master bedroom, and a flush toilet.

Gallier's three "unclaimed treasures," his spinster daughters, lived here until 1917. The Gallier House Museum was opened to the public in 1971 having been painstakingly restored along the lines of the 1868 inventory of Gallier's estate. Note the "summer dress" in several rooms, stylistic tricks employed to combat the brutal heat and humidity. *Mon-Fri 10-3:30, 1132 Royal St.; 504-525-5661.*

Beauregard-Keyes House and Garden *map page 33, E-2/3*

This house possesses one of the most captivating gardens and courtyards in the French Quarter. Built in the Greek Revival style, it dates from 1826. Confederate General P. G. T. Beauregard rented a room here from 1866 to 1867. Later, the prolific writer Frances Parkinson Keyes (rhymes with "eyes") took up residence here.

Ms. Keyes's doll collection and her huge Victorian dollhouse remain special treats for guests. Each Christmas the museum house

(above) A painting of a 19th-century French Quarter residential area by Boyd Cruise. (Historic New Orleans Collection)

The Pontalba Apartments (opposite) are the oldest in the United States (Syndey Byrd).

hosts a Dolls' Tea Party on the second Saturday of December. Children of all ages are invited to bring their dolls along to have tea with the dolls in the collection.

While the house is decorated in a style appropriate to the turn of the century, its beautiful garden is authentic to 1830s New Orleans. The interior courtyard is dominated by a magnificent live oak tree which serves as a gigantic umbrella, keeping the garden 10 degrees cooler than the rest of the French Quarter. If a tour of the house isn't possible, peek through the gate at the garden. *Mon-Sat 10-3, tours on the hour. 1113 Chartres St. at the corner of Ursulines, across from the convent; 504-523-7257.*

Old Ursuline Convent   *map page 33, D/E-3*
The earliest Ursuline Convent and the country's first charity hospital were originally located at 301 Chartres Street, in a townhouse leased to the Sisters of St. Ursula from 1727 until 1734. Here they founded the first convent and the first girls' school in the United States.

The sisters then moved to what is now known as the Old Ursuline Convent when it was completed between 1745 and 1750. Having survived the fire of 1788, it has stood longer than any brick-and-post building of the French Colonial style in the Mississippi Valley. Adjacent to the old convent is the Chapel of the Archbishops erected in 1845. Today it is called **St. Mary's Church,** and it serves as the Military and Hospitalier Order St. Lazarus National Shrine. *1114 Chartres St.*

Old U.S. Mint   *map E-3*
One of the oldest mints still standing is at the back of the Quarter. On the site of one of the city's original five forts, Fort San Carlos, it was designed by William Strickland and begun in 1837. Now part of the Louisiana State Museum system, the building houses the extensive **New Orleans Jazz Collection** and **Mardi Gras Museum.** *1300 Decatur St. at Esplanade near French Market.*

Old Farmers Market   *map E-3*
Old French Market   *map C/D-3*
Meander back to Jackson Square along North Peters and visit the Old Farmers Market between Ursulines and Governor Nicholls. Local chefs, professional and amateur, peruse the garlic-draped stalls 24 hours a day for produce, seafood, and spices. At the corner of Decatur and Dumaine stands the Old French Market, where Creoles have been shopping since the early 1700s.

◆ **UPPER FRENCH QUARTER**
   map page 33
Pat O'Brien's   *map C-2*
Originally the Tabary Theatre, the first Spanish theater in the United States, built in 1791, now houses a famous bar. Today, Pat O'Brien's sells more mixed drinks than any other establishment in the world and is home of the Hurricane, the notorious pink drink which the next day will make you feel as if you'd been hit by one. *718 St. Peter St.; 504-588-2744.*

Court of Two Sisters   *map C-2*
Spanish settlers favored private, shaded interior courtyards and patios. One courtyard

that is particularly lovely is named after two sisters who ran a dry goods store here from 1886 to 1906. The courtyard is now a restaurant. *613 Royal St.; 504-522-7261.*

Historic New Orleans Collection

map page 33, B-2

Stay on Royal Street to visit the Historic New Orleans Collection, housed in seven historic French Quarter buildings. The earliest was built in 1792 and is one of the few existing buildings spared by the fire of 1794. The privately endowed research facility mounts exceptional exhibitions related to the history of New Orleans; a wonderful gift shop specializes in fine historical reproductions. The **Williams Residence,** also in the complex is an elegant 19th-century townhouse restored in the mid-20th century by its then-new occupants, General and Mrs. L. Kemper Williams. *Main entrance at 533 Royal St.; 504-523-4662.*

Antique shops on Royal and Chartres

Both Royal and Chartres Streets are lined with a plethora of shops specializing in fine French and English antiques. Both areas also have many shops offering antique jewelry and porcelains.

Napoleon House *map B-2*

By now you may be ready for a break. Make a detour and turn left at St. Louis to visit The Napoleon House, a quiet place to stop in for a Pimm's cup and a game of chess while enjoying the visual appeal of crumbling plaster and the smell of antiquity. Built in 1814, the French colonial building is topped by the original tile roof

and an octagonal cupola. Napoleon never slept here, but at least he was invited. The original owner, Mayor Girod, was said to have offered his home as a residence for Napoleon should he be able to escape. *500 Chartres St.; 504-524-9752.*

Louisiana State Supreme Court *map B-2/3*

This grand Victorian structure was built 1908–09. After decades of neglect, the building was renovated, and the Louisiana State Supreme Court moved in. Oliver Stone fans may recognize it from the film *JFK,* part of which was shot here. *Covers the entire 400 block of Royal Street.*

New Orleans Pharmacy Museum *map C-2*

The cocktail is thought to have been invented here in the late 1800s, when Antoine Peychaud concocted the first bitters and stirred them into his brandy—along with a little absinthe. The word "cocktail" itself derives from the egg cups, or *coquetiers,* in which Peychaud originally served his mixture, a drink known as a Sazerac. *514 Chartres; 504-565-8027.*

Brennan's Restaurant *map B-2*

Circa 1796, prominent merchant Vincent Rillieux, Edgar Degas's great grandfather, built the home that later became the Banque of Louisiane, hence the "BL" in the balcony rail. The Gordon family purchased it shortly thereafter, hosting Andrew Jackson in 1828. In subsequent decades, chess champion Paul Morphy lived here until his death. The building has housed the popular Brennan's since 1955. *417 Royal St.; 504-525-9711.*

Bourbon Street

Bourbon Street may not be the Vieux Carre's most picturesque byway—it's the only street in the Quarter with neon—but a wander amidst the rowdy crowds and a drink at a noisy club are a part of the New Orleans experience.

Old Absinthe House   *map page 33, A-2*

Although most people do not visit Bourbon Street to savor the architecture, several structures are worth strolling by. The Old Absinthe House, dating from 1874, is thought to be the oldest bar still in operation in the state. Note the Creole-style building that houses it. *240 Bourbon St.; 504-523-3181.*

Hermann-Grima Historic House   *map B-2*

One of the earliest Georgian-style residences in the French Quarter, with the only functioning 1830s kitchen in the city, the house is the scene of fascinating open-hearth cooking demonstrations each Thursday from May until October. Throughout the year many homemade delights are available in the gift shop. Between the first of December and New Year's, the house is decked out Creole-style for the holidays. *818-820 St. Louis St.; 504-525-5661.*

Audubon Cottage   *map C-2*

Artist John James Audubon and his wife Lucy lived here from 1821–1822. It is now part of the Maison de Ville Hotel. *505 Dauphine St.*

(above) The French Market has been a hub of activity since the 1700s.

(opposite) Musicians playing on Royal Street in the French Quarter. (both photos, Syndey Byrd)

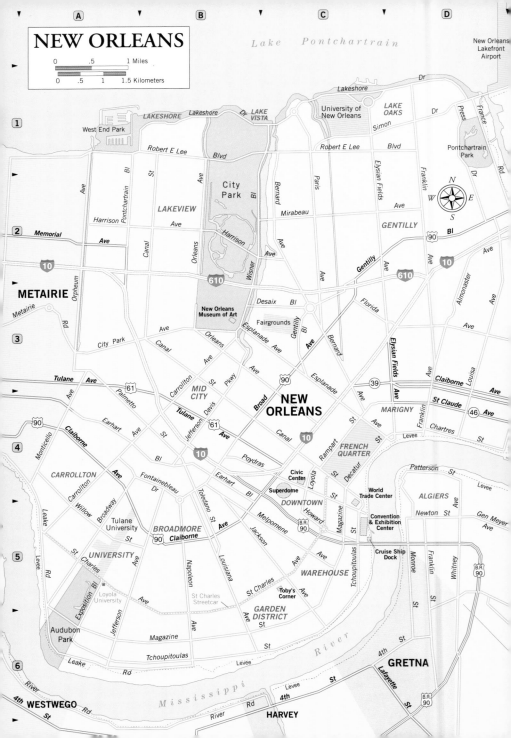

■ GARDEN DISTRICT

JUST A 10-MINUTE RIDE away from the French Quarter on the charming St. Charles Avenue trolley is the Garden District, a historic residential neighborhood whose architecture bespeaks the exuberance of the Southern Belle Epoque of the mid-19th century.

In 1812, the steamboat *New Orleans* arrived in the port of New Orleans, heralding an age of prosperity for the cosmopolitan city. Textile mills in England and France seemed unable to get enough Southern cotton, the sugar industry was thriving, banks were strong, and the port was bustling.

In 1832, a group of real estate developers bought a vast Creole plantation for half a million dollars and carved it up to make a new neighborhood for American belles and bucks excluded socially by the French and Spanish Creoles. Creole society remained rooted in urbanity, exclusiveness, and Catholicism, while the Americans gloried in a 19th-century blend of exuberant excess in decorative arts and graceful, straight-laced decorum. One of the first things that the developers did was to hire a good engineer, Benjamin Buisson, fresh from his service to Napoleon.

Buisson divided the plantation into the pattern of streets that exists today. The oldest home in the area is thought to be **Toby's Corner** at 2340 Prytania Street, which was built in 1838 in the Greek Revival raised-cottage style. The house was eventually sold in a sheriff's sale for $5,000 after the Union occupation in the late 19th century.

The area was to become a 14-block square bounded by St. Charles Avenue and Magazine Street, and by Jackson and Louisiana Avenues.

The beautiful and romantic Garden District is home to many of New Orleans' finest mansions. (Syndey Byrd)

■ CARNIVAL AND MARDI GRAS

In Christian communities around the world, the 40 days preceding Easter comprise Lent, a period of fasting and penitence. It begins with Ash Wednesday, the day many Catholics (and some Protestants) go to church to receive the sign of the cross marked in ash on their foreheads—its purpose being to remind them of their own mortality. For much of the country, the Tuesday before Lent is just that, a Tuesday, but in New Orleans this Tuesday is "Mardi Gras" (literally, "Fat Tuesday") and represents the last gasp of frivolity before 40 days of lenten austerity. The date on which Mardi Gras Day falls is determined by the church calendar—always 41 days before Easter, and as early as February 3 or as late as March 9.

In New Orleans, the term "Carnival" refers to the season of balls and parades that begins on Twelfth Night, or January 6, and continues until Mardi Gras. On January 6, Christmas decorations come down; Carnival colors of purple, green, and gold go up; and the six-to-eight-week season of balls and parades begins. Also on that day, one krewe—the Twelfth Night Revelers—hosts the first ball of the season. (A "krewe" is a club that mounts a ball, a parade, or both.) The high point of

(above) A Mardi Gras float designed and manned by the Krewe of Saturn.

(opposite) Dorothy Love Coates performs at Jazz Fest. (both photos, Syndey Byrd)

NEW ORLEANS

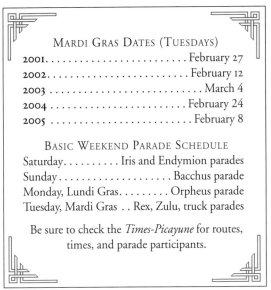

MARDI GRAS DATES (TUESDAYS)

2001 . . . . February 27
2002 . . . . February 12
2003 . . . . March 4
2004 . . . . February 24
2005 . . . . February 8

BASIC WEEKEND PARADE SCHEDULE

Saturday . . . . Iris and Endymion parades
Sunday . . . . Bacchus parade
Monday, Lundi Gras . . . . Orpheus parade
Tuesday, Mardi Gras . . Rex, Zulu, truck parades

Be sure to check the *Times-Picayune* for routes,
times, and parade participants.

Carnival is the parade-filled, four-day weekend that begins on the Saturday before Ash Wednesday and culminates in an all-out bash on Mardi Gras Day with Carnival's main event: the parade of Rex, King of Carnival.

Be sure to make hotel reservations well in advance! For general info contact the Louisiana Office of Tourism, 504-568-5661 or 800-334-8626. Websites: www.nola. com (where you can tune in and watch the revelry live); also www.mardigras.com.

■ NEW ORLEANS JAZZ & HERITAGE FESTIVAL

From the last weekend in April through the first one in May, over 7,000 musicians, cooks, and craftsmen participate in a 10-day event, held in the infield of a racetrack. Performers include internationally known jazz artists, gospel choirs, Cajun and zydeco bands, R&B bands, and many others. The food offerings are impressive and tasty, and the crowd can be as entertaining as the musicians.

Once in the city for "Jazz Fest," you'll find parking to be a nightmare; it's best to stay in a guest house in the back of the French Quarter or on Esplanade, then rent a bike or take a taxi to the fairgrounds. Having the proper equipment is also a must. Don't leave home without a pair of good rubber boots that won't come off even in squishy mud, a rain poncho, plenty of sunscreen, a hat, a long-sleeve cotton shirt for sun protection, and comfortable running shoes. Nighttime concerts, held in air-conditioned venues throughout the city, require a light jacket to combat air conditioning that can make even a crowded club as chilly as a meat locker.

Early January is a good time to book airline tickets, and mid-February is when the rush begins for hotel and restaurant reservations. **Tickets** for everything sell out quickly, so order ahead. *Ticketmaster 800-488-5252 or 504-522-5555. Websites: www.nojazzfest.com; www.offbeat.com; and www.wwoz.org.*

NEW ORLEANS JAZZ

Whether it's Fats Domino's "Walkin' to New Orleans" or Dr. John's version of "Iko Iko," the streets of New Orleans resonate with a funky backbeat laced with African breezes and New World sass. The hometown of Louis Armstrong, Mahalia Jackson, Wynton Marsalis, Harry Connick, Jr., and Terence Blanchard, New Orleans attracts musicians from all over the world who come to sop up inspiration.

If there is one place in the United States that can be credited with being the spiritual birthplace of jazz, it must be the Place des Negres, or Old Congo Square, in what is now Louis Armstrong Park. Here from 1817 until 1857, enslaved Africans were allowed to meet and dance, speaking in their native African tongues and playing their traditional instruments.

One of America's great indigenous art forms, jazz is a musical etouffeé. It emerged from a combination of the syncopated rhythms of Africa and the Caribbean mixed with the melodic structures of classical music; was seasoned with Deep South humidity and oppression; and finally was slathered with the quirky contributions of individual musicians to create the melodic stew. Once its early structures were formed, jazz grew up on the collectively improvised back-of-town ragtime and an unbeatable joie de vivre, bite, and swagger.

The term "Dixieland" was used to connote the syncopated music played by white bands, a distinction made by 1930s jazz critics. Not surprisingly, the jazz played by the Creoles of Color and blacks was rooted more in African and West Indian music, and was therefore more improvisational than Dixieland. Added to the mix were the traditions of Irish, Jewish, and Italian musicians who moved into the urban neighborhoods of their African-American counterparts. Some of the early neighborhood pick-up bands improvised on handmade instruments, such as banjos made of cheese boxes and percussion instruments made from kitchen implements.

The word "jazz" was not applied to the new sound until a good 20 years after the music had already found its way to the ears and tapping feet of New Orleanians, who referred to it with slang terms such as "gutbucket," "ragtime," or "ratty music." The Chicago Musicians' Union angrily used "jass" as a slur against the musicians for playing that dirty New Orleans "jass music."

Today jazz from "trad" to progressive can be heard in the clubs in the French Quarter, Marigny, and Treme. Listen to WWOZ, grab a copy of *Offbeat,* or consult the Friday *Lagniappe* section of the *Times-Picayune* to get the latest schedule. *Website: www.wwoz.org or www.offbeat.com.*

—Bethany Ewald Bultman

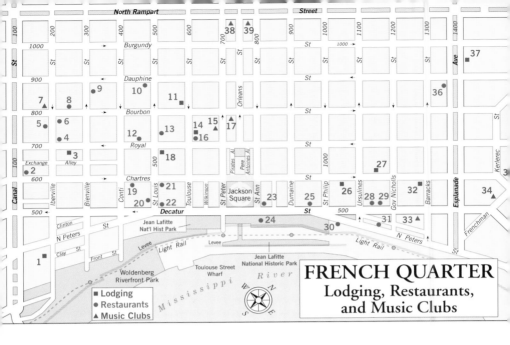

FRENCH QUARTER
Lodging, Restaurants, and Music Clubs

- ■ Lodging
- ● Restaurants
- ▲ Music Clubs

■ HOT SPOTS AND MUSIC CLUBS

Look in the *Times-Picayune* on Fridays and the monthly *Offbeat* for complete listings. Or tune in to WWOZ on local radio (www.wwoz.org on the Web).

Palm Court Jazz Cafe
Best place in town to hear traditional jazz in comfort. *1204 Decatur St.; 504-525-0200.*

Preservation Hall
A living, traditional jazz experience. No food or drink. *726 St. Peter St.; 504-522-2841.*

Storyville District
Fantastic local jazz on Bourbon Street in comfort and style. *125 Bourbon St. (at Iberville); 504-410-1000.*

Funky Butt
A very laid-back atmosphere that features some upcoming and cutting-edge local jazz artists. *714 N. Rampart; 504-558-0872.*

Donna's Bar and Grill
Brass bands play every night. *800 N. Rampart St.; 504-596-6914.*

Fritzel's European Jazz Club.
Popular with French Quarterite jazz aficionados; *733 Bourbon St.; 504-561-0432.*

Snug Harbor
Intimate setting for sitting back and listening to top contemporary jazz performers. *626 Frenchman St.; 504-949-0696.*

Tin Roof Cafe
An emerging jazz club owned by the great local clarinetist Jack Mahue. *534 Frenchman St.; 504-948-3100.*

■ NEW ORLEANS LODGING

$$ For room (🛏) and restaurant (✗) price designations and chain lodgings see page 333.

*(S) = Safer area, although caution is always advised.

Take note: Staying in the suburbs and commuting may be cheaper, but it will entail parking costs and the hassle of fighting traffic. Be skeptical of hotels advertised as being "close to downtown" or "10 minutes from the French Quarter."

B&W Courtyards. 2425 Chartres St.; 504-945-9418 or 800-585-5731 $$ Located four blocks from the French Market in the historic Faubourg Marigny. Nestled behind an unassuming facade are five cozy antique-filled guest accommodations (all with private entrances), two lush courtyards, and a hot tub. The multinational, multi-lingual owners offer a perfect balance of nuturing and privacy.

Columns Hotel. 3811 St. Charles Ave.; 504-899-9308 or 800-445-9308 $$-$$$ The large rooms are reminiscent of those romantic, funky hotels straight out of Tennessee Williams. The interior shots in the movie *Pretty Baby* were filmed in this

Uptown hotel. The 19 guest rooms (nine with private baths) are air-conditioned; some bathrooms feature double bathtubs. Pleasant cocktail lounge. Continental breakfast; Sunday champagne brunch.

Hampton Inn Downtown. 226 Carondelet St.; 504-529-9990 or 800-292-0653 $$ Located in a former Central Business District office building. The 186 rooms have sophisticated modern decor. Exercise facilities, free local phone calls, continental breakfast.

The Hampton Inn Garden District. 3626 St. Charles Ave.; 504-899-9990 or 800-292-0653 $$-$$$

One hundred charming rooms definitely a cut above conventional chain hotels due to the European-style furnishings. Lap pool, courtyard, and petite hospitality room.

THE HOUSE ON BAYOU ROAD

The House on Bayou Road. 2275 Bayou Rd.; 504-945-0992 or 800-882-2968 $$$-$$$$
A petite West Indies–style plantation (c. 1798) nestled on two acres of landscaped grounds in a picturesque historic neighborhood near Esplanade. Eight gorgeous rooms and suites (each with working fireplace); pool and Jacuzzi; and fabulous complimentary breakfasts, including a champagne mimosa brunch on weekends. Car and driver available for hire.

The Josephine. 1450 Josephine St. (near St. Charles Ave.); 504-524-6361 or 800-779-6361 $-$$-$$$
At the fringe of the Garden District, near Jackson Avenue, is an Italianate 1870s mansion with fluted Doric and Corinthian columns. The rooms in the main house have 13-foot ceilings and are resplendent with their "Creole Baroque" decor. Room 1 at the front has a magnificent bed with ivory inlay.

THE JOSEPHINE

The Maison de Ville. 727 Toulouse St.; 504-561-5858 or 800-634-1600 *(S) $$$-$$$$
The hotel is concealed behind wrought iron gates and semi-tropical plants in an 18th-century French Quarter mansion. Each of its 14 rooms, two suites, and seven "Audubon Cottages" are furnished with 19th-century antiques. Rates include a continental breakfast and sherry, port, iced tea, and coffee on the patio in

MAISON DE VILLE

the evening. The outdoor pool is near the Audubon Cottages where Audubon lived in 1821 and Tennessee Williams lived while he was working on *A Streetcar Named Desire.* Parking is $15.00 a night.

MCKENDRICK-BREAUX HOUSE

McKendrick-Breaux House. 1474 Magazine St.; 504-586-1700 or 888-570-1700 $$
Winner of an Historic District Landmark Commission award in 2000, this three-story Greek revival masonry townhouse was built in 1865 and lovingly restored in the 1990s. Seven charmingly furnished guestrooms have fresh flowers, antiques, and state-of the-art plumbing. Complimentary delux breakfast. Special summer and special event rates.

HOTEL MONTELEONE

Hotel Monteleone. 214 Royal St.; 504-523-3341 or 800-535-9595 $$$
Opened in 1886, this gracious 17-story French Quarter belle is still owned by the Monteleone family and has been completely renovated in recent years. Of the 600 spacious rooms, the best views of the river are in those numbered 50, 79, 81, and 82 on floors 7 and up. The beautiful Queen Anne mezzanine ballroom has true Royal Street ambiance. Rooftop pool.

THE OMNI ROYAL ORLEANS

The Omni Royal Orleans. 621 St. Louis St.; 504-529-5333 or 800-THE-OMNI $$$-$$$$
Tops for French Quarter location and New Orleans hospitality. The 346-room hotel was built in 1960 as a replica of the palatial 19th-century St. Louis Hotel. The view from the rooftop pool on the seventh floor is one of the loveliest in the city. Balconies overlooking Royal Street provide an ideal vantage point during Carnival to view the decadence below. Rooms with balconies overlooking St. Louis Street are the most expensive. Inside rooms are smaller and quieter, and the nicest view is from those that overlook the Royal Garden Terrace.

Parkview Guest House. 7004 St. Charles Ave.; 504-861-7564 or 888-533-0746 $$-$$$
Built in 1884, this inn offers 15 rooms with private baths and seven with shared baths. Continental breakfast served daily. Rooms on the east side overlook the oak-lined Audubon Park, have ceiling fans and brass beds; those without the view have nicer decor.

St. Charles Guest House. 1748 Prytania St.; 504-523-6556 *(S) $-$$
There are six backpacker rooms that share one bath and a range of more deluxe rooms that lack only TV and phone. Continental breakfast is served next to the pool. Near Felicity Street streetcar stop.

St. Vincent's. 1507 Magazine St.. Check in at 1415 Prytania St.; 504-566-1515 $
This 19th-century brick orphanage has been converted into a guest house of 31 fresh, cheerfully appointed rooms with private baths and phones. A nice breakfast costs only a few dollars.

THE SONIAT HOUSE

The Soniat House. 1133 Chartres St.; 504-522-0570 or 800-544-8808 $$$-$$$$

Two early 19th-century mansions, the 33 rooms (most with Jacuzzis) brim with a combination of effortless good taste, elegance, and comfort. The owners' care shows in every detail from their restoration of the Creole mansion to the crisp linen on the breakfast tray.

The Windsor Court Hotel. 300 Gravier St.; 504-523-6000 or 800-262-2662 *(S) $$$$
Twice ranked No. 1 by the prestigious *Conde Nast Traveler* Reader's Choice Poll and chosen as one of the top ten in the United States by *Zagat's*—no doubt for its luxuriant courtliness, exceptional five-star restaurant, grand swimming pool, and health club. The nicest views are on floors 13 through 23.

THE WINDSOR COURT HOTEL

The Wyndham Canal Place. 100 Iberville St.; 504-566-7006 or 800-228-3000 *(S) $$$-$$$$
A 438-unit hotel high atop the Canal Place shopping complex; breathtaking views of the river and the city. Popular with conventioneers who might only use the room as a place to shower and sleep.

■ NEW ORLEANS RESTAURANTS

$$ For restaurant price designations see page 333.

Acme Oyster House. *Seafood.* 724 Iberville St.; 504-522-5973 $$
The oyster shuckers here move quickly, the oysters are fat and salty, and the place has the ambiance of a typical, slightly unkempt, local oyster house.

Antoine's. *Traditional Creole.* 713 St. Louis St.; 504-581-4422 $$$$
Owned by the same family for five generations, Antoine's offers over 130 dishes on its vintage turn-of-the-century French menu. Best dishes include pommes de terre soufflée, and a combination of oyster dishes—Rockefeller, Foch, and Bienville—followed by a crème caramel make for one of the finest lunches or dinners in town.

Arnaud's. *Traditional Creole.* 813 Bienville St.; 504-523-5433 $$$$
Jackets are required in this large (six public dining rooms, 12 private) French Quarter institution. Live jazz at Sunday brunch.

Bayona. *Bistro.* 430 Dauphine St.; 504-525-4455 $$$
Chef Susan Spicer has combined her talent and elegant style to create a terrific menu for her own intimate restaurant. From garlic soup to a black beans and shrimp appetizer, her culinary style is clever, not overbearing.

Bella Luna. *Bistro.* 914 N. Peters St.; 504-529-1583 $$$
Enjoy the visual splendor of one of the grandest vistas of the Mississippi and indulge in an elegant array of fresh pastas and seafood creations in this chef-owned restaurant.

Blue Bird Cafe. *Breakfast.* 7801 Panola; 504-895-7166 $
Funky, hippie-chipper service, great eggs, grits, and pecan waffles.

Brennan's. *Breakfast.* 417 Royal St.; 504-525-9711 $$$$
Brunch at Brennan's is one of those high-cholesterol landmark meals to have at least once. Most famous for poached egg dishes, Brennan's claims to serve 750,000 poached eggs a year. Eggs Sardou and Bananas Foster make a tasty way to fritter away the day. (They also serve lunch and dinner.)

Cafe Atchafalaya. *Soul Food.* 901 Louisiana Ave.; 504-891-5271 $
On the fringe of the Irish Channel, this is a nothing-but-plain-food, formica-top neighborhood restaurant. It is the brainchild of a feisty lady from the Mississippi Delta who is as unpretentious as they come. Her daily specials are written on a board on the wall. The vegetable plate is great, but don't expect healthy, California-style veggies. Pluses: the wide range of seafood, the beef brisket, the homemade cobblers, and the ice cream.

Café du Monde. *Coffeehouse/Late Night.* 813 Decatur St. in the French Market; 504-525-4544 $
Good Creole café au lait and beignets (square pillows of fried dough doused in powdered sugar) without much opportunity to form a meaningful relationship with fellow coffee sippers. Open 24 hours a day, seven days a week.

Camellia Grill. *Late Night.* 626 S. Carrollton Ave.; 504-866-9573 $$
The lights are bright enough to elicit a confession and there is often a wait for one of the 29 stools, but the food is worth it. Omelets (especially the potato and onion with chili and cheese on top), hamburgers, pecan waffles, and pecan pie are all close to the best in the world. The beverage of choice is the mocha freeze. Avoid the coffee, unless you happen to like the coffee in Kansas. Clientele includes university types, ball-goers, and after-rounds physicians.

Casamento's Restaurant. *Seafood.* 4300 Magazine St.; 504-895-9761 $
Closed June through August. Best fried and raw oysters in the city. The tile-lined walls are immaculate.

Central Grocery. *Sweets and Snacks.* 923 Decatur St.; 504-523-1620
This tiny Italian market will give any food lover a lot to think about with aisles of olive oil and other imports. Famous for muffulettas—huge sandwiches filled with ham, salami, mozzarella, and marinated, chopped green olives—that can be ordered in quarters and halves.

Clancy's. *Traditional Creole.* 6100 Annunciation St.; 504-895-1111 $$-$$$
Seasoned waiters and dishes like smoked soft-shell crab give this eatery its old New Orleans feel.

Commander's Palace. *Eclectic Creole.* 1403 Washington Ave.; 504-899-8221 $$$$
Excellent food and service keep this restaurant's 12 dining rooms and cocktail courtyard full seven days a week. Luncheon specials are always delicious and well priced. Fish Grieg, oysters Rockefeller, turtle soup, and crab dishes shouldn't be missed. For dessert, crème brûlée, lemon crêpes, and bread pudding soufflé are tops. On a nice day, request a table on the patio or in the upstairs room that overlooks it. Live jazz on weekends.

Coop's Place. *Late Night.* 1109 Decatur St.; 504-525-9053 $
A back-of-the-Quarter neighborhood bar and pool hall with great omelettes and Cajun specialties.

Court of Two Sisters. *Traditional Creole.* 613 Royal St.; 504-522-7261 $$$-$$$$
Upscale French Creole cuisine in an historic setting. Live jazz at brunch, seven days a week.

Domilise's. *Sweets and Snacks.* 5240 Annunciation St.; 504-899-9126 $
French bread stuffed to bursting with fried seafood. A neighborhood institution for close to 80 years.

Donna's. *Late Night.* 800 N. Rampart St.; 504-596-6914 $$
Try a slab of baby back ribs and grand beans as the live brass bands boogie in the background.

Dooky Chase. *Traditional Creole/
Late Night.* 2301 Orleans Ave.;
504-821-2294 $$
Elegant black Creole food. The crabmeat
farci, shrimp Clemenceau, fried catfish,
sweet potatoes, and bread pudding are
all exceptional. Service can become slow
as the hour grows late.

Dunbar's. *Soul Food.* 4927 Freret St.; 504-
899-0734 $-$$
Guests are in for a hard time, having to
decide between some of the best fried
chicken in the city, knock-your-socks-off
mustard greens, fantastic red beans and
rice, and bell peppers stuffed with
shrimp and meat. Don't miss the soul
food breakfast from 7:00 A.M.

Emeril's. *Bistro.* 800 Tchoupitoulas St.;
504-528-9393 $$$
Chef Lagasse wows diners with his own
food laboratory in the Warehouse District
using herbs, cheeses, and fresh produce
culled from his network of farmers—and
Emeril's TV shows have wowed folks na-
tionwide. Go with a few friends and order
six appetizers, then finish off with Creole
cream cheese cake.

Feelings. *Traditional Creole.* 2600 Chartres
St.; 504-945-2222 $$
Away from the bustle of the Quarter, this
venue has been noted for more than 20
years for its updated renditions of Creole
favorites like Chicken Clemenceau.

Felix's Restaurant and Oyster Bar. *Seafood.*
739 Iberville St.; 504-522-4440 $$
A top-of-the-line seafood house. The
oyster shuckers are characters worthy of
starring roles on a sit-com; the cooked
oyster and crab dishes are home-style.

Fiorella's Cafe. *Breakfast.* 45 French Market
Pl.; 504-528-9566 $
French Quarter ladies use the front door
and French Market truckers use the
back, on the market side, where the
hours are earlier. Either way, the food
and atmosphere are as real as it gets.

Gabrielle's. *Traditional Creole/Bistro.* 3201
Esplanade Ave.; 504-948-6233 $$
Plump soft-shell crab, festive sauces,
homemade sausages, and friendly service
reign in this unpretentious chef-owned
bistro at the edge of the French Quarter.
Reservations recommended.

Galatoire's. *Traditional Creole.*
209 Bourbon St.; 504-525-2021 $$$
Oysters en brochette, the Godchaux salad
(not on the 6-page menu), trout alman-
dine or with crabmeat, and the crabmeat
Yvonne are some of the finest seafood
dishes to be found. Best time to go is be-
tween 1:30 and 4:00 P.M. on a Saturday
or Sunday.

Gautreau's. *Bistro/Eclectic Creole.*
1728 Soniat St.; 504-899-7397 $$$
American-Creole cuisine at its finest.
Don't miss the corn crabmeat soup and
the crawfish and crab cakes.

Grill Room. at the Windsor Court *French/
Eclectic.* 300 Gravier St.; 504-522-1992
$$$-$$$$
Luxurious international dining without a
trace of hometown funk.

Johnny's Po-Boys. *Sweets and Snacks.*
511 St. Louis St.; 504-524-8129 $
A good, honest po' boy is actually a rare
find in the French Quarter, but Johnny's
is an exception. Choose from New

Orleans classics such as roast beef and gravy, fried oysters, shrimp, or ham, sandwiched in crusty French bread.

K-Paul's Louisiana Kitchen. *Cajun/ Eclectic Creole.* 416 Chartres St.; 504-524-7394 $$$
K-Paul's chef, Paul Prudhomme, has made Cajun cuisine famous beyond its Louisiana borders. Among the many favorites are blackened fish, sweet potato –pecan pie, creative gumbos, and jalapeño-laced martinis served in canning jars. K-Paul's national recognition has made the restaurant extremely popular with tourists. Reservations accepted.

Lemon Grass Cafe. *Vietnamese.* 216 N. Carrollton Ave.; 504-488-8335 $$
Cozy elegance and continental-flavored Vietnamese dining. Reservations recommended.

Le Salon at the Windsor Court. *Tea.* 300 Gravier St.; 504-596-4773 $$
Overstuffed chairs, live classical music, and an elegant English tea service make an afternoon here a memorable experience.

Mandina's. *Creole/ Italian/ Seafood.* 3800 Canal St.; 504-482-9179 $$
This Mid-City spot is famed for its stiff drinks, seafood, Italian food, and red beans. Waiters wear white coats; the patrons are generally more casual.

Martinique. *Caribbean.* 5908 Magazine St.; 504-891-8495 $$$
This chef-owned bistro features delightful fish dishes and ambrosial homemade ice creams. Lovely dining patio.

Maximo's Italian Grill. *Late Night/Italian.* 1117 Decatur St.; 504-586-8883 $$-$$$
Innovative northern Italian cuisine in a chic bistro with a Roman-style grill and outdoor dining.

Mr. B's Bistro. *Bistro/Eclectic Creole.* 201 Royal St.; 504-523-2078 $$$
This pop version of Commander's Palace, Jr., has remained fresh and innovative since it opened in 1979. Sample the coconut- and beer-battered shrimp, any of the items from the grill, or pasta jambalaya, followed by killer chocolate cake or a custardy bread pudding.

Mother's. *Sweets and Snacks.* 401 Poydras St.; 504-523-9656 $
Since 1938 locals have been lining up for "debris" po' boys made from the roast beef and gravy scraped off the bottom of the roasting pan.

Napoleon House. *Sweets and Snacks.* 500 Chartres St.; 504-524-9752 $
Look beyond the cocktails to partake in this historic spot: try the muffulettas, gumbo, and/or Italian ice cream.

Nola. *Bistro/Eclectic Creole.* 534 St. Louis St.; 504-522-6652 $$$-$$$$
A "Baby Emeril's" sizzling with conversation and lively plates of rich food. Don't be put off by the snooty maitre d'.

Palace Cafe. *Bistro.* 605 Canal St.; 504-523-1661 $$$
The chicken with garlic mashed potatoes, and custardy bread pudding with white chocolate sauce are sinfully delicious. This is another Brennan family restaurant. Live jazz on Sundays.

Peristyle. *Bistro.* 1041 Dumaine St.; 504-593-9535 $$$
Chef Anne Kearney's 56-seat restaurant is a treat, from the fresh flowers and gracious waitstaff to her delectable food. It is also no longer a local secret, since she was named as one of the nation's "Rising Stars of 1997" by the James Beard Foundation. Reservations are a must.

The Praline Connection. *Soul Food.* 542 Frenchman St.; 504-943-3934 $-$$
Cool soul; white, lima, or red beans; stewed or fried chicken; and fantastic pralines. They also operate a lunch spot called **The Praline Connection Gospel & Blues Hall** at 907 South Peter St.; 504-523-3973, where they serve up jambalaya, gumbo, and red beans and rice along with live gospel music on Sundays.

Progress Grocery. *Sweets and Snacks.* 915 Decatur St.; 504-525-6627 $
Next door and similar to Central Grocery, this spot offers gastronomic goodies like muffulettas, etc. Word has it that Progress offers a better deal with a larger selection and lower prices.

Ruth's Chris Steakhouse. *Steak.* 711 N. Broad St.; 504-486-0810
Metairie: 3633 Veterans Blvd.; 504-888-3600 $$$$
When only a well-aged, prime slab of beef will do, this testosterone-affirmative home-away-from-the-car-phone for politicos and sports fans serves the best steak to be found east of Fort Worth. Peppermint-stick ice cream is the perfect complement for such gustatory decadence.

Sid Mars. *Seafood.* 1824 Orpheum, Bucktown near the lakefront; 504-831-9541 $-$$
A meal of boiled crabs on the screen porch at this small fishing enclave is a trip back to a calmer era.

Tujague's. *Traditional Creole.* 823 Decatur St.; 504-525-8676 $$
The second oldest restaurant in New Orleans with the city's oldest standing bar originally was conceived to serve the working class. Today it's noted for the Wednesday lunch special: veggie soup and a hunk of brisket with mashed potatoes. Other days, shrimp rémoulade and the garlicky chicken bonne femme are worth a visit.

Uglesich Restaurant & Bar. *Seafood.* 1238 Baronne; 504-523-8571 $
Some of the best food to be had in the Big Easy—delicious barbecued oysters, potato crabcakes to die for, and legendary po' boys. It's open for lunch only, perhaps for safety reasons. The neighborhood may have character, but it isn't a place for an evening stroll.

Upperline. *Bistro.* 1431 Upperline St.; 504-891-9822 $$$
Nestled Uptown is this charming, cozy bistro, whose culinary style begins with local products and is elevated with Latin, Anglo-Indian, and classic French cooking techniques. All of the crispy duck dishes are perfection, though the one with ginger peach sauce edges out the others.

R I V E R R O A D
by Malia Boyd

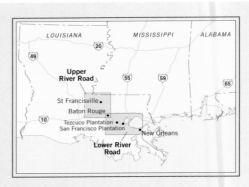

Food & Lodging, page 100
Maps, pages 62-63 and 83

■ TRAVEL OVERVIEW

More than 20 antebellum plantations lie along the Mississippi River above New Orleans. The flat riverside road stretches from New Orleans to Baton Rouge, linking the settlements along the vacherie—a grassy plain of higher ground. We take you through the verdant hills of the area around St. Francisville and on into Mississippi. Many of the architectural treasures along the way, with their pungent histories and insistent ghosts, are open to the public. The narrow roadway follows a high levee so all the structures will be on the passenger side on the east bank of the river, and on the driver's side on the west bank of an upriver excursion.

Along the roads you'll pass yellow-green cane fields, ancient live oaks, hulking chemical plants, squat brick ranch houses, and pre–Civil War mansions. Between Baton Rouge and the Mississippi border, the river becomes your nearby but largely unseen guide, while rolling terrain, punctuated by live oaks and a variety of robust trees, shrubs, and flowers, takes up the open spaces between sleepy towns. In the spring, wild iris blooms in the bayous and the silvery dogwood blossoms in the woods.

Climate: The seasons in this neck of the woods can best be broken into two: the hotter-than-Hades months, and the not-as-hot months. People who are phobic of perspiration had best spend their time somewhere else between late April and late September. Temperatures and humidity routinely hover in the 90s, while heat indexes jauntily step into the 100s. It's a good night when the lows plummet to 85. Moving north might shave a degree or two off the highs and lows, but really and truly, summer here is like a hot, wet blanket. The months of July and August will inevitably bring afternoon showers that locals have come to love for the brief, though admittedly anemic, respite they bring from the relentless heat. The not-as-hot months (October through March or April) can sometimes get downright gorgeous, March and October being particularly fabulous. About then, temperatures will cling to the mid-70s or low 80s during the day with cloudless and blinding blue skies, and air that feels to residents as dry as the Mojave (though people from the desert still might insist they're in a tropical rain forest). In the teeth of winter, temperatures on the lower River Road will remain reasonable with daytime highs in the 60s or low 70s and lows in the 50s or 60s. Further north, though, you will see some good old-fashioned country freezes, but those usually happen in the pre-dawn hours.

Food: The highways and byways of River Road offer those fraternal twins of local cuisine—Cajun and Creole. Dilapidated, family-run roadhouses abound, but some fancy eateries also appear along the way. Fresh-caught and fried catfish, just-made boudin sausages, and golden shrimp po-boys are typical. **See page 100 for restaurant listings.**

Nightlife: Here it's slow and rural. This is the ideal region to rock on a porch swing, roll in the sheets, and read a good long book. Baton Rouge is a mecca for live entertainment due to its two universities and the clubs that cater to their students. It's where Athens, Georgia band REM cut its musical teeth. Check local papers for listings.

Accommodations: Most travelers will find lodging prices pleasingly affordable. The high falutin', fully-restored, white-columned antebellum wonders can go for three figures but are less expensive in the winter. There are a profusion of bed-and-breakfast inns along the route—some more delightful than others. If B&Bs aren't for you, the Holiday Inns in Gonzales and La Place are near the area, as are the plethora of motels in Baton Rouge. **See page 100 for lodging listings; see page 333 for price designations and toll-free numbers for chain accommodations. For a chart of listings by region, see page 334.**

◼ RIVER ROAD HISTORY

In the early 1700s, the areas on both sides of the river in St. Charles, St. James, and St. John the Baptist Parishes became known collectively as the Côte des Allemands, or the German Coast. It was to this drier soil upriver on the west bank from New Orleans that farmers from Alsace and Lorraine first fled after discovering that their one-way passages to the New World had landed them in soggy, mosquito-infested Nouvelle Orleans. By 1724, 60 German households were established in the Côte des Allemands, where they grew crops and raised cattle crucial to the survival of the New Orleans colony.

In 1748, the western Choctaw raided an east-bank German farm, tomahawking the husband to death, scalping the wife, and capturing the daughter and a black

slave. When the other terrified Germans fled en masse to New Orleans for protection, there went the food supply! The French governor finally sent a military detachment to protect German farms. But once the Germans realized how hungry and cowardly the French forces were, most of the Germans abandoned their east-bank farms, opting instead for the west bank (where the Choctaw did not live and to which they could not easily cross). Ever resourceful, the Germans soon reorganized themselves into thriving communities, selling their produce in New Orleans and later opening breweries and bakeries.

Many last names in this part are Gallicized German (not Cajun as most people assume). Hymel (pronounced HEE-MEL) is actually Himmel.

In time this region became home to French and American planters who grew sugarcane and cotton as well as wheat.

■ PLANTATIONS AND SIGHTS

◆ DESTREHAN PLANTATION

map page 62, lower right

Destrehan Plantation is the grand antebellum home nearest to New Orleans on the lower River Road; it lies just eight miles from New Orleans International Airport. Built in 1787, this French Colonial mansion claims to be the oldest plantation in the lower Mississippi Valley. (Actually Parlange Plantation further north in New Roads is older by a few decades.) The contractor for Destrehan was a Free Man of Color, Georges Pacquet, who built the house for Robert Antoine Robin de Logny. De Logny died

Golden Twilight in Louisiana by Charles Giroux, circa 1860. This painting of a homestead along the river in evening is a classic Louisiana scene both in historic times and today. (Roger Houston Ogden Collection, New Orleans, Louisiana)

RIVER ROAD

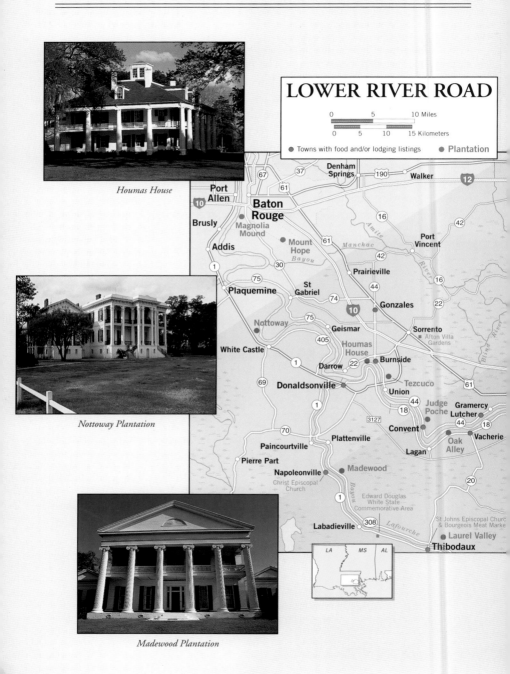

Houmas House

Nottoway Plantation

Madewood Plantation

LOWER RIVER ROAD

| 0 | 5 | 10 Miles |
| 0 | 5 | 10 | 15 Kilometers |

● Towns with food and/or lodging listings   ● **Plantation**

Denham Springs — 190 — Walker — 12

Port Allen — 10

Baton Rouge

67   37   61   16   42

Brusly   Magnolia Mound

Addis   Mount Hope   61   *Manchac*   Port Vincent

Bayou   42

1   30   Prairieville   16

75   St Gabriel   44

Plaquemine   74   10   Gonzales   22

Nottoway   75   Geismar   Sorrento

405   Houmas House   Afton Villa Gardens

White Castle   1   Darrow   22   Burnside

69   Donaldsonville   Tezcuco

Union   61

1   44   Judge Poche   Gramercy

18   Lutcher

3127   Convent   44   18

70   Plattenville   Oak Alley   Vacherie

Paincourtville   Lagan

Pierre Part

Napoleonville   Madewood

Christ Episcopal Church   20

1   Edward Douglas White State Commemorative Area

Bayou   *Lafourche*

St Johns Episcopal Church & Bourgeois Meat Market

Labadieville   308   ● Laurel Valley

Thibodaux

LA   MS   AL

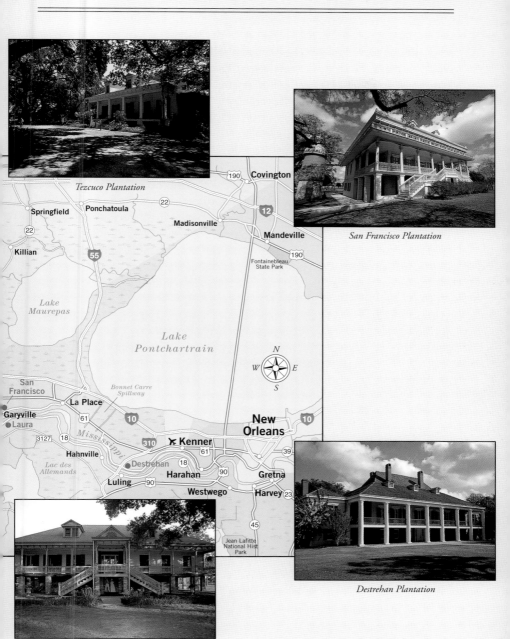

Tezcuco Plantation

San Francisco Plantation

Destrehan Plantation

Laura Plantation

soon after he moved in, leaving the house to his daughter and son-in-law, Jean Noel Destrehan. The construction contract Pacquet signed is still filed away in the courthouse in nearby Hahnville. His pay for the job was a cow and a calf, 18 bushels of corn, some silver, and his choice of a "brute Negro."

By the 1970s, Destrehan was deserted and half demolished. A rumor that pirate Jean Lafitte had hidden some treasure in the walls of the house had led scavengers to rip out the mortar. In 1972, the River Road Historical Society took charge of rebuilding it. The house came to the Society an empty shell but is now in beautiful condition. The Society has also been campaigning to buy back the house's original furniture. Their research-and-recovery mission continues to pay off: all of the furniture is true to the period, and now a quarter is actually original to the house. The best examples are the mahogany secretary and the two oil paintings of Jean Noel Destrehan and his daughter Zelia in the upstairs parlor. The tour begins with an informative video. The guides have been through a rigorous training period and can answer questions that deviate from their rap—an ability than distinguishes them from guides at many other plantations.

If you can swing it, the nicest time to visit Destrehan is during the fall, when the weather in Louisiana has cooled off a bit, and when Destrehan hosts its annual Fall Festival (always the second full weekend in November), with scores of arts-and-crafts booths, live music, food booths, and historical re-enactments. *Daily 9–4; 13034 River Rd. (Hwy. 48), Destrehan; 504-764-9315.*

Up the road about five miles is the **Bonnet Carre Spillway.** The path of the original River Road goes right through the Spillway. It's a basin filled with wildlife and much used by cane-pole fishermen. The Army Corps of Engineers began building the Spillway after a devastating flood in 1927 that threatened New Orleans and ultimately wiped out several downriver communities entirely. When the Mississippi River rises higher than 19 feet at Carrollton, just a few miles from the French Quarter, the Corps is required by federal law to open the Spillway gates. When all of the Spillway bays are open, the mechanism can drain almost two million gallons of water per second from the river—a handy device since all of the area's towns are at or below sea level. (If any of the Spillway bays are open, detour from LA 48, back onto Hwy 61 and up to LA 628, which eventually links back to LA 44 along the river.)

(opposite) San Francisco Plantation, an 1853 Steamboat Gothic mansion. (Brian Gauvin)

◆ SAN FRANCISCO PLANTATION   *map page 63*

On LA 44—and in wacky contrast to the white, ordered splendor of Destrehan—is the colorful, heavily adorned riot known as San Francisco Plantation, which lies just about seven miles up the River Road, midway between New Orleans and Baton Rouge off the I-10. Jazz historians might recall that this is the birthplace of the legendary Edward "Kid" Ory, a Creole of Color who took the same name as the home's white owners after the Civil War.

After a major and ultra-costly renovation of the plantation finished in 1860, the second owner and his young wife sarcastically began referring to their home by the name of Sans Frusquin, a French phrase for something like "without two pennies to rub together." The name was changed by a later owner to the less embarrassing and more familiar "San Francisco."

Inside and out, the house is like a slightly faded circus wagon. But the ceiling frescoes, as well as the great *faux bois* (false wood) and *faux marbre* (false marble) detailing are worth the price of admission. (These decorative effects require much painting skill and patience: just *try* rendering a painted surface indistinguishable from a real piece of wood or marble—grain, imperfections, and all.)

Between 1974 and 1977, millions were spent to restore the house with fanciful period carpets and furnishings. *Open daily 10–4:30 Mar–Oct, 10–4 Nov–Feb; on River Rd .(Hwy. 44) in Garyville; 504-535-2341 or 888-322-1756.*

Laura Plantation, an 1805, West Indies–style, Creole plantation house. (Brian Gauvin)

If you've only time for a short trip out of New Orleans, the "two-fer" of Destrehan and San Francisco will probably take only four to five hours door-to-door.

◆ LAURA PLANTATION   *map page 63*

A few miles upriver of Veterans Memorial bridge lies Laura Plantation, a wonderfully restored West Indies–style Creole plantation house built in 1805—one of the few left in the country. Laura's colorful exterior and stories are what make a visit a magical experience, even though she's not one of the grande dames of River Road. Using details culled from written plantation records found in the National Archives in Paris, the memoirs of Laura Locoul (after whom the property is named), and even some oral history, owners Sand and Norman Marmillion have crafted a riveting tour intimately portraying those whose lives and labors created Laura.

Laura's French-speaking slaves made an important contribution to the cultural history of the plantation and, ultimately, to generations of American children. They told stories about a clever, mischievous rabbit known as Compair [sic] Lapin and his wacky companion, Compair Bouki. In the 1870s, the grandson of a major River Road planter recorded the stories in their original French patois. In 1894,

Tar Baby author Alcée Fortier included "The Tale of the Piti Bonhomme Godron" in his book *Louisiana Folktales*. A decade later the moniker "Brother Rabbit" (from the French "Compère Lapin") was shortened to "Br'er Rabbit," and his madcap adventures were recorded by Joel Chandler Harris in *Uncle Remus Tales*. Soon, they were read as bedtime stories all over the English-speaking world; eventually they were made into the seminal Disney movie *Song of the South*.

A recent conversation with manager Norman Marmillion shed light on both Creole history (such as that at Laura) and on Acadian traditions as well. Marmillion is related 16 different ways to Creole families, among them the Bourgeois family, one of the original Acadian families expelled from Canada by the British.

At Laura Plantation you can visit the original slave cabins, barns, and four 19th-century Creole cottages. The site is surrounded by sugarcane fields; the historic Creole–style landscaping includes a formal French-style *parterre* and cottage vegetable garden. Web: *www.lauraplantation.com; tours daily from 9–4; 2247 Hwy. 18, Vacherie; 225-265-7690.*

Senagalese slaves brought colorful folktales to America. On Louisiana plantations, these stories became French "Compair [sic] Lapin" tales; in the English colonies similar "Br'er Rabbit" stories were told. Here the fox encounters the Tar Baby in Uncle Remus *by Joel Chandler Harris.*

◆ OAK ALLEY PLANTATION   *map page 62*

Built in 1839, this majestic Greek Revival plantation home has 28-exterior Doric columns, mirroring the eponymous lane of 28 massive, moss-draped 250-year-old live oaks. Though planted 90 feet apart, the oaks in this quarter-mile row are so vast that their branches caress each other and nearly blot out the sun with their fullness. So large and imposing was the house and its alley that steamboat captains used it as a landmark by which to navigate the river and changed its name from Bon Sejour (a Good Visit) to the more literal Oak Alley.

The home was built for Jacques Telesphore Roman, the brother of the governor of Louisiana. It fell on hard times for many years—including those during which an owner's children were allowed to gallop their horses down the alley of oaks, right through the front doors and out the back. To its credit, the tour at Oak Alley offers a few funky, unexpected facts from the rituals of antebellum life. Did you know, for example, that in the mid-1800s makeup was made of colored beeswax? During the winter, when the fires were lit, young women had to sit and shiver far from the fire—or else use a side table with a flip-up top as a heat shield—if they didn't want their faces to melt into their laps.

Oak Alley, a grand plantation home built along the Mississippi River, is fronted by a quarter-mile row of enormous live oaks. (Syndey Byrd)

The magnificent oaks of Oak Alley are as much an attraction as the house itself. (Brian Gauvin)

Okay, so the tour guides dressed as Southern belles are a bit hokey, and, unlike the guides at Laura, they tend to forget here that the plantation was built and run by African slaves. Nonetheless it's worth a visit to this slice of commercialized Louisiana culture. And you can treat yourself to a mint julep before or after the tour, and lounge for a spell on the shady grounds. The site has ample parking and a dinner theater, and it operates as a B&B (see page 106). *Daily tours from 9–5:30 Mar–Oct and 9–5 Nov–Feb; 3645 LA 18, Vacherie; 225-265-2151 or 800-442-5538.*

◆ GRAMERCY AND LUTCHER   *map page 62*

The village of Gramercy, so named by some nostalgic New Yorkers, and Lutcher, once a big cypress mill town named after a mill owner, are now most famous for the yearly conflagrations called the Christmas Eve bonfires. Conventional wisdom says the fires, built alongside the river in 20-foot-high pyramids, are to light the way for Papa Noël. The tradition is said to have been brought over by Catholic French and German settlers in the 1880s. Historians trace the custom even earlier to a Celtic winter solstice celebration.

Locals start gathering wood in the swamps on the Friday after Thanksgiving. Building the fires is a source of pride among local families, and it's a skill that's

RIVER ROAD

These wooden towers are lit on Christmas Eve, creating bonfires along the Mississippi River and lighting the way for Saint Nick. (Syndey Byrd)

been passed down through generations. The town fire departments oversee the festivities and have special dispensation to build their own larger and more distinctive pyres. Over the years, the Lutcher Fire Department has built models of everything from the *Mayflower* to a giant alligator to a scale model of Lutcher High School. The fires are spread every 150 feet along 10 miles of the river bank, and nearly 50,000 people each year make the pilgrimage to watch them burn.

If you don't care to drive out to the bonfires, you can get an incendiary view of them from the river, aboard the *Creole* or *Cajun Queen* riverboats. They leave from a dock in the French Quarter, and passengers can eat, drink, and be merry all the way up and back for the all-inclusive price of $125. The bar is open, the food is only so-so, but the views are magical. *Information for both: 504-524-0814.*

❖

An exemplary small-town museum is the **St. James Historical Society Museum,** a small turn-of-the-19th-century pharmacy packed with antiques and pictures from residents' pasts. Also on the grounds are the old Post Office, a locomotive, train station, an 800-year-old sinker cypress log, and several other quaint curiosities.

Don't miss the video on Perique tobacco farming. Perique is a strain of strong tobacco that few Americans can smoke unblended. The area between Lutcher and Paulina used to be a the prime location for farming Perique. Today there are only about 30 acres still under cultivation and most of it is shipped out to heartier lungs in Greece. *Open Mon–Fri, 8–4; 1988 LA 44, Lutcher; 225-869-9752.*

◆ CONVENT *map page 62*

One of the more striking aspects of this stretch of the River Road is the juxtaposition of the yellow-green undulation of the vast sugarcane fields and the metallic menace of the Road's many chemical plants.

Coexisting with cane and chemicals in Convent is one much loved restaurant and two religious sites of note: Manresa Retreat House and St. Michael's Church.

RIVER ROAD

Hymel's

This roadhouse, with its hearty seafood specialities, is beloved by two generations of Louisianans; *8740 LA 44.*

Manresa Retreat House

Manresa was built in the early 1830s as the College of Jefferson, an alternative to Northern and European boarding schools for the sons of local planters. Most of it burned in 1842, but the main building was rebuilt with hopes of an imminent reopening. It reopened briefly in the late 1850s only to be turned into a Union Hospital during the Civil War. After changing hands between private ownership, the Marist Fathers, and the Jesuits, the property was opened as a retreat for Catholic and non-Catholic laymen in 1930 and remains so to this day.

Lourdes Grotto

A mile up the river is St. Michael's Church and its Lourdes Grotto. The outside of the church is fairly unremarkable red brick. Inside, statues of Michael the Archangel and Joan of Arc stand guard over a pipe organ and a hand-carved altar from Paris. But the real draw is the grotto, which is behind the main altar. The brainchild of Christophe Colomb, Jr., it was built in 1876 to commemorate Bernadette Soubiroux's 1858 vision at Lourdes. First the parishioners took a sugar kettle and clinkers made from bagasse (bagasse is the cellulose remnant of sugarcane after the juice has been taken); then they added thousands of clamshells to make the grotto. It's believed to be one of the first such grottos in the country.

❖

If you're interested in hopping across the Mississippi River to visit Donaldsonville, take the Sunshine Bridge just outside of Union, Louisiana, back to the West Bank, and head up the winding path of the river about 10 miles on LA 18. To skip Donaldsonville, stay on the River Road, LA 44, through Romeville and Union. Burnside is about five miles or so past the town of Union.

■ DONALDSONVILLE   *map page 62*

Along the roadway, historical markers note the sites of the first Acadian settlements and of the church of St. Jacques de Cabahonce, established in 1757.

Donaldsonville (pop. 8,600), named for a man who purchased the land from an Acadian widow in 1806, may have peaked as a town when it was briefly selected to be the state capital in 1825. But true to their reputation for extreme inefficiency, Louisianans took four years to move the political center from New Orleans, and Donaldsonville got to enjoy only one legislative session before the capital was moved north to Baton Rouge.

One little known fact about Donaldsonville is that it was once home to a substantial Jewish community, though today only vestiges remain. Even its synagogue, once the spiritual home to 70 families, is today a hardware store. There is, however, a Jewish cemetery, Bikur Sholim, tended by an elderly Jewish man.

If hunger pangs get the better of you here, you're lucky to be in Donaldsonville. Pop over to **Lafitte's Landing**, which has been getting acclaim ever since chef John Folse reopened it in 1999. (The first Lafitte's Landing burned in 1998.) There you can tuck into Cajun and Creole favorites, and if you get a little sleepy you can check into rooms upstairs in **Bittersweet Plantation** *(see page 101).*

At a 1938 county fair in Donaldsonville, boys peek at a peep show, and a snake-eater entertains the crowd. (photo by Russell Lee, Library of Congress)

The African-American Museum at Tezcuco describes the lives and contributions of blacks to plantation life and the Civil War. (Syndey Byrd)

◆ TEZCUCO PLANTATION   *map page 62*

As you get off the Sunshine Bridge, returning to the east bank from Donaldsonville, head northwest toward Burnside and Darrow. Technically in Darrow, Tezcuco Plantation is actually just south of Burnside, another of those barely-there River Road towns.

The first owner of the 1855 house, Benjamin Trudeau, a Mexican War veteran, named Tezcuco after a lake in Mexico. (Tezcuco is Aztec for Resting Place.) The Greek Revival main house is small as plantation houses go, but the interior is notable for its masterful plasterwork and original *faux bois* details. The many outbuildings and formal garden make Tezcuco worth seeing; there's a lovely B&B here, too. *Open daily from 9–5; 3138 Hwy. 44, Convent/Darrow; 225-562-3929.*

Tezcuco, now privately owned, is the only plantation on River Road dedicated to explaining the role of blacks in the plantation system, the Civil War, and Reconstruction. **The River Road African American Museum and Gallery** is housed in one of the buildings on the plantation grounds. Though small and folksy, it packs a pretty good historical punch with original documents, photos, and artifacts taken from the lives of slaves in 1858 in Ascension Parish and the surrounding areas. It also includes a registry of African-American Civil War veterans from 1890. *Open Wed–Sat 10–5, Sun 1–5; Tezcuco Plantation; 225-562-7703.*

◆ BURNSIDE AND HOUMAS HOUSE *map page 62*

After Tezcuco, continue northwest on Highway 44, to Burnside—but don't blink or you might miss it. Before it became Burnside, it was home to the Houmas Indians, who had begun settling the area in the early 1700s. Their tribal land was a smallish space that ran from Burnside to a point near the Houmas House Plantation, and inland from the river for about a mile. In 1776, they sold their land to two men—Alexandre Latil and Maurice Conway—and by 1784 most of the Indians had left the area.

Burnside was named after an Irish immigrant, John Burnside, who in the 1850s and '60s was known as the "Sugar Prince" of Louisiana, owning 18,200 acres of cane and corn and 500 slaves to work them. In 1858, Burnside bought Houmas House and its 10,000 acres for $1 million. Built in 1840, the mansion has Doric columns on three sides and a hipped, dormered roof.

Mr. Burnside is perhaps best remembered, though, for talking Union troops

With its imposing columns and fine prospect, Houmas House is a classic example of an antebellum plantation home. (Syndey Byrd)

The graceful grand ballroom at Nottoway Plantation, where belles and their beaus once danced the night away. (Syndey Byrd)

out of destroying or appropriating any of his vast holdings during the Civil War by convincing the people who mattered that as a British citizen, he was immune from such actions. They acquiesced, Houmas House was spared, and today, after a grand restoration by the Crozat family in 1940, you can tour Houmas House and its formal gardens. *Open daily 10–5 Feb–Oct; and 10–4 Nov–Jan; 40136 Highway 942; Burnside, 225-473-7841.*

◆ NOTTOWAY PLANTATION   *map page 62*

Nottoway is one of those imposing grand belles that delight the camera lens. Two miles north of the town of White Castle, it was completed in 1859. At 53,000 square feet, it is purported to be the South's largest surviving plantation home. But who's measuring? These days Nottoway is open for day tours and is also a full-service inn and banquet facility *(see page 107). Open daily 9–5; 30970 LA 405; 225-545-2730.*

■ NAPOLEONVILLE   *map page 62*

Off the beaten path of River Road, Napoleonville (pop. 850) is nonetheless worth a trip if you have time for a day jaunt. To get there, take LA 1 out of Donald-sonville and follow it south down the bayou about 13 miles. If you decide to head out straight from New Orleans, take LA 90 West, till you get to 308, then head north, reversing the order of this section.

In Napoleonville, on Bayou Lafourche, is a noted example of Gothic Revival architecture, **Christ Episcopal Church** (1853). Under pressure from the Anglican Church in London, Southern parishes were encouraged to adopt medieval English architecture, and this is a prime example.

◆ MADEWOOD   *map page 62*

Just 2.2 miles south of Napoleonville, this lovely mansion was designed in the Greek Revival style by the famed Irish-American architect Henry Howard in 1846, and restored to a fine polish in 1964. The white-columned house is open for tours, but if you want to enjoy the full impact of Madewood, experience a night in one of its rooms. There is just the right patina of frumpiness to make you relax. It's like spending the night at a great auntie's home, where hand-crocheted quilts cover canopy-sheltered four-posters; in one room dolls lie tucked into an-tique doll beds. Waterford crystal chandeliers capped by elaborate ceiling medal-lions tinkle in the breeze. Guests assemble for wine and cheese in the library, then move on to a candlelit dinner round an imposing oak table decked with crystal candelabra. Afterwards, it's coffee and brandy in the drawing room *(see page 103)*.

On the mansion's walls are framed photos of the family with various Republi-can bigwigs; one is of the present owner with Bill Clinton at Oxford, back when they were Rhodes Scholars together. Out back are giant oak trees dripping with moss, an ancient cemetery, and a huge cauldron in which sugarcane was boiled down. Service is "y'all come back," and rural Louisiana fare is prepared by family retainers. *Tours from 10–4:30 daily; 4250 Highway 308; 800-375-7151.*

❖

There are several bayou crossovers between Napoleonville and Thibodaux, but it's best to take the first one you see after leaving Madewood, to assure you get over to the east side of the bayou before you hit Thibodaux, which is about 15 miles away.

The kitchen at Madewood Plantation, which can be seen on a tour of the house.
One of the most magnificent of the River Road plantations, Madewood's
front prospect can be seen on page 62. (Syndey Byrd)

RIVER ROAD

■ THIBODAUX *map page 62*

No more than a few minutes from Napoleonville and an hour from New Orleans, Thibodaux (pop. 15,700) remains a working cane town with a distinctly Acadian flavor nestled on the banks of Bayou Lafourche.

St. John's Episcopal Church

In the heart of downtown is the live oak–shaded St. John's Episcopal Church, originally organized by Bishop Leonidas Pope (later a Confederate general) in 1843. It was designed by Henry Howard, architect of the Pontalba Apartments in New Orleans.

Wetlands Acadian Cultural Center

Thibodaux is home to the Wetlands Acadian Cultural Center which provides you with everything you ever wanted to know about the Acadians. Consider it the equivalent of Cajun Cliff Notes, with Cajun language, history, culture, music, and food vividly chronicled in pictures, along with audio, videos, and artifacts. Run by the National Park Service, the center is staffed by helpful, well-trained guides. *Open daily at 9; closing time varies; 314 St. Mary St.; 504-448-1375.*

Bourgeois Meat Market

A town landmark is Bourgeois Meat Market, which has been cranking out fresh boudin, andouille, stuffed pork chops, and other spicy meats since 1891. *543 W. Main St. (Hwy. 20).*

Rienzi

A little south of Thibodaux on LA 308 just past the Howard Johnson's on the left, is Rienzi, which is closed to the public but

has a noteworthy genesis: Queen Maria Louisa of Spain ordered the house built in 1796 and intended to use it as her refuge in the event Napoleon Bonaparte defeated Spain.

Laurel Valley Village

Further down Highway 308, Laurel Valley Village looms in lonely, almost desolate, relief against acres of waving cane. It is the largest, turn-of-the-19th-century cane plantation complex in the country. While its general store and museum are open to the public, the rest of the massive sprawl

Laurel Valley Fall Festival. (Syndey Byrd)`

can be seen only on a prearranged tour. Like St. James Parish Historical Society Museum, the General Store has that homespun, chock-a-block feel, as crafts and photos compete for shelf and wall space. *10–3 Tues–Sun; Hwy. 308 two miles south of Thibodaux; 504-446-7456.*

■ BACK BY THE RIVER

If you decide that you don't have a day for Thibodaux and Napoleonville, take LA 22 from Burnside east to **Sorrento,** for a hokey but fun pit stop at the Cajun Village. This conglomeration of restored plantation outbuildings is home to the **Ascension Parish Tourist Commission,** the ideal place to stop for brochures and directions for the parish. You're guaranteed to have more fun in some of the other buildings. The Coffee House features cafe au lait and beignets for the weary or sugar-starved. Around the back there's a mini-bayou stocked with real live alligators behind a sturdy chain link fence.

■ BATON ROUGE *maps pages 62, 83*

If you plan to visit Baton Rouge, leave off River Road at Sorrento and choose one of two express routes: the I-10 West or US Highway.. 61 North. If you are stubborn, you could stick with the circuitous path of River Road, but the asphalt is potholed and neglected, the scenery is no great shakes, and the going is snailish. At Baton Rouge, the River Road ends—but the river doesn't.

Compared with other River Road towns, Baton Rouge sticks out like—well, a bright red stick. The name literally means "red stick" in French and is believed to have been coined by French explorer Sieur d'Iberville upon seeing an Indian territorial marker—a cypress pole smeared with animal blood—marking the boundary between the lands of the Bayougoulas and the Houmas.

Baton Rouge has been the state capital since 1849. Today it's the home of Jimmy Swaggart and his Bible college, as well as singers Joe Tex and Johnny Rivers. Multimillionaire rapper Master P lives in the exclusive Country Club of Louisiana, and the city is the nation's most inland deepwater port, the fifth largest port in the country.

As you drive into Baton Rouge (pop. 231,000), strip malls and billboards dominate the landscape, and there's nothing immediately visible that makes you want to stop and spend the day. Nonetheless there are several points of interest, best seen by driving up to them, having a look, then getting back into your car and driving to the next one. If you do feel like stretching your legs, tour the capitol, check out the few restaurants and shops nearby, then walk the quarter mile or so on the road by the river to the **Old State Capitol Spanish Town Historic District.** This area was laid out in 1805 by Don Carlos de Grandpere, and several houses dating from the mid-1800s are still standing: the Presbyterian Minister's Cottage, Grace-Persac House, Prescott-Dougherty House, and Potts House.

Louisiana State Capitol

If you want to pinpoint one thing that Baton Rouge symbolizes today, it's state politics—and it's a brand usually reserved for wily rulers of Third World countries. As the saying goes: "Here in Louisiana, we don't tolerate corruption… we demand it."

The tomb of populist governor Il Duce–Senator Huey P. Long, stands in front of the State Capitol—a building he commissioned—only to be assassinated in it three years its completion in 1932. *Open daily 8–4:30. Take I-10 to 110 North; Exit 1E, follow signs to State Capitol Dr.; 225-342-7317.*

The capitol remains a symbol of Long's undeniable power, and his incomprehensible arrogance. Long had to browbeat members of the legislature into approving its construction, at a cost of $5 million during the depths of the Depression. At 34 stories it is the tallest state capitol in the United States—but only because Long, upon finding out that Nebraska's capitol was taller, changed the plans to add 50 feet to its top. This is a petty, almost absurd, example of Long's desire to keep his state's edge at all costs. But occasionally his maneuvers were more cunning. For instance, Long also demanded that the bridge over the River in Baton Rouge be built with a 65-foot clearance, a few feet shy of the necessary draw for ocean-going vessels, thus preventing this big-ticket traffic from taking any business upriver of the port of Baton Rouge.

The magnificent foyer of the Louisiana State Capitol; and the exterior of the tallest state capitol in the nation. (Syndey Byrd)

Old State Capitol   *map page 83, C-3*
Officially the **Center for Political and Governmental History,** but more commonly known as the Old State Capitol, this building located on the high bluffs of the river, is a monument of the romantic Gothic Revival style and has earned its share of sniggers over the years. When reconstruction began on the building after a fire partially destroyed it during the Union occupation, a young Mark Twain wrote, "It is much more pathetic to see this architectural falsehood undergoing restoration... when it would have been so easy to let dynamite finish what a charitable fire began."

In its present incarnation, the building houses various multimedia displays on Louisiana politics and government. Here you can see the gun with which Huey Long was shot by Carl Austin Weiss on September 8, 1935, along with various news clippings, all set to foreboding background music. *Open Tues–Sat 10–4, Sun 12–4; 100 North Blvd.; 225-342-0500.*

Rural Life Museum and Windrush Gardens   *map page 83, C-3*
Located on the 450-acre Burden Research Plantation, this museum and garden are the legacy of Steele Burden, a Renaissance man who noted that in the mid-20th-century rush to save the actual plantation homes of Louisiana, the complex infrastructure of plantation outbuildings and rural Louisiana society was in fact being bulldozed. To remedy this, Burden purchased and painstakingly moved an entire plantation store, a schoolhouse, a rural church and graveyard, an overseer's house, slave cabins, and an Acadian trapper's cottage to his property.

He restored them, then opened the whole complex to the public. A five-minute video introduces the village in context. Then it's up to you to see what real life was like for common folk in the 19th century. *Open daily from 8:30–5; just off the I-10 on Essen Lane, on the New Orleans side of town; 225-765-2437.*

Magnolia Mound Plantation
map page 62; also map page 83, C-3
Poised on a natural ridge facing the river, Magnolia Mound Plantation is one of Louisiana's oldest wooden structures unscathed by famished termites, fire, or the wrecking ball of progress. It was built circa 1791 on 950 acres, with architectural modesty of the Creole style (a hybrid of Spanish and French styles nurtured in the intemperate climate of the Caribbean) by Irish merchant John Joyce. Perched atop brick piers to raise the building above the mud and flood, the home is constructed of a mud-over-moss mortar smudged between chunky cypress posts. Sadly, Joyce lived to see only a few indigo harvests before drowning in 1803. His Creole widow soon remarried a French planter who'd come to Louisiana with the Marquis de Lafayette's entourage. The new master of Magnolia Mound set about fancying up the place with European elements, though the most significant features remain the Louisiana-made furnishings, the original kitchen, and its adjacent kitchen garden.

Today the fascinating former plantation and its 16 acres of majestic live oak trees is open for tours. *Tues–Sat 10–4, Sun 1–4. Directions: take I-10 to LA 30 (Nicholson Dr.), 2161 Nicholson Dr.; 225-343-4955.*

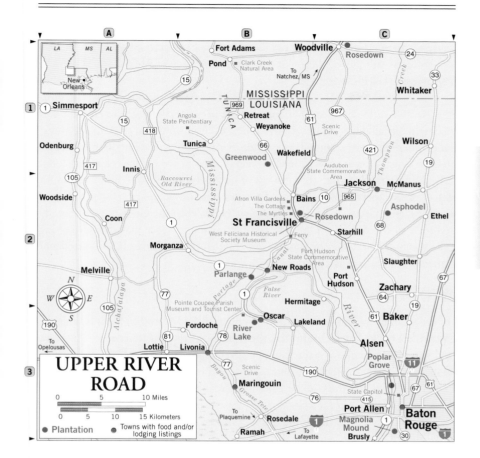

UPPER RIVER ROAD

◆ POPLAR GROVE PLANTATION   *map above, C-3*

Poplar Grove Plantation, directly across the river from Baton Rouge, is one of the state's most exotic architectural treasures. Originally used as the Bankers' Pavilion for the World's Industrial and Cotton Centennial Exposition in 1884 in New Orleans and designed by noted architect Thomas Sully, Poplar Grove was essentially Victorian but with heavily Oriental motifs—coiling dragons, cypress carved to resemble bamboo, and a pagoda-like roofline. In 1886 the building was purchased by Poplar Grove owner Horace Wilkinson, who floated it upriver on a barge to the sugar plantation. The plantation has remained in the family ever since and is now owned by Horace's great granddaughter, Ann. The family operated the lands as a sugar plantation for nearly 100 years, ceasing major operations in 1982, though some cane is still grown there. *Visits by appointment only; 3142 North River Rd., Port Allen, LA; 225-344-3913.*

During World War II, German prisoners of war were kept in camps in Louisiana. Rented out to locals as labor, many of the prisoners were used to cut cane and maintain outbuildings at plantations in the area. One of the barracks and commissaries where they were housed still stands in Port Allen. This forgotten fact came to light when a former POW from Rommel's Afrika Korps began seeking his long-lost camp on the Internet. (For reasons of national security the POW s never knew exactly where they'd been interred.) Turns out, this German had labored for some time at Poplar Grove. In an oddly nostalgic twist, when the German POW recently returned to the plantation, he told the Baton Rouge paper that though cutting cane was hot, hard work, he was just grateful that he had been treated so well and remembered his time as a prisoner fondly.

■ UPPER RIVER ROAD   *map page 83*

To get a handle on just how mightily commercial the Mississippi River is, visit the **Port Allen Lock.** The lock connects the Mississippi to the Intercostal Waterway, and you can stand above it watching massive barges pass through the deep water. Finished in 1961, the locks are 84 feet wide and over a thousand feet long, shortening the distance to the Gulf by 160 miles. *Open 8–4; best to call ahead to let them know you're coming. Off LA 1 South, follow signs to the Port; 225-344-8272.*

The quickest way to leave the heavy industry of Port Allen behind is also to leave the Mississippi behind—if only for awhile. Take Highway 190 heading northwest until you come to the LA 1 junction. Along LA 1, the territory rapidly becomes more rural, and after only a few miles, what looks to be a river appears to your right. But wait! It's not the Mississippi. It's not even a river. Called **False River** (originally Rivière Fausse), it's a 22-mile-long oxbow lake.

◆ NEW ROADS   *map page 83, B-2*

At the northern tip of the lake is New Roads (pop. 5,400), the Pointe Coupee parish seat, a mere six-block settlement in 1822 when it was established at the end of the new road linking False River with the Mississippi River. Although it didn't get its charter until 1894, the history of the area of New Roads, and much of Pointe Coupee Parish, is far older—and *très français.*

French Canadian explorers and brothers Sieur d'Iberville and Sieur de Bienville first came across the area in 1699. By the 1700s, French speakers were coming in droves first to hunt and trap, then as planters who grew tobacco and sugarcane. By mid-century, the wealthier French Creole planters had begun building grand plantation houses. Unfortunately, not many of the grand old manses are left—about five in town and about six more in the surrounding area.

For such a small town, New Roads has a surprising number of bed-and-breakfasts, and it's a wonderful place for an overnight. There are few more calming, smile-producing pastimes than watching boats and ripples in the waters of False River from the deck of an overnight hideaway. Of the six B&Bs in New Roads, three are in historic homes: Pointe Coupee B&B (also known as Samson House), Mon Cour, and Jubilee. All deliver a folksy, laid-back experience *(see page 103)*.

RIVER ROAD

Parlange Plantation *map page 83, B-2*

The most beloved, and also the oldest plantation in the parish, Parlange is still a 2,000-acre working plantation, worked by the seventh and eighth generations of the very same family—the Parlanges. The fine cypress main house was built by the Marquis de Ternant in 1750, and the walls have more than their fair share of stories to tell. During the tour you can find out how then-mistress Virginie de Ternant Parlange played hostess to both Union and Confederate officers, in a wily bid to save her home during the Civil War. Or how Virginie's granddaughter posed in the buff for painter John Singer Sargent, resulting in the scandalous portrait *Madame X*—which now hangs in New York at the Met. *Tours by appointment only; 8211 False River Rd.; 225-638-8410.*

Pointe Coupee Parish Museum
map page 83, B-3

This modest building stands in stark contrast to the grandeur of Parlange. A typical home of 18th-century French settlers, the basic structure has two rooms and is a mere 30 by 17 feet, divided into two rooms. The spaces between the dovetailed timbered walls are filled with "bousillage," a mixture of mud, horsehair, and moss that acts as weatherproofing.

The tourist center can supply you with brochures for nearby historic houses and B&Bs, and a self-guided walking tour brochure of the town. In previous incarnations the building has served as a private home, a jailhouse, a hospital (albeit a very small one), and the *garde mangé* (larder) for the Parlange Plantation. One room has a changing exhibit, the other displays everyday items of rural Creole life: from a husk broom to old clothes to sad old ticking mattresses and bedsteads. *Open daily 10–3; 8348 False River Rd.; 225-638-7788.*

River Lake Plantation *map page 83, B-2/3*

About three miles up False River Road from the museum is Cherie Quarters, a worker's community at the River Lake

Plantation, just across the river from Baton Rouge, in Oscar, Louisiana. The plantation house was constructed in 1795 by Antoine Decuir, a wealthy planter, for his mistress, Sophie Deslondes, a Free Woman of Color. Decuir's legitimate three-year-old daughter inherited the property—2,000 acres of sugarcane and 200 slaves— in 1829.

It was in a tin-roofed former slave cabin on this property that famed author Ernest Gaines was born in 1933 and it was his life here that vividly lives on in Gaines's fiction,

such as *The Autobiography of Miss Jane Pittman, A Gathering of Old Men,* and *A Lesson Before Dying.* Gaines's family were the descendants of seven generations of the plantation's slaves. His grandmother, Miss Zuma, was the white owners' legendary cook until her retirement. River Lake Plantation is privately owned; occasionally visits can be arranged by the docents at the Pointe Coupee Museum, who may be willing to call ahead to see if a visitor would be welcome.

❖

One of the loveliest drives in the Gulf South is taking Highway 77 north from Plaquemine to Livonia along Bayou Grosse Tete. The drive is shaded by historic live oaks and passes the remains of a 19th-century sugar factory and several unmarked plantation homes. One popular dining experience is a meal at **Joe's Dreyfus Store Restaurant** in Livonia on Highway 77 South; *(see page 103).*

Leaving New Roads, get onto LA 10 and follow the road to the **New Roads–St. Francisville Ferry,** which leaves every half hour. This point on the river seems so empty that you can't imagine when you get to the other side there'll be anything much there. But disembark the ferry (the short ride costs a dollar) and follow the road as it curves into town, and you'll be delighted with what you find.

■ ST. FRANCISVILLE   *map page 83, B-2*

You have now left French Creole Louisiana for the heartland of Anglo-Southern plantation country. The town's about 25 miles north of the Baton Rouge airport and 60 miles south of Natchez. To get an overview of local events in the region, grab a copy of the locally published *Country Roads* magazine (free), available at many St. Francisville businesses.

St. Francisville (pop. 1,800) is an ideal place for an overnight stay. Between the Audubon Pilgrimage in the spring and a major gardening symposium in the fall, the area can be thronged with visitors. If you come up for a day, take the walking

Miss Emily sells peanuts and pralines—the latter one of Louisiana's favorite sweets—at the ferry crossing between St. Francisville and New Roads. (Syndey Byrd)

tour, lunch at the local favorite Magnolia Cafe, and finish up with a leisurely stroll through the churchyards and cemeteries on the far end of Ferdinand Street.

◆ HISTORY

While many of the histories of St. Francisville seem to pick up when John James Audubon came to town in the 1820s, interesting things actually started happening there much sooner. The parish of West Feliciana was home to the aggressive Tunica tribe when white men arrived in the area in the 1700s. The parish was handed back and forth between the French, Spanish, and English several times, before the area that became St. Francisville was settled in 1785 by Capuchin friars.

The town was officially established in 1807—under Spanish rule—by an American named John Johnson. Spanish origins notwithstanding, men like Johnson and other residents (many of whom came from the Carolinas) of St. Francisville clung stubbornly to their Anglo-Saxon-Calvinist roots. In fact, when it looked like the town would remain under Spanish control after the Louisiana Purchase, citizens took matters into their own hands and declared themselves the Free and Independent Republic of West Florida. After 74 days, the U.S. Army marched in and claimed the town as part of the original Louisiana Purchase, to the great pleasure and satisfaction of residents. Since then—especially when compared with its neighbor New Roads—St. Francisville has been all Anglo all the time. Despite the early questions of national allegiance, St. Francisville grew rapidly after 1807; roads and houses sprung up, a newspaper was established, a courthouse erected, and crops planted. By the 1820s, thanks to the determination of its people and the fecundity of its land, St. Francisville had become an enchanting, wealthy town, and a cultural and religious center for the area.

◆ ST. FRANCISVILLE SIGHTS

West Feliciana Historical Society Museum
This is the best place to start exploring St. Francisville. Pick up a walking/driving tour map (the town is so small and walkable, that unless the weather's bad, we recommend spending the day on foot) that takes you mostly along Ferdinand and Royal Streets, touring some of the more than 140 structures that merited inclusion on the National Registry of Historic Places. Though the tour will give you only a small taste, nearly all the houses in the area have fascinating tales to tell. *Open Mon–Sat 9–5, Sun 9:30–5; 11757 Ferdinand St.; 225-635-6330.*

Seabrook

Owned by the town's most passionate historian, Libby Dart, Seabrook started its life in 1810 as a typical Creole cottage with two rooms, a center fireplace, and no front gallery. Seven years later Georgian style was imposed on the house. This private home is on the tour described above. *9889 Royal St.*

Evergreenzine

The unusual name is Anglicized Yiddish, and the house was built by a German Jew named Adolph Teutsch in 1885. In the late 19th and early 20th centuries, St. Francisville had a flourishing Jewish population, with its own synagogue and cemetery. Many of the St. Francisville Jews arrived in the 1870s, while planters and residents struggled to rebuild the economy after the Civil War. In this climate of limited economic resources, many of these newcomers set up retail businesses and extended to the planters credit secured by their cotton crops. The growing and planting seasons continued apace, fueled by Jewish money, and slowly St. Francisville recovered from the war. The death of the cotton industry by the early 1920s, followed by the Depression, wreaked havoc on many Jewish businesses. Most of the town's Jewish population left for better opportunities in larger cities. Today, besides Evergreenzine and a few old mercantile buildings, the only trace of the town's Jewish community is the Hebrew Rest Cemetery. Descendants of the St. Francisville Jews send money for the cemetery's upkeep, and a Catholic woman in her 80s, whose father was Jewish, is the caretaker. *11875 Ferdinand St.*

Other Historic Structures Around Town

While it's fun to hear some of the stories, in St. Francisville you always come back to the beauty and abundance of the structures themselves.

There's the Victorian Gothic **St. Francisville Inn**, built in the 1880s and sheltered in a tranquil park of Spanish moss–draped oaks, and nearby the simple but pleasing **Methodist Church** (1899). Don't miss the **Grace Episcopal Church** (1858) on Ferdinand Street, an English Gothic–style brick church beneath a canopy of green. The organ inside dates from 1860 and is one of the oldest still in use in the country. Read the gravestones for a poignant glimpse into local history. For example, the Masonic emblem on the grave of Lieutenant Commander John E. Hart: a truce was declared during the Civil War shelling of the town so that Hart, a Union officer, could receive a Masonic burial. Ironically, it was his brother Confederate Masons who carried out the request.

Rosedown Plantation   *map page 83, B-2*

The picture-postcard vista of the oak alley leading to the classic Greek Revival Rosedown Plantation (1835) is not to be missed. The 28-acres of formal gardens were inspired by gardens the original builders saw on their honeymoon in France. Today, the Rosedown garden is considered one of the most important historic gardens in the country.

A wing of the house was added in 1844 to hold a massive Gothic bedroom suite which was to be presented to Henry Clay,

RIVER ROAD

had he won the Presidency in 1844. Clay lost and the presidential-scale furniture remained at Rosedown. The home offers B&B accommodations. *East of town on Rte. 10; (see page 105).*

Tunica Hills Wildlife Area *map page 83, B-1* Magnificent Tunica Hills is northwest of St. Francisville, on the ridges overlooking the Mississippi River. The entrance is down a long gravel road, but it's worth the effort.

Hiking here is pleasant and in March and April the hills are bright with flowering dogwood *On LA 66 in Tunica; no phone on site but try the Pond Store 601-888-4426. For area information:web www.saint-francisville.la.us or call 800-789-4221.*

JULIA SANDERS' FLORA GUIDE: TUNICA HILLS

Louisiana Copper Iris
Iris fulva
Crosses with Louisiana blue iris to create many beautiful Louisiana iris hybrids. Blooms March to April. Found in ditches, bayous, and fresh marshes of Mississippi River floodplain.

Oak-leaved Hydrangea
Hydrangea quercifolia
A shrub of varying size. Flower petals dry and turn pink, remaining on bush into fall. Blooms April to June. Grows on sides of ravines and embankments throughout Tunica Hills.

Afton Villa Gardens. (Syndey Byrd)

◆ NEARBY PLANTATION HOUSES

Just outside of St. Francisville are dozens of fantastic plantation houses to discover.

Afton Villa Gardens

A gatehouse and iron gates greet you as you approach this French-Gothic-Victorian whimsy begun in 1849 by David Barrow for his wife-to-be, a Kentucky belle. Sadly for visitors, the house burned in 1963, and the fire took with it turrets, Dresden-china doorknobs, and opulent stained glass. But Morell and Genevieve Trimble bought the property in the 1970s and created a stunning ruin-garden of a place. Today it offers visitors a boxwood maze, a reflecting pool, and droves of azaleas and daffodils in which to delight. *Open Mar–June and Sept–Oct 9–4:30 ; 9247 Hwy. 61; 225-635-6773.*

Butler Greenwood

This is one of the oldest houses in the area, construction having begun in 1796 by Samuel Flower, a Quaker medical doctor who came down from Pennsylvania in a covered wagon and chose to settle in this lovely, hilly wilderness just a few miles from St. Francisville. Currently the eighth generation of Flower's family inhabits the house. Besides the fantastic 12-piece Victorian rosewood parlor set which still bears its original red upholstery, there's a titillating collection of Mardi Gras invitations, Sèvres vases, and oil portraits of the family on the walls. This B&B has six charming, dog-friendly guest houses and acres of grounds on which to roam. *Open for tours Mon–Sat 9–5, Sun 1–5; two and a half miles north of town, 8345 LA 61; 225-635-6312.*

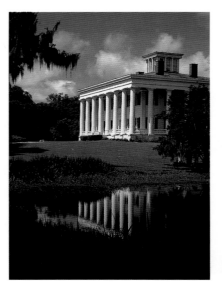

Greenwood Plantation. (Syndey Byrd)

Between 1968 and 1984 the owners rebuilt and renovated the house. Today the copper roof covers a mix of period antiques and reproductions, crowned by details such as silver doorknobs and hinges on all the doors. To spend a day at the massive Greenwood is to experience the grandeur and wealth of the antebellum South. Guides wear antebellum costumes.

Directions: Six miles north of St. Francisville on Hwy. 61, turn west onto Hwy. 66. Follow Hwy. 66 to Highland Road and turn left at the sign for Greenwood Plantation. *Open Nov–Feb 10–4; Mar–Oct 9–5; 6838 Highland Rd.; 225-655-4475.*

The Cottage (1795-1859)

One of Louisiana's oldest plantation complexes, this site's outbuildings—the school, milk house, carriage house, and slave cabins—are of particular interest. *Five miles north of St. Francisville on Hwy. 61, then right on Cottage Lane; 225-635-3674.*

Greenwood

Greenwood is a near-perfect reproduction of its Greek Revival predecessor—you'd never know it's not the original. At its peak, Greenwood was a working plantation encompassing 12,000 acres worked by 750 slaves. But in 1960, lightning struck, and the building burned to the ground in three hours. It was a horrific loss.

A staircase that seems to float down the foyer at Greenwood Plantation. (Syndey Byrd)

The Myrtles

Built in 1796, this house derives its name from the forest of crepe myrtles that surround it. Over the years, various owners festooned the home with verandas, lacy wrought iron, and crystal chandeliers. That's not what The Myrtles is noted for, however: it's been featured on numerous tabloid television programs as America's Most Haunted House. It's a B&B, so you can decide for yourself. *Open for daily tours; one mile north of Rte. 10; 7747 LA 61; 225-635-6277.*

Audubon State Historic Site and Oakley *map page 83, C-1/2*

Painter John James Audubon spent a few months in Oakley back in 1821, and rumors have been flying ever since. Audubon was hired as a tutor by Oakley's Scottish-born owner James Pirrie. He was to teach Pirrie's comely young daughter Eliza such valuable life skills as drawing, music, dancing, and hair braiding. (French and mathematics were also in Eliza's curriculum, but they were the responsibility of others). Audubon departed abruptly a mere four months later, and people still wonder why. It wasn't that the job was too demanding—it left him with time to complete more than 30 paintings of birds he encountered in Oakley's 100-acre forest. He even had time to paint wingless animals, such as the portrait of Eliza that hangs today in Rosedown, the family home of her daughter-in-law.

Audubon remains a presence at Oakley: first-edition prints of his work are displayed throughout the house, and the wooded

The Myrtles is often described as America's Most Haunted House.

acres of the surrounding Audubon State Historic Site are atwitter with birds. It's a nice place for a picnic, if you care to take out lunch from the Magnolia Cafe in town and picnic amid the oaks and shrubs of Audubon's one-time home.

The house itself, completed in 1808 and decorated in 1820s Federalist style, is interesting in its own right. It is four stories tall and raised in the Caribbean style to attract and distribute the anemic breezes that barely alleviate the region's oppressive heat. Inside, the light fixtures, dating from the late 1600s to the 1800s, are particularly interesting. *Open daily 9–5; 11788 Hwy. 965 (off Hwy. 61); 225-635-3739.*

RIVER ROAD

■ JACKSON *map page 83, C-1*

Fifteen miles from St. Francisville and 30 from the Baton Rouge Airport, Jackson (pop. 4,100) lies just over the parish line in East Feliciana. The charming town is a relatively unsung cousin to St. Francisville, brimming with historic buildings, a 19th-century college, and even its own winery.

Established in the early 1800s, just a few miles from what would be the parish seat in Clinton, Jackson bloomed with cotton, as well as traffic and trade from the Clinton and Port Hudson Railroad. By the late 19th century, the town was crowded with several general stores, three colleges, and a plethora of Greek Revival buildings. But as with St. Francisville, the boll weevil arrived to work its sinister magic on cotton crops and the town rapidly declined. Luckily, almost 125 historic buildings have been preserved.

Walking Through Town

A walk through town—with attention to the names and dates highlighted on plaques —will satisfy the need for a dose of everything from Greek Revival to Spanish mission-style to Victorian architecture.

Centenary College Historic Site

Once the apex of higher learning in East Feliciana and the surrounding parishes, Centenary is now a state commemorative area and its well-preserved buildings offer a glimpse into 19th-century education. Centenary started out as the College of Louisiana in 1826, and after a closing, a merger, and a move, eventually settled on its present site as Centenary College of Louisiana. Just before the Civil War, the college had 250 students and 11 faculty members conversant in such subjects as rhetoric, Greek, French, astronomy, and logic. During the War, the college, like so many others, closed, and possession of it was batted back and forth between Union and Confederate troops. After the war, the school struggled to regain its former enrollment and by the early 1900s it moved to Shreveport, where Centenary College continues today. A tour of the college will give you a pretty good historical knowledge of student life and the quality of education, not just in Jackson, but in the state as a whole. *3522 College St.; 225-634-7925.*

Local Wineries

If you haven't acquired a taste for juleps, how about some fine Louisiana wine? The wine industry here is young and growing. It took an act of the state legislature in the late 1980s to make wine production legal. Now there are six vineyards: Pontchartrain Vineyards in Bush, Hungarian Harvest in Albany, Amato in Independence, Lynn Creek in Bernice, Casa de Sue in Clinton, and Feliciana Cellars in Jackson. The latter two wineries are within a 15-mile radius.

Feliciana Cellars Winery bottles 10 types of muscadine wine; *1848 Charter St./LA 10; 225-634-7982.* Casa de Sue makes several versions of muscadine wine, as well as the odd bottle of blueberry wine. *14316 Hatcher Rd.; 800-683-5937.*

About muscadines: Fruit wines almost always tend to be sweet. Remember Boone Farms Strawberry Hill? But the much-maligned muscadine grape is capable of producing wines in the full range from very dry to lip-curlingly sweet. Wine connoisseurs don't usually trip over each other trying to grab the last bottle of muscadine, but the folks at Feliciana and Casa de Sue consider their wines pretty darn successful.

■ ANGOLA PRISON RODEO   *map page 83, A/B-1*

Angola, or more accurately the Louisiana State Penitentiary at Angola, is home to a history that's worth noting. And with the recent opening of the **Louisiana State Penitentiary Museum** on its grounds, a trip to Angola is a fascinating, disturbing trip into the bowels of the penal system. *End of Hwy. 66; 225-655-2592.*

Twenty-six miles from St. Francisville, Angola is ideally situated to keep prisoners caged, bounded as it is by the Mississippi River on three sides and the Tunica Hills on the fourth. It earns its keep as an 18,000-acre working farm that produces wheat, soybeans, and corn among other things.

Convict poker. Last man to leave the table wins the pot. (Syndey Byrd)

If you happen to be in the area during any Sunday in October, then you should not miss the **Angola Prison Rodeo.** Begun in 1964, it is one of only three prison rodeos in the country and hands-down the best. People flock to see events like the Bust Out, where six prisoners (many of them lifers) sit atop six angry bulls trying to be the last man on; the Wild Horse Race, where teams of three inmates try to grab onto an unbroken horse, mount it, and ride it across a finish line; and the Buddy Pick Up, where an inmate who's never ridden a horse before negotiates an obstacle course that includes picking up a buddy standing on a barrel at the other end.

But what everyone waits for are the two main events: the Guts and Glory Challenge, where prisoners try to snatch a poker chip worth $100 from between the horns of a 2,000-pound bull; and Convict Poker, where four men sit at a card table as a similarly large bull charges the table. Last man at the table wins the pot. Each rodeo rider is listed in the program by his name and his sentence. *Every Sunday in October; information: 225-655-2592.*

■ CLARK CREEK NATURAL AREA   *map page 83, A&B-1*

A worthy detour for the naturalist is this natural area, with its 30-foot rock "Woodville" waterfall. Just over the border in Mississippi, it isn't easy to find. It's not even on many maps. Locate Pinckneyville (to the south) and Fort Adams (to the north), get on LA 969, turn off on LA 66 toward the Tunica Hills and Angola. The area is about 15 miles to the west of Woodville, Mississippi, on LA 66, near the hamlet of Pond (pop. 5). From the other direction, go three miles north of St. Francisville, turn left on LA 66; after 13 miles turn right onto LA 969 for seven miles. Turn left at the pond.

You know you're in the right pew when you get to the **Pond Store,** located on the hill. It's been there since 1881, as has some of the merchandise—or so it appears. For a couple of bucks the owners will give you a tour of their house and the store. Grab whatever food you may need before heading into the 700-acre Clark Creek Natural Area. A 1.78-mile well-maintained gravel path gives access to six of the park's 50 waterfalls, which range from 10 to 30 feet high. Another 2.6-mile path takes you looping through the preserve. Plants and trees are well marked. There is also a labyrinth of primitive trails. Beware: these are challenging, not just because of the thick foliage, ridges, and hills, but also due to the threat of cottonmouth snakes and poison ivy. The Pond Store has a cabin. **Desert Plantation Bed & Breakfast,** three miles away, sits on a thousand-acre plantation and has its own walking trails and a pool (*see page 107*).

JULIA SANDERS' FLORA GUIDE: CLARK CREEK NATURAL AREA

Coral Bean

Erythrina herbacea

Flowers are a source of nectar for hummingbirds. Bean pods open to reveal bright red seeds. Blooms April through June. Abundant along portions of Clark Creek trails.

Rose Mallow

Hibiscus militaris

A cousin of okra, cotton, and tropical hibiscus. Blooms May to October. Grows to six feet tall in ditches, fresh marshes, and other wet sites.

■ ALONG HIGHWAY 61

Highway 61 (also known as the Blues Line), celebrated in so many blues and honky-tonk songs, makes the 1,500-mile trek from Thunder Bay, Canada, to the corner of Tulane Avenue and Broad Street in New Orleans. The road winds from St. Francisville towards the Mississippi border. On the stretch of road between St. Fran and Natchez there is a private prison and various yellow brick Jehovah's Witness Churches built in the "God's Little Ranch House" style. Many on the Louisiana side of the border sell fireworks in their front yards before Fourth of July and New Year's. In the spring the woods along the way are sugared with white dogwood blossoms and the road is bordered by breeze-rippled clover.

As the hills get a bit more pronounced, you will pass **South of the Border,** the landmark roadhouse that recently celebrated its 50th birthday. It's your last chance to eat good gumbo, play video poker, and buy a lottery ticket. In the old days, it was an illegal gambling hall, last stormed by the Feds in 1968.

◆ To Woodville, Mississippi   *map page 83, C-1*

Though officially neither on the River Road nor the Natchez Trace, Woodville (pop. 1,300) is a charming town on Hwy. 61 between St. Francisville and Natchez (or the farm-to-market highway, LA 66). It's the first historic town over the Mississippi border and the county seat of Wilkinson County, sitting on the southwestern corner of the state. Its fertile alluvial soil is called loess, a sugar-fine loam. It has a peculiar quality of standing in sheer walls for generations, then letting go in hunks taking all trees and buildings poised on it, toppling tons of earth upon whatever happens to be beneath.

This stretch of Highway 61, passes telephone poles and the random satellite dish, the gently rolling meadows, grazing cattle, and pecan groves. As William Faulkner said, "The past is never dead, as a matter of fact, it's not even past." Woodville is a genteel, old-time Southern town, with a fine courthouse square.

Rosemont, a simple wooden center-hall cottage built in 1814, was the childhood home of Confederate president Jefferson Davis. It remained in the Davis family until 1896 and contains some of the original Davis family furnishings. Tours give the feel of a working plantation with outbuildings, the Davis family cemetery, the rose garden, and the lovely wooded grounds. *From Hwy. 61, turn east on Hwy. 24. Continue one mile (north side of the road); 601-888-6809.*

Country roads and rural churches abound near the River Road. (Syndey Byrd)

■ RIVER ROAD FOOD & LODGING

by James Fox-Smith

☎ For chain lodgings see toll-free numbers on page 333.

$$ For room (☎) and restaurant (✕) price designations see page 333.

Baton Rouge
map page 83, C-3

✕**Chalet Brandt.** 7655 Old Hammond Hwy. at Jefferson Hwy.; 225-927-6040 $$$$
This Swiss-French restaurant has long set the standard for fine dining in the city; As a matter of fact, it's worth a trip to Baton Rouge just to eat here.

✕**The Chimes.** 3357 Highland Rd.; 225-383-1754 $- $$
Situated at the north gates of LSU, The Chimes teems with students, ex-students, and faculty at all hours, testimony to the interesting, reasonably priced menu, good daily specials, and often, live music. Huge range of specialty and imported beers, 30 of which are on tap.

✕**Desirée's.** 450 Main St.; 225-336-0685 $- $$
Every weekday Baton Rouge's business types swarm here to be pampered by white-aproned waiters serving inventive dishes with French, Creole, Asian, and Mexican influences. Menu changes weekly. Good bloody Marys, if you don't have to hit the road again. Lunch only.

✕**Di Giulio Bros.** 2903 Perkins Rd.; 225-383-4203 $$-$$$
This snug Italian bistro is the epitome of a neighborhood place. Through a hub-bub of conversation and Italian opera, waiters thread their way between tightly packed tables bearing tasty Italian fare. Pastas, pizzas, fine fresh seafood, and a terrific osso buco are all to be found. If there's a long wait, you can go to the bar across the road and they'll call you.

✕ **Mulate's.** 8322 Bluebonnet Blvd.; 225-767-4794 $$
For those in search of an exuberant Cajun experience without leaving the city, Mulate's offers a recreated Cajun-style dance hall, complete with dance band five nights a week. The menu includes all the Cajun mainstays—etouffée, jambalaya, gumbo, crawfish—and you can generally find someone who'll teach you the basics of a Cajun two-step or waltz.

Burnside *map page 62*

✕**The Cabin Restaurant.** Hwy. 22 at Hwy. 44; 225-473-3007 $-$$
A monument to recycling, this cleverly constructed building consists of salvaged materials from various Louisiana plantations. Elements from slave cabins, a distillery, even a cypress water cistern have been incorporated, resulting in a unique eating environment. Good hearty Cajun, Creole, and Southern specialties at reasonable prices, too.

Convent

map page 62

⊞ **Tezcuco Plantation.** 3138 LA 44; 225-562-3929 $-$$$

In testament to its name—which is an old Aztec word meaning Resting Place, Tezcuco welcomes visitors with wooden rocking chairs and porch swings, gracing the front porches of 11 cottages lining a small street leading up to the classical Greek Revival mansion. Breakfast is delivered by maids driving golf carts.

HYMEL'S RESTAURANT

✕ **Hymel's Restaurant & Bar.** 8740 LA 44 (between San Francisco and Tezcuco) 225-562-9910 $-$$

A seafood favorite for generations, Hymel's began as a dance hall 40 years ago, serving oysters on the half shell. In this classic Louisiana roadside diner, fourtops are layered with newspaper and a sheet of butcher paper—perfect for devouring the marvelous boiled, broiled, and fried seafood that keeps the tables full all week long.

Donaldsonville

map page 62

⊞ **Bittersweet Plantation.** 404 Claiborne Ave.; 225-473-1232 $$$$

Two luxuriously appointed suites are but a stagger up the staircase from Chef John Folse's acclaimed restaurant Lafitte's Landing, which occupies the lower floor (see below). You'll find luxuries like a central fireplace and antique-style sleigh bed topped with old-fashioned quilts alongside TV, CD player, exercise equipment, and kitchen facilities.

BITTERSWEET PLANTATION

✕ **Lafitte's Landing at Bittersweet Plantation.** 404 Claiborne Ave.; 225-473-1232 $$$-$$$$

Following a devastating fire that destroyed the world-renowned Lafitte's Landing restaurant near the foot of the Sunshine Bridge in 1998, Chef John Folse relocated the restaurant into his own home of 20 years. The fare is masterful: Cajun- and Creole-inspired delicacies of great complexity, served with impeccable attention to detail.

RIVER ROAD
FOOD & LODGING

RIVER ROAD
FOOD & LODGING

Gonzales (St. Amant)
map page 62

Rosewood Plantation. 10254 LA 431; 877-767-3007 or 225-675-8838 **$$**
A recent reproduction that pays tribute to Louisiana's antebellum architecture, Rosewood was reconstructed from salvaged materials from 40 plantation homes. Twenty-two suites in the main house, cottages, and side buildings offer a variety of accommodation choices. Full breakfast.

ROSEWOOD PLANTATION

✕ Sno's Seafood. Corner of Hwy. 74 and Hwy. 61; 225-647-2632 **$$**
Amid the wood-panel-and-wallpaper of a decades-old roadhouse cheery with the hubbub that only a local family place ever seems to have, waitresses distribute huge platters of delicious fried seafood to the hungry faithful. Steaks, sandwiches, and salads too.

Jackson
map page 83, C-1

The Lodge at the Bluffs on Thompson Creek. LA 965 at Freeland Rd., (six miles east of US 61); 888-634-3410 **$$**
Situated a moment's walk from the Arnold Palmer–designed Bluffs Golf Course, the Lodge can offer complete golfers' packages as well as overnight accommodations. Thirty-nine suites, a restaurant open daily (three meals), swimming pool, croquet, and tennis courts offer various diversions along the pretty banks of Thompson Creek.

Milbank. 3045 Bank St.; 225-634-5901 **$$**
This c. 1835 townhouse is a place of tall white columns and deep, cool double galleries. Two rooms feature en suite bathrooms, period antiques, and queen-sized beds. Another suite includes two bedrooms, shared bath, and sitting room. Full breakfast.

MILBANK

☷ **Old Centenary Inn.** 1740 LA 10; 225-634-5050 $$
In the heart of Jackson's historic district, the inn's eight rooms include one sporting a superbly recreated wagon bed and another with a sleigh bed that really lives up to its name. Antique furnishings are balanced by sleek modern amenities—private baths with jacuzzis, cable TV, and VCRs. A hearty breakfast may be taken in the lobby, in the ballroom, in the courtyard, or on your private balcony.

OLD CENTENARY INN

Livonia   *map page 83, B-3*

✕ **Joe's Dreyfus Store.** 2731 Maringouin Rd. (LA 77) about one mile south of LA 190 in Livonia; 225-637-2625 $$$ (no credit cards)
When Joe and Diane Major opened a restaurant 10 years ago in an 1870's general store, they would explain where it was by saying "at the old Dreyfus Store." The name stuck. Today, everybody for miles around knows how to get to Joe's. Expect luscious interpretations of Cajun and Creole classics, along with magnificent fresh seafood. A must.

Lutcher   *map page 62*

✕ **Nobile's Restaurant.** 2082 West Main St.; 225-869-8900 $
This family-owned-and-operated eatery specializes in local River Road fare, serving seafood, gumbos, soups, steaks, and po' boys in a casual setting. The menu makes the best of what's available from local fields and farms year round.

Maringouin   *map page 83, B-3*

✕ **Ox Bow Restaurant.** 6813 False River Dr.; 225-627-5285 $$
A recent move up the road to cozier quarters hasn't compromised chef Philip Plaisance's fare, which has been luring those traversing the shores of False River for 10 years. Kung pao oysters with garlic-ginger dipping sauce or corn-and-crab bisque are frequent offerings from the daily-changing carte du jour.

Napoleonville   *map page 62*

☷ **Madewood.** 4250 Hwy. 308; 504-369-7151 or 800-375-7151. $$$$
Built of brick and hand-carved cypress wood (hence the name "Made Wood"), this National Historic Landmark is today

acknowledged as one of the best preserved examples of Greek Revival architecture in Louisiana. The eight rooms provide a glimpse of old world graciousness in a setting removed from modern conveniences. There is wine and cheese every evening in the library. Breakfast and dinner, served in the formal dining room by long-time family retainers, are included in the price.

MADEWOOD

New Roads *map page 83, B-2*

☎ **Jubilee Bed & Breakfast.** 11704 Pointe Coupee Rd.; 225-638-8333 $-$$
Airy, spacious cypress cottage stands on tall piers, testimony to the fact that its construction predates that of the Mississippi River levee. Prior to 1880, Spring floods would turn the home into an island for months. Cozy attic rooms, all with fireplaces, share a book-lined common sitting room. Or try the private cottage with double jacuzzi. Swimming pool. Full breakfast.

MON COUR

☎ **Mon Cour.** 7739 False River Dr., Oscar; 225-638-9892 $$-$$$
The pineapples on the gateposts are a traditional Louisiana symbol of welcome. Three acres of secluded grounds surround an impressive home with two elaborate third-floor suites that share a fabulous balcony overlooking False River. Cozy book-lined ground floor rooms are another, less pricey option. Five-minute drive from downtown New Roads.

POINTE COUPEE B&B

☎ **Pointe Coupee B&B.** 405 Richey St.; 225-638-6254 $$
Guests enjoy the cozy atmosphere of this small B&B situated on a quiet street in

New Roads' historic district. Pretty garden and tasteful antiques, within easy walking distance of restaurants and False River.

✗ **Satterfield's.** 108 East Main St.; 225-638-5027 $$
Fresh fried seafood, tasty Cajun and Creole standards served with a view. A lofty second-floor dining room with wraparound terrace affords diners sweeping views of False River.

✗ **Ma Mama's.** 124 West Main St.; 225-618-2424. $$
"Recipes passed down from a long line of Mamas" contribute to the New Orleans –style cuisine, ambience, and decor of this small bistro across the road from False River.

St. Francisville
map page 83, B-2

⌂ **Butler Greenwood.** 8345 US 61, north of St. Francisville; 225-635-6312 $$
A half-mile of driveway winds through sinuous live oaks before depositing you at the door of this 200-year-old English planter's cottage, still occupied by the family who built it. Accommodations are in six private cottages: two original, four added. All are comfortable, dog friendly, romantic, and imaginatively decorated with more than a touch of whimsy.

⌂ **Green Springs.** 7463 Tunica Trace; 800-457-4978 or 225-635-4232 $$-$$$
Five authentic shotgun houses have been transported to this leafy hideaway in the

Tunica Hills and impeccably renovated as luxurious private cottages. Additional suites in the main house and various amenities provide many possibilities to choose from. Huge Southern breakfast, wooded walking trails, even a 2,000-year-old Indian mound.

⌂ **Rosedown Plantation.** 12501 LA 10; 225-635-3332 $$-$$$
Enjoy the extensive formal gardens and a self-guided tour of the 1850s plantation while relaxing in modern comfort in the B&B. Private bath, canopied beds, tennis courts, and pool.

⌂ **Shade Tree Inn.** Royal St. at Ferdinand St.; 225-635-6116 $$-$$$
One of St. Francisville's most renowned B&Bs. Adirondack-style rusticity, a lovely setting in the town's historic district, exquisite interior design, and most luxuries imaginable. Very private. Repeatedly described as magical.

SHADE TREE INN

✕**Club South of the Border.** US 61 just south of the Mississippi border; 225-635-3071 $-$$

Fifty years ago, this roadhouse did a roaring trade, thanks to the fact that the Mississippi county over the state line was dry. Today they're still coming for burgers, steaks, and fried seafood, alongside some interesting variations like crawfish Nyma (fried green tomatoes topped with crawfish in cream sauce). The waitresses still call you "hon."

✕**Kean's Carriage House.** On the grounds of the Myrtles Plantation, 7747 US 61; 225-635-6276 $$$

Intriguing eclectic fare is fitting for a restaurant on the grounds of what is reputed to be "America's Most Haunted House." Offerings include imaginatively treated meats, fish, and poultry on a menu that changes with the seasons. Sunday brunch, too.

✕**Magnolia Cafe.** 5687 E. Commerce St.; 225-635-6528 $

This one-time gas station has been the first and foremost lunch spot for most St. Francisvillians for almost 20 years. Great, fresh daily specials join a huge menu of just-made soups, salads, burgers, sandwiches, seafood, and Mexican fare. Homemade cookies every day. Serves dinner Thursday through Saturday.

Thibodaux   *map page 62*

🛏 **Danserou House.** 506 St. Philip St.; 504-447-1002 or 888-746-0122 $$$

Beginning its life in the 1840s as a large single-story cottage built in the 1840s, this house was extensively reconstructed to a splendid Second Empire–Italianate design in 1861. The three-story inn has a restaurant on the first floor and the second floor, four rooms fluffed up with antiques and lacy things.

✕**Danserou House.** 506 St. Philip St.; 504-447-1002 or 888-746-0122 $$-$$$

An impressive wine list sporting labels from California, Oregon, Australia, and Europe accompanies the Danserou House's extensive menu. You'll find everything from classic Southern plantation food to modern dishes in the French creole tradition. The sunset prix fixe menu is great value.

✕**Holiday Inn.** 400 East First St.; 504-446-0561 $$

Great breakfasts have a hometown flavor. As a matter of fact, locals swear by the restaurant. Rooms are typical motel fare - clean and quiet.

Vacherie   *map page 62*

🛏 **Bay Tree Plantation.** 3785 Hwy. 18 (River Rd.); 800-895-2109 $-$$$$

The choice of B&B suites in this c. 1850 French Creole cottage has recently been augmented by the addition of a new private cottage on the grounds. The Mississippi River levee in front; sugarcane in back; Oak Alley Plantation next door. Full breakfast.

⊡ **Oak Alley Plantation.** 3645 Hwy. 18 (River Rd.); 800-442-5539 $$
Viewed through its incomparable boulevard of live oaks, Oak Alley must be one of the most immediately recognizable—and photographed—Louisiana landmarks. This National Historic Landmark is open for tours, or you can install yourself in one of five turn-of-the-last-century cottages on the grounds. Full breakfast.

OAK ALLEY PLANTATION

White Castle *map page 62*

⊡ **Nottoway.** 30970 Hwy. 405; 225-545-2730 $$$-$$$$
Nottoway Plantation is such an extraordinary example of antebellum grandeur that the makers of *Gone With the Wind* tried, unsuccessfully, not once but three times to secure it as a location for their film. It is open for guided tours during the day and for overnight stays in one of the plantation's 13 B&B rooms. A huge plantation breakfast is served in the Magnolia Room on the first floor of the mansion. Randolph Hall, on the grounds of the plantation is open daily, serving Cajun and Southern dishes. www.nottoway.com.

NOTTOWAY

Woodville, Miss. Area
map page 83

⊡ **Desert Plantation.** 411 Desert Ln. (call for directions); 601-888-6889 $$
One thousand wooded acres surround an 1810 plantation mansion, providing bird-watchers, flower-pickers, and roamers with endless possibilities for wandering the nature trails. Suites are furnished with period pieces. Enormous country breakfasts, with optional evening meals available. Swimming pool.

⊡ **The Forest.** contact 601-639-4591 or www.forestretreat.com for details $$
Deep in the Homochitto State Forest on a dirt road accessible only by all-terrain vehicle. Three isolated cabins combine zen serenity with air-conditioned comfort and adorable furnishings. Lofts recommended only for the agile. Ideal for birders or those seeking solitude.

A C A D I A N A
by Stanley Dry

■ HIGHLIGHTS *page*

Food & Lodging, page 159
Map, page 120

■ TRAVEL OVERVIEW

Twenty-two parishes (read "counties") make up Acadiana, the Cajun heart of Louisiana. The "French Triangle," as it is sometimes called, stretches across southern Louisiana from the Texas border to New Orleans and tapers up to Avoyelles Parish in the center of the state.

Here we'll confine ourselves to central Acadiana, an area that will whet your appetite for all things Cajun. This section of Acadiana has been the epicenter of the cultural movement that has led to the rebirth of Cajun pride. It is also home to many of the best restaurants and music clubs in the entire Gulf South. To make the most of a visit here, stroll the streets of the charming small towns of New Iberia or Breaux Bridge, hire a local fishing guide, amble into the bayous, or linger in a local cafe. Almost every town has a bar where you can dance the night away. Just ask any local and they can tell you were to find the fun.

Travel: One of the Gulf South's busiest and most beautiful highways is the elevated portion of I-10 between Baton Rouge and Lafayette that passes over the 3,000-square-mile Atchafalaya Basin, America's largest overflow swamp. Be advised speed limits are strictly enforced. The highway is heavily patrolled both by car and plane. Figure about two hours or more (depending on traffic and construction delays) driving time between New Orleans and Lafayette. The Atchafalaya River Floodway, often referred to as "The Swamp Expressway" is 17.9 miles long.

Highway 90 between New Orleans and Lafayette is now four-lane. This route, which passes through the southern portion of the Atchafalaya Basin, is an alternative to the interstate preferred by some. Allow two-and-a-half to three hours' driving time between New Orleans and Lafayette.

On two-lane highways, going is slow and sometimes treacherous during the sugar cane harvest, when trucks overflowing with cane clog the roads. "Grinding season," as the harvest is called locally, runs from late September until the end of December.

Climate: As in much of the Gulf South, there are two principal seasons in Acadiana; the long hot summer and the few months a year that are not summer. Daytime summer temperatures range from the high 80s to the high 90s, but the humidity often pushes the discomfort index well above 100. In summertime, afternoon showers are frequent. Temperatures in the spring and fall, particularly March to May and September through October can be quite mild and pleasant. Winter temperatures alternate between extremes brought on by warm winds from the Gulf and cold fronts from the north. Temperatures often go into the 60s or 70s during the day, then drop into the 30s or 40s at night. When the temperature plunges, the high humidity creates a damp cold. At any time of the year, bring an umbrella and a light sweater or jacket—the umbrella for rain, the sweater or jacket for air conditioning. Rayne holds the state record for the heaviest snowfall—24 inches in 1895. Lafayette Parish had the state's highest monthly rainfall of 38 inches in 1940.

Food and Lodging: Cajun food is one of the principal attractions of the area, and appetites are well served by a variety of restaurants, ranging from simple plate lunch cafes and seafood patios to fancy dinner restaurants. It is possible to get a bad meal in Cajun country, but you'll have to work pretty hard to find one.

There are particularly nice accomodations to be had in the charming towns of Breaux Bridge and New Iberia; and houseboats to be rented in the Atchafalaya Basin. Chain hotels and motels are also available.

For restaurant and lodging listings, see page 159; see page 333 for price designations and toll-free numbers for chain accommodations. For a chart of listings by region, see page 334.

ACADIANA

■ ACADIAN HISTORY

Exiled from present-day Nova Scotia in 1755 for refusing to swear allegiance to the British crown, the French-speaking Acadians wandered for decades looking for a new home. Their search took them to various colonies along North America's eastern seaboard, to England, to France, and to present-day Haiti. Between 1765 and 1785, groups of these people settled in Louisiana, which was then under Spanish rule.

By the time of the Acadians' arrival, lower Louisiana already had a diverse population that included American Indians, French, Spanish, German, English, Swiss, Welsh, African slaves, and free people of color. With the passage of time, Acadians intermarried with other ethnic groups, including Anglo settlers and 19th-century immigrants from France. Remarkably, given the plurality of cultures and the original minority status of the Acadians, the Acadians absorbed the others and their Cajun culture became the dominant one.

Acadians are the largest French-speaking minority in the United States, with half a million of the country's three-quarter million Acadians living in Louisiana,

Fifth-generation Cajun cowboy Johnny Richard of Abbeville, poses with the saddles he makes and sells. (Syndey Byrd). His family has long raised cattle in the bayou country, not unlike that near Lake Martin near Breaux Bridge (Brian Gauvin).

Historians generally attribute the triumph of the Cajun culture to the close-knit family structure that characterized the original Acadian settlers and their desire to recreate on the Louisiana frontier the society they had been driven from in Nova Scotia. The Acadians were a hardy band of farmers, ranchers, and fishermen who proved themselves skilled at adapting to very different conditions in their new homeland. The original settlers were, by all accounts, not highly materialistic; they were more intent on establishing their own society where they could maintain their culture and engage in a self-sufficient lifestyle without outside interference.

Though of French descent, the Acadians had not been partisans of France in Nova Scotia (some, after all, had fled French religious persecution) and had skillfully managed to establish their own niche between French and British forces. The experiences of those exiled Acadians who were sent back to France to live for years under deplorable conditions before making their way to Louisiana only strengthened their anti-French sentiment.

Once settled in Bayou Teche country, the Acadians found themselves in conflict with uppity French landowners and cattle barons who were already firmly entrenched. Many Acadians responded by migrating further west to the isolated prairies of southwest Louisiana.

The Acadians did not remain a monolithic society for long. In the 1770s, some came to embrace the materialism of their new homeland, including the ownership of slaves. By 1810, one of the state's largest slave owners was an Acadian. In the antebellum period, Acadian society became increasingly complex and stratified as upwardly mobile Acadians sought to mimic the pretensions of the Creole grandees.

The reactions of Acadians to the Civil War followed class lines. Wealthy planters and slave owners supported secession, while non-slaveholding small farmers and ranchers did not, viewing the war as an elitist cause. Following the Civil War, Acadian society became increasingly divided into the rich and the poor, the landed gentry, merchants, and professionals who renounced their Acadian heritage and imitated the Anglo-American elite (the "genteel Acadians," as they have come to be called) and the landless sharecroppers. Increasingly, negative stereotypes were ascribed to the newly impoverished French-speaking Cajuns. Some historians estimate that the isolated Acadian parishes fell into a recession that lasted from the Civil War until World War II.

Beginning with legislation in 1916, a movement began to forcibly Americanize the Cajuns through compulsory education and the prohibition of the French language in the schools. Cajun assimilation accelerated with the construction of new highways and an influx of Anglo-Americans lured by the burgeoning oil business. The intrusion of the outside world with its "Americanizing" forces increased after World War II. After 1953, when the U.S. government authorized offshore drilling, Cajuns found themselves working side by side on the rigs with English-speaking men from all over the country. Not until the late 1960s, with the beginning of the French renaissance and the movement toward cultural preservation, did the term "Cajun" begin to lose its negative connotations.

■ CAJUN COOKING

Given the great diversity of cultures present in Acadiana, it is not surprising that Cajun cuisine is a kind of gumbo that reflects various ethnic influences. And while it's impossible to state with certainty how modern Cajun cooking evolved or which groups contributed what to the mix, we do know that today's Cajun food is very different from the diet of the Acadians in Nova Scotia or the Creoles in New Orleans. Fried foods and boiled or one-pot dishes are common to both, but the ingredients available to the Acadian settlers in Louisiana were very different from those in Nova Scotia.

"Bland" is not a term one would apply to Cajun food. Cajun cooking today has gained an undeserved reputation for being excessively spiced with cayenne pepper. While it is true that some dishes are highly spiced, most are not, even though many are seasoned at a level several notches above the American norm. Onions, garlic, bell pepper, and celery are commonly used as seasoning vegetables, and various forms of smoked pork find their way into many dishes.

Many restaurants in Acadiana specialize in one type of food or another, and residents think nothing of making a road trip to eat at a favorite spot. Restaurants featuring boiled seafood (sometimes called "seafood patios")—crawfish, crabs, and shrimp—in an informal atmosphere are extremely popular, especially on Friday nights. Some restaurants, particularly in Abbeville, specialize in oysters, others feature fried seafood, and every town has its little "plate lunch" spots that offer a main dish, rice, and a vegetable or two plus dessert for a fixed price.

One-pot dishes such as crawfish or shrimp etouffée and various stews or fricassees of crab, poultry, pork, or beef yield a rich "gravy" that is sometimes more esteemed than the main ingredient. All of these dishes are served with generous amounts of steamed rice. Interestingly, rice, which has come to characterize so much of Cajun cooking, did not become a staple of Cajun food until the early

20th century, after the commercial cultivation of rice began on the prairies. Prior to that, corn was the staple in Acadiana, as wheat had been the Acadians' staple in Nova Scotia. Ducks, geese, venison, and various game birds are highly esteemed in Acadiana, but wild game cannot legally be on restaurant menus.

The greatest dish in the Cajun repertoire is gumbo. Seafood or chicken and sausage are the versions most commonly found on restaurant menus, the former containing crab and oysters; chicken and sausage gumbo is made with chicken and either fresh or smoked sausage.

Boudin is a sausage made of seasoned ground pork and rice (many versions also contain liver). Widely available at grocery stores, meat markets, convenience stores, and gas stations, it is often eaten as a snack, sometimes with gratons or cracklins (fried pork skins) and always with a cold beer. Andouille ("AN-doo-EE") is a spiced and smoked pork sausage—unlike the andouille ("on-DWEE") of France, which contains chitterlings—frequently used in gumbos and other cooked dishes. Various other items of Cajun charcuterie include head cheese, chaurice (a smoked sausage), and tasso (spiced, smoked pork, used for seasoning).

Lester Bourgeois at his well-known meat market (see page 78) in Thibodaux, proudly exhibits his sausages and meats. (Syndey Byrd)

Zachary Richard, whom some call the "Mick Jagger of the Cajun world," performs at the Festival Acadien. (Syndey Byrd)

■ CAJUN MUSIC

Visitors to Acadiana are far more likely to hear French sung than spoken. In addition to food, Acadiana is best known for white Cajun music and the zydeco music of black Creoles. And when music is played, everyone—from toddlers to old ladies, priests to mechanics—dances.

Like jazz, the other music form native to the area, Cajun music and zydeco are open to many interpretations. While both are predominately "can't stop dancing" music sung in French, Cajun music stems from French and German musical traditions. Zydeco grew out of the musical traditions of West Africa, the hollers of the fields, and the guitar rifts of R&B. Both were shaped by the varied cultures of south Louisiana. Ethno-musicologist Barry Jean Ancelet describes a wide variety of cultural influences on the early development of Cajun music, citing contributions from Louisiana Indians, black Creoles, the Spanish, Santo Domingan refugees, even Anglo-Saxons. In particular, students of the two genres point to a fertile period of musical exchange between black and white sharecroppers who worked side-by-side in the early 20th century, a sharing that parallels the development of the region's cuisines.

Both Cajun and zydeco are accordion-dominated dance-oriented musical forms. Historians doubt that the Acadian exiles brought musical instruments with them, but they did bring their folk songs. By the early 19th century they were acquiring fiddles, and after the Civil War, German accordions. But without instruction manuals or with instructions only in German, the Louisiana musicians made up how they thought they should be played, including a lot of hip-wigglin'.

A dozen or more radio stations have some Cajun programming scheduled during the week. These have major Cajun music and talk:

KJEF (1290 AM, 927 FM; Jennings)   KRVS (88.7 FM; Lafayette)

KEUN (1490 AM; Eunice)   KJJB (105.5 FM; Eunice)

KBON (101.1 FM; Eunice)

To experience the "real deal," go to **Randol's** and **Prejean's** in Lafayette; **Mulate's** and **La Poussiére** in Breaux Bridge (1301 LA 347), and **Whiskey River Landing** on the Henderson levee. Or attend the Saturday night French "Rendez-Vous des Cadiens" radio broadcast from the Liberty Theater in Eunice. Next day, try live morning dance from 9 A.M until 1 P.M. at **Fred's Lounge** on Sixth Street in Mamou or listen to it broadcast live on KRVS.

Mulate's, in Breaux Bridge, is considered one of Cajun music's best venues. (Syndey Byrd)

Playing the signature instruments of zydeco—the accordion and the frottoir—two musicians jam in the back seat of a car near New Iberia in 1938. (Library of Congress)

■ ZYDECO MUSIC

Folklorist Nicholas Spitzer describes zydeco as a mixture of Afro-American blues (tunes, texts, tonality), Afro-Caribbean rhythms, and Cajun dance songs. In the 1930s, zydeco phraseology often repeated "la-la" and "bazar" giving the style some early nicknames. The expression "les haricots (lay-ZAH-ree-COE) ne sont pas salés" —"the beans aren't salty"—is often cited as the source for the name zydeco. Barry Jean Ancelet sees the expression as a metaphor for hard times, when folks couldn't afford salt pork to season their stewed snap beans.

The 20-to-30-pound pearlized and gilded accordion is a jewel in the zydeco crown, but not the only one. The hip-grinding thunder of the syncopation comes from the "frottoir," or rubboard—a corrugated metal washboard worn like a vest and scraped with a pair of hearty kitchen spoons or bottle openers. The original ones were literally the ice drip pans the musicians borrowed from their mamas' old ice boxes. More recently, Grammy Award–winning zydeco legends Clifton and

Cleveland Chenier of Opelousas created a wearable model which allows freedom of movement. Added to these instruments is an electric guitar, whose pulsating sound drives the music into the bloodstream: you can hear the dancers echo the guitar's staccato clap with their stomping heels.

Zydeco club patrons are predominantly black. Observe proper juke joint etiquette—never dance with someone else's mate and watch where you spill your beer. (Check listings in local papers for times.)

Hamilton's Place

The mother lode of zydeco: Hamilton's has the rural look it had when it was a true country bar, before the town grew up around it; *1808 Verot School Rd. in Lafayette; 337-984-5583.*

Ed Sid O's

Nathan & the Zydeco Cha Chas and Buckwheat Zydeco often play here; *1523 N. St. Antoine in Lafayette; 318-237-1959.*

Richard's Club

Kermon Richard's, Richard's Club is a hotbed of zydeco in a remote location, west of Opelousas. *US 190 W in Lawtell; 337-543-6596.*

Slim's Y-Ki-Ki

A legendary zydeco club near Opelousas on LA 182.

Patrons schmooze while listening to zydeco at Slim's Y-Ki-Ki Club near Opelousas. (Syndey Byrd)

■ LAFAYETTE *map page 120, B-2*

Lafayette (pop. 110,000) is the largest city in Acadiana, a shopping, medical, and entertainment hub for the surrounding area and the administrative base for the offshore oil and gas industry. A boomtown, it's adorned with malls and more concrete than greenery. It also has restaurants of every description, a thriving arts community, and an active club and concert scene.

Lafayette was once an agricultural center, as the Regal Yam, who reigned in nearby Scott, testifies. (courtesy of the Dinkins Collection)

More importantly, Lafayette has been the center of the remarkable French renaissance that began in the late 1960s and continues today. The signs of it are everywhere, from downtown street markers in French, to the popularity of Cajun cooking, Cajun and zydeco music, and, most importantly, the resurgence in pride among the Cajun people themselves. Lafayette's two major festivals—**Festival International de Louisiane** in April and **Festivals Acadiens** in September—are outgrowths of the French cultural movement and represent its two primary goals: to understand and preserve Cajun heritage and culture, and to foster ties between Acadiana and other French-speaking communities all over the world. Recently, the Louisiana World Congress of Acadians assembled more Acadians in Lafayette than have been together since their expulsion from Canada in 1755. Eighty-two separate Acadian family reunions were held around the Acadian religious holiday, The Feast of Assumption.

For most of Lafayette's history, the town was a sleepy agricultural center. Beginning in the 1950s, with the development of the Oil Center, a modern mixed-use office and retail complex targeted to oil and gas companies, the city began to change. With that growth has come sprawl, urban ills, and rush-hour traffic jams. Lafayette's street patterns defy comprehension. The fastest route from one area to another is often through a maze of residential and back streets off the main thoroughfares that only a native would know.

In recent years a downtown revitalization program has turned central Lafayette into an attractive place to stroll and browse in shops and galleries. In the spring, Lafayette explodes with color when the azaleas, widely planted throughout the city, come into bloom.

ACADIANA

◆ LAFAYETTE SIGHTS

Acadian Cultural Center

The best place to start a visit to Lafayette is at the Acadian Cultural Center, conveniently located across the street from the airport. The center's museum provides a good introduction to the history and culture of the region. The exhibits make extensive use of photographs with explanatory panels; there are also tools, musical instruments, models of Acadian houses, kitchen artifacts, recordings of Cajun jokes told in French and English, and the like. In the theater, a film depicts the expulsion of the Acadians from Nova Scotia; some find it over-dramatized and sentimental. *Daily 8-5, free; 501 Fisher Rd.; 337-232-0789.*

Vermilionville

Adjacent to the Acadian Cultural Center is Vermilionville, a re-creation of an early 19th-century village located in a 23-acre park. Guided tours are available, or you can see it on your own with the aid of an interpretive brochure. Some of the structures are originals that were moved to the site, others are re-creations. Cooking classes and demonstrations of Acadian crafts such as weaving, blacksmithing, and sewing are held in the buildings, and music performances are given twice daily.

Vermilionville will give you an understanding of the architecture of the period, including the use of *bousillage,* a mixture of mud and Spanish moss (and sometimes horse hair) that served as wall insulation.

A word of warning: some might find Vermilionville a touch sanitized and incomplete. *Daily 10–5; 1600 Surrey St.; 337-233-4077 or 800-992-2968.*

Acadian Village

Acadian Village, located on the east side of Lafayette and virtually impossible to find without a map, is another re-creation of a 19th-century Acadian settlement. Apart from the general store and the chapel, all of the houses are originals built in the early and mid-1800s that were moved to the site.

One interesting home at Acadian Village is the **birthplace of state senator Dudley J. LeBlanc,** a colorful man affectionately known as "Coozan Dud." He was a long-time advocate of Cajun pride, a populist politician who championed the poor, and the founder of the Happy Day Company in Lafayette, which produced Happy Day Headache Powders, Happy Day Mamou Cough Syrup, and Dixie Dew Cough Syrup. But Coozan Dud's most famous product was Hadacol, a high-alcohol tonic that was credited with every sort of medical miracle imaginable. When asked what Hadacol was good for, Coozan Dud liked to reply, "for me, about a million a year." The exhibits in the LeBlanc house include memorabilia from the days of the Hadacol Caravans, LeBlanc's traveling medicine shows that featured movie stars and country musicians such as Hank Williams.

In addition to the homes, an art gallery features a series of paintings by Lafayette artist George Rodrigue depicting central events in the Acadian/Cajun experience, as well as rotating exhibits of other local artists.

ACADIANA

The Mississippi Valley Missionary Museum, located on the grounds of Acadian Village, focuses on Native American culture. A recreated **doctor's office and museum** will make you thankful for the miracles of modern medicine. *200 Greenleaf Dr.; 337-981-2364.*

Lafayette Museum/ Mouton House

In the central section of the city, The Lafayette Museum/Alexandre Mouton House contains exhibits relating to the history of the city. The original house belonged to Jean Mouton, the city's founder. The house was enlarged by his son Alexandre, Louisiana's first Democratic governor and a leader of the vigilante movement of the mid–19th century. Among the exhibits are costumes from Lafayette's Mardi Gras royalty, King Gabriel and Queen Evangeline (who take their names from the Longfellow poem) and a quilt stitched by Abraham Lincoln's mother. *Open Tues–Sat 9–5, Sun 3–5; 1122 Lafayette St. near Convent St.; 337-234-2208.*

Cathedral of St. John The Evangelist

An imposing Dutch-Romanesque structure built in 1916, this is the cathedral for the Diocese of Lafayette. It stands on the land Jean Mouton donated in 1821. Behind the church is Cathedral Cemetery, and to the right of the church is the **Cathedral Oak,** estimated to be between 400 and 500 years old; its branches spread 145 feet. The tree is vice-president of the Live Oak Society. Membership in the group is restricted to the oldest and most beautiful live oaks in Louisiana. Dues are 45 acorns per year. *914 St. John's St.; 337-232-1322.*

University of Louisiana at Lafayette

ULL boasts of more than 15,000 "Ragin' Cajuns." Signs on campus read "Alligator Habitat–Keep Pets on Leashes." The university faculty includes some of the world's authorities on local culture, history, and anthropology. Check the listings in the *Times of Acadiana* for lectures and campus events. *University Circle; 337-482-1000.*

USGS National Wetlands Research Center

Ecologists at the center conduct important research on our national wetlands. Louisiana contains 25 percent of the vegetated wetlands and 40 percent of the tidal wetlands in the 48 coterminous states. The state also leads the nation, and possibly the world, in coastal erosion and wetland loss. The center's exhibits include a man-made wetland with native plants and animals. Tours are available by appointment, which should be made at least 10 days in advance. *Located in the University's Research Park; 700 Cajundome Blvd.; 337-266-8655. www.nwrc.usgs.gov.*

The chapel at Acadian Village is a popular place for weddings. (Syndey Byrd)

ACADIANA

■ BREAUX BRIDGE: "CRAWFISH CAPITAL" *map page 120, B/C-2*

It's only eight miles from Lafayette to friendly, lovely Breaux Bridge (pop. 6,500) on LA 94 (locally known as the Breaux Bridge Highway). Just outside Lafayette, you pass a Carmelite Monastery and the headquarters of the Roman Catholic Diocese in an unexpectedly hilly landscape formed by ancient meanderings of the Mississippi River. A few miles further, the road straightens out and runs over the more familiar flat south Louisiana landscape. One of the state's many salt domes is situated off the highway.

This road used to be home to a number of bars and clubs that offered "short-term female companionship" as well as liquor, but these days it seems pretty tame, almost bucolic. Cattle and horses graze in the lush, green fields, residences and small businesses pop up here and there, and the only visible reminder of its shady past is a forlorn adult video store housed in a mobile home.

As you come into the outskirts of Breaux Bridge (founded in 1829 by a woman named Scholastique Breaux), **Mulate's** restaurant and dance hall is on the right. In the 1980s, Mulate's became a beacon for tourists in search of Cajun food and music. There have always been numerous clubs in the area that feature Cajun and zydeco music, but many of them are in out-of-the-way places and most offer music only on the weekends. Then along came Mulate's in its modern reincarnation (it had existed as a local joint for decades). It was easy to find, had a safe, family atmosphere, offered food and live music nightly. Add to that the owners' flair for promotion, and not surprisingly, it was an overnight sensation. As other accessible venues for local music have developed, Mulate's no longer has a monopoly, but it is still a reliable spot for Cajun music and dancing.

Take a right on LA 31 at the intersection just past Mulate's and go to Rue Pont (Bridge Street), where a left turn will bring you into the **historic district.** The **Bayou Teche Visitors Center** is just down the street before the bridge. Actually the bridge is how Breaux Bridge got its name. The town used to be called La Pointe. Locals preferred to refer to the place as where Agricole Breaux (pronounced "Bro'") built a bridge across Bayou Teche.

Not that many years ago, this was an area of unenticing abandoned storefronts. Visitors would flock to Mulate's at the edge of town, then depart without even making a trip downtown. Today, the area is home to antique shops, bed and breakfasts, and great places to eat. And, as benefits the Crawfish Capital of the World, the town hosts the **Breaux Bridge Crawfish Festival,** held the first weekend in May, one of the most popular festivals in all of south Louisiana.

■ ATCHAFALAYA WETLAND   *map page 120, C/D-1/6*

With the growth of the commercial crawfish industry in the 1960s, the little village of Henderson, just down the road from Breaux Bridge, became the center of crawfish processing. A cluster of tourist-oriented businesses has grown up around the interstate exit. The town itself straddles LA 352 between the exit and the Atchafalaya Basin levee.

When you reach the end of the highway at the levee turn right and follow the blacktop, taking particular note of the "Substandard Road" sign. This is the west protection levee of the Atchafalaya Basin, built as a WPA project in the 1930s to avoid a repeat of the disastrous 1927 flood. The adventurous can drive it all the way to Morgan City (about 70 miles)—hopefully in a sturdy, all-terrain vehicle.

The Atchafalaya Wetland is North America's last great free-flowing river-basin swamp, a watery expanse about 100 miles long and 30 miles wide. It is laced with lakes and bayous and clumps of land that may appear to be islands, but have the consistency of coffee grounds even though they have thick cypress and willow trees sprouting from them. The casual visitor can often see herons, white-tailed deer, even alligators. There are several commercial boat launches located along the levee just outside **Henderson** *(map page 120, C-2)*.

Boaters glide through the Atchafalaya Wetlands, land of bayous, cypress trees, birds, and alligators. (Syndey Byrd)

Wetland Boat Tours:
Touring the Atchafalaya Basin in a 17-seat pontoon boat, you'll have a chance to glimpse swamp life, usually including alligators, up close. Those following are near Henderson *(map page 20, C-2)* but it's best to call for directions. Try **Angelle's Whiskey River Landing,** 337-228-8567 or **McGee's Landing,** 337-228-2384. McGee's has a restaurant and bar built out over the water with good views of Henderson Lake, once home to groves of giant cypress that were thousands of years old. Today, clusters of stumps are the only legacy left us by greedy timber barons.

More personalized tours of the Basin and nearby Lake Martin in smaller boats are offered by Lafayette-based **Atchafalaya Experience Swamp Tours.** The owner, Coerte Voorhies, also owns Bois des Chênes, a Lafayette bed-and-breakfast, from which the tour departs: *338 N. Sterling St., Lafayette; 337-233-7816.*

Other landings along the levee offer cabins right on the water and houseboat rentals. Staying overnight on a houseboat deep in the basin is unforgettable, especially for birders. The time before dawn is ghostly still—"as if every living being is listening to the silence of God" says bayou native Gerard Sellers. Houseboats are for rent at **Cypress Cove Landing,** *800-491-4662.*

(above) An alligator drifts through shallow dark waters. (Brian Gauvin)

(previous pages) Bayou scene: egrets and a great blue heron in flight. (Brian Gauvin)

Julia Sanders' Flora Guide: Acadiana

| **Painted coreopsis** | **Passion flower, maypop** |
| *Coreopsis tinctoria* | *Passiflora incarnata* |

This colorful annual readily reseeds in the wild and in the garden. Blooms April through June. Plentiful in Acadiana, sometimes covering roadsides, fields, and other open areas.

A vine with beautiful and unusual flowers and edible fruit. Blooms May to September. Can be found growing on fences and sunny places throughout the region.

■ LAKE FAUSSE POINT STATE PARK   *map page 120, D-3*

About 15 miles down the west Atchafalaya levee road is Lake Fausse Point State Park, where you can rent a cabin, take a hike, or rent a canoe. It isn't easy to find. It is also accessible from St. Martinville, but it's more than 20 slow miles out of town. (From St. Martinville, take LA 96 east. After about two miles take a right onto Rte. 679. At Coteau Holmes, make a left onto Rte. 3083. Beware that the paved road ends at Levee Rd. Turn right and follow the road for seven miles.) *For details on renting comfortable lakeside cabins, tent platforms, and canoes see page 163; 5400 Levee Rd.; 337-229-4764 or 888-677-7200.*

■ SCENIC ROAD AND CYPRESS ISLAND PRESERVE   *map page 120, C-2*

One of the loveliest drives in an area known for its pretty drives is further west of the Atchafalaya Basin at Lake Martin, three miles south of Breaux Bridge off Highway 31. The Nature Conservancy maintains this stretch of gravel road leading to its Cypress Island Preserve at Lake Martin, the largest white ibis rookery in the world. It is also home to thousands of roseate spoonbills, egrets, and herons, which flock to the nearby crawfish ponds.

ACADIANA

■ BAYOU TECHE   *map page 120, C/D-4*

Two roads lead from Breaux Bridge to St. Martinville (pop. 7,100) 13 miles away, one on each side of Bayou Teche. The western road is the more traveled, the black-topped LA 347 on the east is more scenic. Teche is a Native American word for snake, and a glance at a map will reveal how apt the name is. About 5,000 years ago, the main channel of the Mississippi River flowed along the course of Bayou Teche. Settlement patterns along the bayou followed those of other waterways in south Louisiana. Because boats were the principal (if not only) means of travel, water frontage was essential for settlers who needed to receive supplies and ship crops and livestock. As a result, land grants were long and narrow, running back from the bayou, with each grant receiving a small amount of water frontage.

The road runs between Bayou Teche and expansive fields of cane, shaded at points by large live oaks draped with Spanish moss. The road makes a sharp turn at the small town of **Parks,** and a little further down the road you'll come to the St. Louis Catholic Church. To the side of the church is the **Dauphine Club,** a week-end mecca for zydeco musicians and dancers. Just below Parks you pass **St. John's Plantation.** The home is private, but it's worth a brief stop to view the house and grounds from the road. The sugar mill is set back off the highway.

In old-time Acadiana, moss was used to stuff mattresses and to chink log walls. In the 1940s, Elemore Morgan demonstrated how to go about moss collection. (Louisiana State Univ. Press)

FISHING IN THE BAYOU

*A*t noon I drove down the dirt road by the bayou toward my dock and bait shop. Through the oak trees that lined the shoulder I could see the wide gallery and purple-streaked tin roof of my house up the slope. It had rained again during the morning, and the cypress planks in the walls were stained the color of dark tea, the hanging baskets of impatiens blowing strings of water in the wind. My adopted daughter Alafair, whom I had pulled from a submerged plane wreck out on the salt when she was a little girl, sat in her pirogue on the far side of the bayou, fly-casting a popping bug into the shallows.

I walked down the dock and leaned against the railing. I could smell the salty odor of humus and schooled-up fish and trapped water out in the swamp.

꿏ꕉ ꕉꕉ

"*W*rong time of day and too much rain," I said.

"Oh, yeah?" she said.

She lifted the fly rod into the air, whipping the popping bug over her head, then laying it on the edge of the lily pads. She flicked her wrist so the bug popped audibly in the water, then a goggle-eye perch rose like a green-and-gold bubble out of the silt and broke the surface, its dorsal fin hard and spiked and shiny in the sunlight, the hook and feathered balsa-wood lure protruding from the side of its mouth.

Alafair held the rod up as it quivered and arched toward the water, retrieving the line with her left hand, guiding the goggle-eye between the islands of floating hyacinths, until she could lift it wet and floppinginto the bottom of the pirogue.

"Not bad," I said.

—Sunset Limited, James Lee Burke, 1998

■ ST. MARTINVILLE   *map page 120, C-3*

St. Martinville is a delightful old colonial settlement, founded as the Poste de Art-takapas in 1756. The town is built around the lovely **St. Martin de Tours Catholic Church** and square. The congregation dates from 1765; the present church was completed in 1844 and serves as the mother church of the Acadians. Worshippers are called to prayer by three bells named Marie Angeli, Auguste, and Stephanie. *133 S. Main; 337-394-6021.*

In recent years, the charming, two-story buildings downtown, with their second-story balconies, have been spiffed up, and the old opera house has been restored. A number of restaurants, a bakery, and antique stores are ranged around the church square.

Le Maison DuChamp, built in 1876, is one of many graceful and historic buildings surrounding St. Martin Square in St. Martinville. (Brian Gauvin)

Le Petit Paris Museum

Adjacent to the church, this museum celebrates local Mardi Gras royalty. To the side of the church is a bronze statue of Emmeline La Biche, (known as Evangeline) donated by the actress Dolores Del Rio, who played title role in the movie *Evangeline,* filmed here in 1929. Perhaps it was the attention of Hollywood that resulted in the naming of the first state park after a mythic Acadian. Ironically, the park, dedicated five years after the release of the movie, is located on a Creole plantation where there is no record of an Acadian ever setting foot. *Adjacent to St. Martin de Tours Church at 133 S. Main St.; 337-394-7334.*

Acadian Memorial

Located on the bayou behind the church, in what was originally a market building, is the Acadian Memorial, honoring the exiles from Nova Scotia. One wall is inscribed with the names of Acadian refugees who arrived in Louisiana; the opposite wall is covered with a large mural depicting their arrival. *Behind St. Martin de Tours; 337-394-2258.*

Adjacent to the memorial is the **St. Martinville Cultural Heritage Museum,** which focuses on the history of African Americans in the area.

Evangeline Oak

The Evangeline Oak, long St. Martinville's biggest tourist attraction, is just past the museum, on the bank of Bayou Teche. It is a rather unspectacular tree by live-oak standards, but it is the mythical meeting place of Evangeline and Gabriel in Longfellow's epic poem *Evangeline.*

During the annual pepper festival the hot-pepper-eating contestants line up under it to compete. So many people have stood under the oak to be photographed that the heavy foot traffic has endangered the tree and visitors are now asked to stay on the sidewalk. Most days local musicians will be playing nearby.

The Evangeline Oak was an important spot in Huey Long's rise to power. *(See page 185)* In 1927, during his successful campaign for governor, as he was seeking the south Louisiana vote to augment his solid standing in the northern portion of the state, Long made one of his most celebrated speeches beneath the famous tree:

And it is here, under this oak where Evangeline waited for her lover, Gabriel, who never came. This oak is an immortal spot, made so by Longfellow's poem, but Evangeline is not the only one who has waited here in disappointment. Where are the schools that you have waited for your children to have, that have never come? Where are the roads and the highways that you send your money to build, that are no nearer now than ever before? Where are the institutions to care for the sick and the disabled?

The Romero Brothers can often be found performing in front of the Evangeline Oak in St. Martinsville. (Brian Gauvin)

Evangeline wept bitter tears in her disappointment, but it lasted through only one lifetime. Your tears in this country, around this oak, have lasted for generations. Give me the chance to dry the tears of those who still weep here!

The romantic Evangeline legend is only one of the myths that have surrounded St. Martinville. The town was long thought to have been the site of the first Acadian settlement, but modern scholarship puts that site closer to Loreauville, further down Bayou Teche. Similarly, St. Martinville has been called "Le Petit Paris" in memory of a supposedly golden age ushered in by the arrival of French aristocrats fleeing the French Revolution. But again, modern historical research has found the aristocrat claim baseless.

The office of Henri Clay Bienvenu's weekly, the *Teche News,* is on Main Street near the church square. It's worth a stop to buy a copy of the paper, which will give you a good sense of contemporary life in the small towns of St. Martin Parish. *214 N. Main St.*

Longfellow-Evangeline State Historic Site

This 147-acre park, north on Highway 31 from the downtown area, features a two-room interpretive area with a worthwhile exhibit of photographs and artifacts depicting 19th-century life. An Acadian homestead and a Creole plantation home show the contrast between how the wealthy and the poor lived. *1200 N. Main St.; 337-394-3754 or 888-677-2900.*

Highway 31 follows Bayou Teche for several miles, then cuts abruptly south to the town of New Iberia, and then meanders through lush, green fields of sugarcane and shaded canopies of stately live oaks. The bayou takes a more leisurely route, slithering east to Loreauville, then south, before looping back toward New Iberia. This is the country local writer James Lee Burke describes so evocatively in a series of popular novels, including *Sunset Limited* and *A Stained White Radiance,* featuring the detective Dave Robicheaux, a man who, tormented by his own private demons, derives emotional sustenance from this serene bayou world.

At the outskirts of New Iberia (pop. 31,800), gracious dwellings with large landscaped lawns are interspersed with mobile homes, creating a jarring juxtaposition of rich and poor that defines the entire region.

In addition to sugar, Iberia Parish depends on offshore oil and gas, and her prosperity rises and falls with the price of black crude. Most of the companies that constitute the backbone of the industrial sector are located at the Port of Iberia south of the city and along the 25-mile stretch of Highway 90 between New Iberia and Lafayette.

■ NEW IBERIA *map page 120, C-3*

Founded by settlers from Malaga, Spain, in 1779, during the Spanish colonial period, New Iberia thrived and grew prosperous off numerous sugar plantations that developed in the area. Spanish names such as Romero, Miguez, and Lopez are common, but Spanish as a spoken language is not. Only when Mexican laborers are brought in for planting and harvesting cane in the fall does one hear Spanish on the streets of New Spain.

The newest immigrants to the area are from Southeast Asia, principally Vietnam and Laos. Three Asian grocery stores on Hopkins Street have greatly increased the range of foodstuffs available to local residents.

The city boasts an impressive gift from Spain: a seven-foot-tall **statue of the Roman Emperor Hadrian** (A.D. 117-138). (Hadrian was born in what is today Spain, then known as Iberia). It stands at 301 East St. Peter, at Weeks.

The **downtown business area**, which abuts the Historic District, was largely rebuilt after an 1899 fire. In recent years, the area has been spruced up. The art deco **Evangeline Theatre,** resplendently restored, now serves as a venue for theater and cultural events. Several galleries and antique shops make for good browsing. **Books Along The Teche** stocks autographed copies of James Lee Burke's novels.

The Historic District on East Main Street in the center of town contains a number of interesting homes in a variety of styles including Victorian, Steamboat Gothic, Queen Anne Revival, and Georgian Revival, built in the 19th and early 20th centuries. A slow drive or walk along the live-oak-shaded street is as tranquil an experience as one could imagine. Most of the homes are private, but several have been turned into charming bed-and-breakfasts.

The oldest and most notable home in the district is **Shadows-on-the-Teche,** which is open to the public. Built in 1834 by sugar planter David Weeks, the plantation home and gardens on Bayou Teche were preserved in this century and donated to the National Trust by Weeks Hall, the great grandson of the original inhabitants. *317 E. Main St.; 337-369-6446.*

Hall often entertained literary figures and Hollywood celebrities such as Sherwood Anderson, Mae West, and Henry Miller in the home. ("Tomorrow I'll tell you about my stay in New Iberia. It's a book in itself," Henry Miller wrote to Anaïs Nin in 1941.) Weeks also employed Willie Geary "Bunk" Johnson, the renowned coronet player, as a yardman at Shadows-on-the-Teche.

The Episcopal **Church of the Epiphany** (1856) is one of the oldest brick

JAZZ GREAT "BUNK" JOHNSON

Willie Geary "Bunk" Johnson, born in New Orleans in 1880, was working as a professional musician by the time he was 15. Johnson traveled the country playing with Jelly Roll Morton and Buddy Bolden, and is the musician who taught a young Louis Armstrong how to place his mouth on the coronet to emulate their smooth rifts or licks.

New Iberia was a hotbed of jazz in the early 20th century, and in 1914, "Bunk" Johnson came to this city on the banks of the Teche to perform with Gus Fortinet's Banner Band, the most commercially successful jazz band outside of New Orleans. After falling in love with the band leader's daughter, Maude, Johnson decided to make New Iberia his home. But jazz didn't pay the bills and Johnson's teeth were soon in such bad shape, that he could barely play the horn.

In 1932, Johnson's instrument was smashed in a fight at a concert in Rayne, and Bunk gave up music for 10 years, taking a job as a yard man at one of the historic homes in the area, Shadows-on-the-Teche. Johnson was famous for his devotion to the owner's English setter. Feeling "Spot" was too much of a lady to eat canned dog food, Bunk cooked special meals for her consisting of seasoned hash and yellow grits served with black coffee.

In 1937, Louis Armstrong played in New Iberia and rediscovered his mentor. In 1942 he asked jazz historian Bill Russell if he could arrange to have Johnson fitted with new teeth. Once that was accomplished, Louis Armstrong presented his Johnson with a new trumpet and the opportunity to tour with his band in 1944.

Johnson died in 1949 and is buried in St. Edward Cemetery. A Bunk Johnson Memorial Plaza has been constructed at Hopkins Street and Babb Alley, and the musician is celebrated annually at the Bunk Johnson/New Iberia Jazz, Arts & Heritage Festival in the spring.

—Stanley Dry

The garden at Shadows-on-the-Teche, where the famous jazz coronet player Bunk Johnson worked as a gardener. (Syndey Byrd)

Lush, green rows of sugarcane line a country lane in Louisiana. (Syndey Byrd)

Gothic Revival churches in Louisiana, and the earliest non-residential building in New Iberia. During the Civil War it had the distinction of serving as both a hospital and a prison. *303 W. Main St.; 337-369-9966.*

♦ OTHER STOPS AND THINGS TO DO

Some of the most creative and elegantly prepared regional cooking in the entire Acadiana region is served in New Iberia. For ideas about places to eat see page 163. For shoppers, the **Konriko Company Store** in central New Iberia offers a variety of local products, as well as a tour of the country's oldest rice mill (where Bunk Johnson also worked). There's a video on Cajun Cuisine. *Mon–Sat; 309 Ann St.; 337-367-6163 or 800-551-3245.*

The **Olivier Plantation Store**, located about seven miles south of town on LA 83, still contains most of the store's original fixtures as well as displays of period merchandise from the turn of the century. The shelves are stocked with a beguiling variety of goods, from Victorian greeting cards to windup tin toys and oil lamps. *Open Sat 10–5; Sun 12–6; 6703 Weeks Island Rd.*

In recognition of the area's most important crop, New Iberia's biggest celebration is the **Sugar Cane Festival** held in late September. It's part country fair and part *fais do do. (see page 339).*

In this portion of Acadiana lie expansive fields of sugarcane. The landscape changes dramatically during the year, depending on the height of the cane. After the fall harvest, the barren fields stretch out to the horizon. By summertime, the lush green cane is thick and high, giving the landscape a closed-in, tropical feel. Between New Iberia and the town of Franklin, you'll see the M. A. Patout Mill, the largest sugar mill in the state. South of Bayou Teche on LA 329, the road traverses marshland that extends to the Gulf of Mexico.

■ AVERY ISLAND AND TABASCO SAUCE *map page 120, C-4*

The exit for the Avery Island is clearly marked, and a few miles down the road, Avery Island comes into view, rising 150 feet above the flat landscape, like a small mountain plunked down in the marshlands. The island covers about 2,500 acres.

Formed by a large salt dome that rose up through lighter layers of rock and soil, Avery Island was a source of salt for Native Americans as early as A.D. 1000. The first European colonists settled the island about 1790. In 1862, John Marsh Avery discovered the solid rock salt, which was used to supply Confederate troops until the salt works were destroyed the following year by the Union army. There is a

The Tabasco Sauce label is the second oldest trademark in the United States. The pepper sauce has been made on Avery Island by the McIlhenny family for more than a century. (Syndey Byrd)

ACADIANA

productive salt mine on the island, but it's pepper—Tabasco Pepper Sauce—and not salt that has made Avery Island famous the world over. The Tabasco Country Store offers Louisiana merchandise.

A tour of the **Tabasco factory** includes an informative video about Tabasco, including its history and an explanation of how the sauce is made. It is a fascinating story, full of ritual and surprising details, such as the fact that each year the McIlhennys store a batch of the precious pepper seeds in a New Iberia bank vault to insure continuity in the event of a natural disaster. Tabasco is the second oldest food trademark in the United States. One of the changes that has

Chili peppers, the key ingredient in Tabasco Sauce, are still grown on Avery Island. (Syndey Byrd)

occurred on Avery Island is the makeup of the labor force. Most of the workers who pick peppers today are Vietnamese women. *As you cross onto the island, the road stops right before the factory; 337-365-8173 or 800-634-9599.*

◆ JUNGLE GARDENS AND BIRD CITY   *map page 120, C-4*

Jungle Gardens features the most complete collection of camellias in the world with nearly 1,000 varieties. They bloom in the cooler months. The gardens are particularly nice in the spring when the azaleas are in bloom and when egrets nest on the bamboo-covered platforms in the lake. **Bird City,** a 250-acre Eden, is one of the largest egret rookeries in the world. Each year egrets return in droves to this lake to mate. By late summer, the trees surrounding the lake are white with nesting egrets. *Adjacent to the Tabasco plant. Open daily; 337-369-6243.*

ACADIANA

ACADIANA

■ JEFFERSON ISLAND   *map page 120, B-4*

Take the Avery Island Road back to Highway 14 and head west. A big sign for Rip Van Winkle Gardens and Rip Van Winkle Drive will take you to Jefferson Island, first settled about 1772 by Joseph Vincent Carlin, a native of Italy who had come to Louisiana with the French army. The island was known by a number of names (including Orange Island) before Joseph Jefferson bought it in 1870. One of the most renowned stage actors of his day, Jefferson gained his fame playing the part of Rip Van Winkle. Today, outdoor concerts and plays are occasionally given here.

Jefferson Island is a salt dome with an interesting recent history. In 1980, a drilling rig punctured the cap of the dome beneath the Lake Peigneur, causing water to fill the mine. There's no more salt mining, but the lake is beautiful, as are the 25 acres of semi-tropical gardens that surround it. Known as the **Rip Van Winkle Gardens,** they were first developed in 1917 with a formal Elizabethan garden, a lovely rose garden, and winding footpaths.

Within the gardens, a good restaurant, **Cafe Jefferson,** overlooks the tranquil lake, and lovely accommodations. *5505 Rip Van Winkle Rd.; 800-375-3332.*

■ JEANERETTE   *map page 120, C/D-4*

LA 182 follows Bayou Teche for 15 miles from New Iberia to the small town of Jeanerette (pop. 6,750). This is a good place to learn something about the sugar-cane industry that dominates the area. None of the sugar mills is open to the public, but if you're in the area during the grinding season, which runs roughly from late September into December, the **Jeanerette Sugar Coop** at the edge of town will be in operation 24 hours a day.

Since you can't go inside the mills, it's worth a stop at the **Jeanerette Museum** (Le Petit Musée), further along LA 182, where you can watch two informative videos that explain 200 years of the harvesting and processing of cane into sugar. *500 E. Main St.; 337-276-4408.*

The biggest issues locally have to do with how the cane is harvested and transported to the mill. The traditional practice involves burning the cane in the fields after cutting to get rid of foliage and cut down processing costs. The cane is then loaded into wagons or trucks and hauled to the mill. Heavy smoke creates health problems, and slow-moving tractors pulling cane wagons create traffic problems.

Enter the combine harvester, which makes burning unnecessary and results in

The Japanese Tea House in Rip Van Winkle Gardens is a peaceful place to while away a warm afternoon. (Syndey Byrd)

Sugar refineries such as this one in Jeanerette process the region's major agricultural product. (Syndey Byrd)

less trash on roadways. Farmers have been slow to change the way they harvest cane, but pressure is mounting to stop the burning and clean up the highways. And there is information about a footnote in World War II history when POWs from Rommel's Afrika Korps worked in the adjacent cane fields *(see page 84).*

■ FRANKLIN   *map page 120, D-4/5*

The Chitimacha Indian Trail follows the curve of Bayou Teche, becoming St. Mary 326, which loops back to LA 182 in Baldwin. Continue east and turn onto St. Mary 28 (Irish Bend Rd.), which again follows the contortions of the bayou, as the main highway takes a more direct route to Franklin (pop. 9,000). As the names "Franklin" and "Irish Bend" suggest, this area was settled by Irish and English planters. These newcomers amassed huge landholdings and were culturally different from their Creole and Cajun neighbors to the west. This area was the scene of the Battle of Irish Bend in 1863 when Confederate troops surprised Union forces, inflicting heavy casualties in fighting described at the time as "sharp, obstinate, and bloody." The Old South legacy lingers here in ways more obvious than it does in the places you have previously visited; yet in reality you are less than 60 miles from the bustle of Lafayette.

(opposite) Steen's Syrup Mill is the largest sugarmill remaining in Cajun country. In this photo, owner Charley Steen poses in front of his syrup "cans," an Abbeville landmark. (Brian Gauvin)

The den at Oaklawn Manor is adorned with Audubon prints. (Syndey Byrd)

Oaklawn Manor

Oaklawn Manor is one of many grand plantation homes (almost all of them private) in the Franklin area. Built in 1837 by Alexander Porter and currently owned by popular Republican governor Mike Foster and his wife, Oaklawn is open to the public. This was the site of one of the meetings between Foster and David Duke, former Ku Klux Klan leader and neo-Nazi, during the 1995 gubernatorial election. Subsequent to those meetings, Foster paid Duke $150,000 for the use of his mailing list and Duke withdrew from the governor's race.

The home contains eclectic furnishings from several periods, including a stunning hand-blown Venetian glass chandelier. Beneath an artist's proof of *Blue Dog,* one of a series of paintings by Lafayette artist George Rodrigue, sit two blue dogs carved in wood, one of them sporting a black Harley Davidson vest. Other objets d'art include several hardhats painted with nature scenes. *Call for directions: sign on Irish Bend Rd., 3296 E. Oaklawn Dr.; 337-828-0434.*

Martin's Bar and Grocery

Not far past Oaklawn Manor, you'll come across a weathered, unpainted building with a tin roof and a Jax beer sign outside. Originally a general merchandise store built in the 1800s, it now looks straight out of a Walker Evans photograph. Stop for a cold beer and a chat with the old-timers who hang out there. *2518 Irish Bend Rd.*

Grevemberg House Museum

Coming into Franklin, Irish Bend Road takes you through a poor section of town to the 1851 Greek Revival Grevemberg House.

The tour guides are extremely well informed and hospitable. The furnishings are from the 1860s, though not original to the house. Several rooms feature very interesting reproductions of period wallpaper. A charming children's room is filled with antique toys, including a wood-and-brass double-barreled cap shotgun. The canvas-covered floor is painted with scenes from Mother Goose nursery rhymes.

In one room of the house are framed coats of arms painted by Col. Francis C. Grevemberg, reform governor Robert Kennon's superintendent of police in the early 1950s. Grevemberg is remembered for his relentless crusade against gambling and vice in Louisiana. His troopers conducted highly publicized raids against illegal operations and dumped thousands of slot machines in the Mississippi River. Some recall the feuds that developed between the state police and local sheriffs during this period. The Opelousas area, which had a reputation as a hotbed of vice at the time, was ruled by St. Landry Parish sheriff "Cat" Doucet, who took a lenient view of human frailties. It is said that Grevemberg's troopers would raid a brothel on Saturday night and arrest all the prostitutes. On Sunday morning, the sheriff would release them. When asked why, he would reply, "Those girls had to go to mass." *Open daily 10–4; 407 Sterling Rd.; 337-828-2092.*

Franklin Historic District

Continue on to LA 182 where a left turn will take you through downtown Franklin and the historic district. Large live oaks

Built on the edge of a sugarcane field, Martin's Grocery on Irish Bend Road evokes a bygone era.
Stop by for a little shade and a snack. (Syndey Byrd)

draped with Spanish moss line both sides of the street, while graceful white lamps stand like sentries along the neutral ground. Descriptive brochures of the most architec-turally significant homes in the district are available from the tourist information office on US 90. The Franklin Historic District contains some 420 structures of note.

A shrimp boat is highlighted against the setting sun. (Brian Gauvin) Shrimping is a way of life in Cajun country. Above, the Knights of Peter Claver crown the Baby Shrimp Queen at the Delcambre Shrimp Festival. (Sydney Byrd)

■ DELCAMBRE   *map page 120, B-4*

West of Jefferson Island *(see page 140)*, you'll find State Highway 14 makes a sharp curve and Delcambre (pop. 2,000) just ahead. The town is home to a large shrimp fleet that is partially visible when you cross the bridge over the Delcambre Canal. Take the first left after the bridge, cross the railroad tracks and drive along the docks. On the right is a little park and pavilion where the Shrimp Festival is held in August. On the left, along the canal are the fixtures of an active fishing village: brightly colored shrimp boats, an ice house, fuel docks, retail and wholesale seafood markets and the like. Delcambre is not a pretty town; it's a gritty place, rough around the edges, with a few small supermarkets, a number of bars, and a population that is sometimes just hanging on, as making a living from commercial fishing becomes increasingly difficult.

■ ERATH   *map page 120, B-4*

Erath (pop. 2,250), founded in 1899 by August Erath, a Swiss immigrant, is the home of Cajun musician D. L. Menard, a Grammy-award nominee sometimes called the "Cajun Hank Williams." Stop signs are in both English and French, as befits a town that is, officially, a bilingual entity. Before the first church was built in Erath in the early 1900s, the citizenry celebrated mass in the local lumberyard.

Acadian Museum

The Acadian Museum (Musée Acadien), housed in the old Bank of Erath building in the center of town, is the most interesting small museum in the entire region.

The guiding force behind the museum is Warren Perrin, chairman of the Acadian Heritage & Culture Foundation, which administers the museum. Perrin has petitioned England and demanded a formal apology for the expulsion of the Acadians from Nova Scotia.

The museum is filled with photographs, mementos, and historical artifacts donated

Acadian Museum. (Syndey Byrd)

by local people. A clipping file and a collection of video and audio tapes are available for research purposes. In the front room are several excellent interpretive panels that explore the history of Erath, including one that acknowledges the problems the town experienced with racial integration. This is one of the few candid acknowledgements of racial tensions to be found in the Gulf South.

The Acadian Room is devoted to the history of the Acadians in Nova Scotia, and the Cajun Room focuses on Cajun life in Vermilion Parish.

The museum has a homey feel. It's a very intriguing place that draws you in—like sifting through a century of family history in your grandparents' attic. There's even documentation of pop star Madonna's Cajun roots. *To visit, drive by to see if it's open. No phone onsite. 203 S. Broadway.*

Museum Café and Music

Next door is the Museum Café (Café Musée), which, in addition to offering food and drink, has become almost an annex to the museum. Cultural programs are often held there, and Cajun musicians hold a jam session every other Saturday. *102 Edwards St.; 337-937-0012.*

On alternate Saturdays, a jam session is held at **Touchet's Kitchen and Bar** on US 167 between Abbeville and Maurice.

A mural graces a parking lot in Abbeville, a charming and historic Cajun town. (Syndey Byrd)

ACADIANA

■ ABBEVILLE *map page 120, B-4*

Another six miles west on LA 14 and you're in Abbeville (pop. 13,000), founded in 1843 by a Catholic priest. Although the town is only 15 miles from Lafayette, it feels a continent away. It is certainly one of the loveliest small towns in all of Acadiana. The well-preserved downtown area is dominated by the white-columned **Vermilion Parish Courthouse** designed by Louisiana architect A. Hays Town. This may be the only courthouse in the world where you can buy books of "Boudreaux and Thibodeaux" jokes (sort of the Cajun Abbot and Costello) in the clerk of court's office. Across the street at 309 Pere Megret, ladies can shop at Beverly Sellers while the guys grab a beer at Black's. During the Christmas season carriage rides are often offered.

As you come into the downtown area, the highway becomes a one-way street and winds around the courthouse. After another block, the street winds around Magdalen Square to the large and imposing **St. Mary Magdalen Catholic Church.** To the left of the church is the **C. S. Steen Syrup Mill,** easily identified by the huge yellow cans of syrup out front, each holding 16,682 gallons of sweet nectar.

◆ OYSTERS, RICE FARMS, AND CATTLE RANCHES

More people in Acadiana probably come to Abbeville to eat oysters than for any other single reason. Two of the oyster emporiums, **Black's** and **Dupuy's**, are located across from the church, and the third, **Shucks**, is across the bridge, only a few blocks on the other side of the Vermilion River. Abbeville has been an oyster town for longer than anyone can remember, back to the days when oyster men brought their catches up the river from Vermilion Bay and sold them from sheds along the river. Although these days the oysters originate in beds along the Louisiana coast and are delivered by truck, they are no less delicious.

Today, rice is the largest cash crop in Vermilion Parish, but the large sprawling parish is an agricultural and fisheries paradise. Shrimp, menhaden (an industrial fish used in pet food), crabs, oysters, catfish, and crabs are important catches. Crawfish farming, alligator farming, and trapping add to the mix, as do sugarcane and soybeans. Vermilion Parish is also Louisiana's largest cattle-raising parish.

Cattle ranching is nothing new in this area. Many of the early Acadian settlers had been small cattle ranchers in Nova Scotia, and cattle ranches or *vacheries* were a natural on the prairie grasslands and marshes of southwest Louisiana. In fact, the cowboy tradition among Cajuns and black Creoles goes back further in Acadiana than it does in Texas. As early as 1773, Cajun ranchers were driving longhorn cattle to New Orleans. Prior to that, the Spanish were driving cattle from Opelousas to New Orleans.

Today, the trail drive survives here and in other parts of Acadiana in the form of trail rides—recreational horseback outings that last for a day, a weekend or longer. The passion for horses and horse racing has earned Acadiana a reputation as "the cradle of jockeys." Some of the nation's top jockeys, such as Marlon St. Julien, Randy Romero, Eddie Delahoussaye, and Kent Desormeaux, to name a few, have come from southwestern Louisiana. Until fairly recently, dirt tracks (bush tracks, as they were called) were common throughout Acadiana. Youngsters got started in racing as young as 10 years of age, and by the time they graduated to the bigger tracks, they were already seasoned veterans.

Abbeville's two principal festivals are the **Cattle Festival** in early October and the **Giant Omelette Festival** in early November. At the latter, chefs prepare a 5,000-egg omelette. *(See pages 339 and 340.)*

■ RICE LANDS AND DUCK HUNTING

West of Abbeville on LA 14, the land opens up, and cane gives way to rice and crawfish. Rice in Louisiana occupies more than 600,000 acres at 5,000 pounds per acre. Some of the crawfish are harvested from permanent ponds, but many more come from fields that are flooded after rice has been harvested. This rotation gives farmers two annual crops instead of one.

Three miles south of Kaplan on LA 35, rice farmers regularly convene at **Suire's Grocery and Restaurant** to trade their tales of duck hunting and rice growing in Cajun French over steaming bowls of gumbo.

The rice fields and, further south, the marshes, are prime duck and goose hunting country. (A little further west is the town of **Gueydan,** which calls itself the Duck Capital of America and hosts the Duck Festival in August.) Duck hunting is an important economic, as well as sporting, activity that draws hunters from around the country.

■ KAPLAN AND CAJUN MUSIC   *map page 120, A-3/4*

Local communities are proud of the musical talents they have nourished. As you come into Kaplan, a small town (pop. 5,200) founded in 1903 by Abrom Kaplan, a young Russian Jewish immigrant, you'll see a sign announcing that this is the home of Cajun musician Sammy Kershaw and zydeco musician Cedric Benoit.

The town is also home to the **Rooster Pit,** a cock-fighting arena so popular that children have birthday parties here. (Cock fighting is legal in Louisiana, as they are classified as poultry and do not come under animal rights statutes.) Kaplan is one of the few places in the United States that celebrates Bastille Day. The festivities include a mock storming of the Bastille.

■ CROWLEY: RICE CAPITAL   *map page 120, A-2*

Just outside Kaplan, LA 13 will take you 18 miles north to Crowley (pop. 14,000), the Rice Capital of America. You'll pass through fields of rice and pastures filled with cattle and their companions, the white cattle egrets who feed on the insects the cattle stir up. The rice fields are particularly beautiful in midsummer, at the beginning of the harvest, when they've turned from green to gold.

ACADIANA

Crystal Rice Plantation (just south of Crowley) belongs to Operation Quackback, a conservation program for ducks and geese. Members leave water on some of the fields in the fall and winter to provide a resting place for migrating waterfowl. The plantation was founded in 1890 by Sol Wright who later developed an improved strain of rice called Blue Rose. The tour includes a museum housed in an 1848 Acadian cottage, an automobile museum, and a look at the current agricultural and aquacultural operations. This is a good place to see how 1,600 acres of rice fields are turned into crawfish ponds after the rice harvest. *Directions: 6428 Airport Rd. (just past Muskrat Rd.). Turn left and drive down to the Crystal Rice Plantation; 337-783-6417.*

❖

Louisiana Highway 13 will not engrave itself on your memory. Note the blue Hurricane Evacuation Route signs. The cane is out of the fields by Thanksgiving so the land seems almost strip-mined. The highway goes right into Crowley's tree-lined historical district filled with imposing late 19th- and early 20th-century homes. It's sort of like Kansas meets Mobile. The architecture has a very midwestern feel to it, and for good reason. Crowley was settled by midwesterners after its founding in 1887. These new settlers, who were experienced in raising wheat, brought capital and established large commercial rice farms on the prairie. The city has more than 200 buildings listed on the National Register. It also has its share of pawn shops and a main street dominated by a satellite dish.

Long ago, slaves from the rice growing regions of Africa brought high prices because of their experience diking, draining, and flooding rice fields. Acadian settlers often planted a small plot of "providence" rice in low-lying areas, so called because they didn't irrigate the rice, and the success or failure of the crop depended on rainfall. These plantings were for the family's own use, and in the early 20th century rice was secondary to corn as a staple in their diet. With the arrival of the railroad and the Anglos in the late 1800s, commercial rice production on a large scale transformed the prairies, and rice became an integral part of Cajun cooking. Crowley's major celebration is the Rice Festival in October.

In more recent years, Crowley was where one of Louisiana's colorful governors, Edwin Edwards, established his law practice and began a political career that made him Louisiana's first Cajun governor in modern times. In 1989, Edwards divorced his wife of 40 years, and soon after was elected to a fourth term as governor under the slogan, "Vote for the Crook–It's Important." Edwards married 29-year-old Candy Picou, who soon found herself to be the wife of a con—Edwards was convicted in the year 2000 of 17 counts of federal racketering.

■ RAYNE: FROG CAPITAL *map page 120, A-2*

From Crowley, take US 90 East five miles to Rayne (pop. 10,000), which calls itself the Frog Capital of the World. By now, you've no doubt realized that people take great pride in their local lore. Rayne's identification with frogs goes back to the late 19th century, when frogs were shipped by the barrel to northern cities where they were in great favor among restaurant goers. On Labor Day weekend, Rayne hosts the Frog Festival, where you can sample various preparations of frog legs and see the crowning of the Frog Queen. But at any time of the year, you can enjoy the frog murals that grace the sides of buildings in the downtown area.

When you come into Rayne on US 90, you'll find a cluster of antique stores around the railroad tracks. Many of the murals are along LA 3, which runs through the center of town. On the front of the newspaper office is a mural of frogs in the print shop putting out the paper. A little further up is a whole block of frogs—a newsboy frog, a girl frog rolling a hoop, a frog barber and so on. There's a frog mural on the side of the police station, and even one on the I-10 underpass.

Just to the north of Rayne is an area called **Roberts Cove**, which was settled by German immigrants in the late 1800s. The settlement's heritage is celebrated each October at the **Roberts Cove Germanfest** which features German cooking, dancing, and singing. The Waldfohrtshappelle (Church in the Woods) is a small pilgrimage chapel that looks like a dollhouse, built in 1890 by members of the Benedictine Order. German farm families still come to pray for good crops and a successful duck hunt. *7166 Roberts Cove via LA 98 North.*

■ GRAND COTEAU *map page 120, B-1*

Grand Coteau (pop. 1,100) is only about 10 miles north of Lafayette, but it seems to be in another world. The interstate runs over gently rolling hills, a sudden departure from the flat prairie and marshland to the south. This little village is filled with buildings that are listed on the National Register of Historic Places. Unfortunately, a junkyard on Main Street gives an unfavorable early impression, but get beyond that and the town reveals itself along narrow shaded streets.

St. Charles College, a Jesuit novitiate where priests study for their first two years, is located here. The college is also a Jesuit Spirituality Center that holds retreats for Catholic laypersons. When a retreat is in progress, visitors are not allowed on the grounds.

ACADIANA

The serene **St. Charles Borromeo Catholic Church**, reminiscent of a white clapboard New England church, dates from 1879. Most of the paintings in the church were done by Erasmus Humbrecht, an itinerant artist who also executed paintings for the St. Louis Cathedral in New Orleans. At the rear of the church is an unusual bell tower. Behind the church is a cemetery striking in its simplicity. Rows of marble tombstones mark the resting places of Jesuit priests who are buried there. Unlike the cemeteries further south, where tombs are the rule, the burials here are below ground. *By appointment; 174 Church; 337-662-5279.*

The centerpiece of Grand Coteau is the **Academy of the Sacred Heart**, both a day and a boarding school for girls that dates from 1821. Tours of the formal gardens and the school are available from guides who are extremely knowledgeable. The tour includes a museum with handmade nun habits and a press for making communion wafers, as well as the **Shrine of Saint John Berchmans**, where a miracle occurred that has been recognized by the Vatican. (In 1866, when a dying young woman said a novena to John Berchmans, he appeared to her in visions and she recovered—although she died within the year.) Students often visit the shrine and petition for their own miracles when faced with a difficult exam. On the

Rayne's obsession with frogs, extends to this mural on the face of the police station. Opposite, the 1879 Church of St. Charles in Grand Coteau. (Syndey Byrd)

school grounds is a cemetery where nuns were buried. Like the Jesuit cemetery, it is elegant in its simplicity—the graves are marked by iron crosses with small marble plaques. The oak alley leading to the school once ran for more than a mile to St. Charles College. The Jesuit priests walked under the towering oaks to the school to conduct mass.

For such a tiny place, Grand Coteau is blessed with two good places to eat. The **Kitchen Shop and Tea Room** offers primarily beverages, baked goods, and desserts, while **Catahoula's** is a full restaurant with creative south Louisiana cooking *(see page 161)*.

■ OPELOUSAS: YAM CAPITAL   *map page 120, B-1*

A quick 12 mile drive further north on I-49 will bring you to the town of Opelousas (pop. 18,200). The city was settled by French hunters and trappers about 1720. In the colonial period, the town was the site of a trading post. The District of Opelousas later became Poste de Opelousas, a civil and military jurisdiction. The third oldest town in Louisiana, it has a good deal of interesting architecture. A map listing the significant architecture is available from the tourist information office coming into town or at the Opelousas Museum.

The **Jim Bowie Museum** is actually a corner of the **tourist information office.** It gives a fascinating look at the life of native son and Louisiana legislator, Jim Bowie, who died fighting at the Alamo. *Open daily 8–4; 828 E. Landry; 337-948-6263 or 800-424-5442.*

The **Opelousas Museum and Interpretive Center** offers a variety of exhibits on local history and famous local personages such as Olympic gold medalist Rod Milburn. One of the displays contains a hat belonging to Cat Doucet, the notorious local sheriff who was in power during the 1950s and '60s, when Opelousas was a wide-open town with a deserved reputation for gambling and prostitution. Opelousas natives chefs Paul and Enola Prudhomme are also honored in the museum. The white-enameled wash basin that was used to bathe Paul when he was a child is on display here. *Tues–Sat; 329 N. Main St.; 337-948-2589 or 800-424-5442.*

❖

Sweet potatoes, soy beans, cattle, and corn are important agricultural crops in this area, but it is the sweet potato that has come to be identified with Opelousas. Billing itself as the Yam Capital of the World, Opelousas celebrates the crop with its Yambilee Festival in late October. The highly prized sweet potato variety is the

ACADIANA

beauregard, a Louisiana hybrid that is moist and sweet. Louisiana harvests six million bushels of sweet potatoes annually, but they have been called yams since the first slaves began calling them "naymai" after the similar African dietary staple (to which Louisiana yams have no relation whatsoever).

Several important food producers are headquartered here, including Tony Chachere's, Lou Ana Foods, and Savoie's. **The Palace Cafe,** across the street from the courthouse, is a favorite local spot that has been around since 1927, featuring dishes as diverse as crawfish etouffée and baklava.

◆ ZYDECO COUNTRY

Opelousas and the surrounding area are in the very heart of zydeco country. The late Clifton Chenier was born on a farm near Opelousas, and Slim's Y-Ki-Ki, one of the legendary zydeco clubs dating from 1949, is located here on Highway 182. On the Saturday before Labor Day, The Original Southwest Louisiana Zydeco Music Festival takes place on the Southern Development Foundation Farm in Plaisance, near Opelousas.

Patrons loosen up listening to Nathan Williams and the Zydeco Cha-Chas at the El Sidos Club in Lafayette. (Syndey Byrd)

■ EUNICE   *map page 120, A-1*

It's only about 20 miles southwest of Opelousas across the flat prairie on Highway 190 to Eunice (pop. 11,200). On the way, you'll pass Richard's ["Ree-SHARDS"] Club in Lawtell, a mecca for zydeco lovers. On the outskirts of Eunice is the Savoy Music Center which hosts a jam session every Saturday morning. Cajun musician and accordion,-maker Mark Savoy and his wife Anne, also a musician and the author of *Cajun Music: a Reflection of a People,* are important figures in the Cajun cultural preservation movement. Savoy's handmade "Acadian" accordions are in great demand. *Open Tues–Sat; 4413 US 190 East; 337-457-9563.*

Eunice was founded in the 1890s by C. C. Duson who named the town after his wife. Eunice Duson's statue stands in the town square today. Eunice has the feel of a Western town sitting out on the prairie under a big sky. Parking is head-first-into-the-curb, and a section of the downtown area has been turned into a kind of pedestrian mall. Eunice is well known for its Mardi Gras celebration, when costumed celebrants ride out into the countryside to beg for gumbo ingredients. The city also hosts the World Championship Crawfish Etouffée Cookoff in March. You can sample one of the winning etouffées at Mama's Fried Chicken on US 190. Four places of interest in Eunice are conveniently located within blocks of each other in the downtown area.

Prairie Acadian Cultural Center
The emphasis here is on the Acadian prairie experience. Informative videos are available on such subjects as music, Mardi Gras, wildflowers, crawfish, cooking, and alligators. Visitors are invited to choose what they would like to see. On Saturday afternoons, the center hosts music programs and cooking demonstrations. *Open daily; 250 West Park Ave. at Third; 337-457-8490.*

Eunice Museum
Housed in the former train depot where in the 1890s C. C. Duson auctioned off the lots in his town, this museum features a number of exhibits of local life, including Mardi Gras masks and costumes from the Eunice Courir du Mardi Gras, as well as photographs and biographies of Cajun musicians. Visitors are offered free coffee. *220 South C. C. Duson Dr.; 337-457-6540.*

Cajun Music Hall of Fame & Museum
Next door is the Cajun Music Hall of Fame and Museum. The exhibits include memorabilia, photos, and biographies of musicians, old recording equipment, and instruments that once belonged to prominent Cajun musicians. *240 South C. C. Duson Dr.; 337-457-6534.*

■ ACADIANA FOOD & LODGING

☎   For chain lodgings see toll-free numbers on page 333.

$$ For room (☎) and restaurant (✕) price designations see page 333.

Abbeville
map page 120, B-4

✕ **Black's Oyster Bar.** 319 Pere Megret; 337-893-4266 $
Restaurant and oyster bar in a small but beautiful old department store. Boiled crawfish, in season, and a wide variety of seafood dishes. Be prepared for a wait on Friday and Saturday nights.

BLACK'S OYSTER BAR

✕ **Dupuy's Oyster Shop.** 108 S. Main.; 337-893-2336 $
One of a trio of oyster restaurants in Abbeville specializing in oysters on the half shell, fried oysters, and other seafood dishes. Since each restaurant has its vocal partisans, sample all three and decide for yourself.

✕ **Richard's Seafood Patio.** 1516 S. Henry St.; 337-893-1693 $
Popular "seafood patio" that features boiled crabs, crawfish, and shrimp in season in a very casual atmosphere. The restaurant has recently added fried and grilled seafood to its menu. Claims to be the "original crawfish patio since 1957."

✕ **Shucks!** 701 W. Port St.; 337-898-3311 $
Opened in the mid-90s by the family that had previously run Dupuy's Oyster Shop. Wonderful oysters on the half shell, fried oysters, and oyster loaves are the specialty here, but the menu offers a wide variety of fried and broiled seafood, as well as seafood gumbo and oyster stew. Don't miss the pralines after dinner. Closed the month of July.

Breaux Bridge Area
map page 120, C-2

☎ **Best Western.** 2088-B Rees St., Breaux Bridge; 337-332-1114 or 888-783-0007 $

☎ **Chez des Amis.** 912 Main St., Breaux Bridge; 337-507-3399 $$
The newest venture of Dickie and Cynthia Breaux, who own Cafe des Amis. Two rooms with furniture handcrafted from exotic woods and handcut metals, adorned with the work of local artists. Rates include a full breakfast for two at Cafe des Amis.

☎ **Maison des Amis.** 111 Washington St., Breaux Bridge; 337-507-3399 $$
Charming, restored 19th-century home on the bank of Bayou Teche. Formal gardens, a gazebo, a fountain, and herb garden provide pleasant surroundings for enjoying the evening air. Rates include a full breakfast for two at Cafe des Amis.

MAISON DES AMIS

☎ **Houseboat Adventures.** Cypress Cove Landing, 1399 Henderson Levee Rd., Henderson; 337-228-7484 or 800-491-4662 $$$
An air-conditioned houseboat with generator, living quarters, kitchen, bath, hot water, TV, and barbecue pit is towed to a location in the Atchafalaya Basin. Each boat sleeps four to eight. Rental includes a small boat with motor.

✕ **Cafe des Amis.** 140 E. Bridge St., Breaux Bridge; 337-332-5273 $$
Popular meeting place in Breaux Bridge for breakfast, lunch, dinner, or just a cup of coffee. Situated in a restored general merchandise store and filled with works

of art, the restaurant features such hard-to-find Cajun dishes as coush coush (a breakfast cereal) and gateau de syrop, as well as creatively prepared seafood, poultry, and meat dishes.

CAFE DES AMIS

✕ **Mulate's.** 325 Mills Ave., Breaux Bridge; 337-332-4648 or 800-422-2586 $$
Live Cajun music and a small dance floor are the principal attractions of this popular down-home, checkered-tablecloth restaurant. The menu is long on fried seafood, as well as baked duck and fried alligator. Seafood gumbo is one of the most reliable dishes.

MULATE'S

Eunice *map page 120, A-1*

⛏ **Best Western.** 1531 W. Laurel Ave.; 337-457-2800 or 800-962-8423 $

⛏ **The Seale Guesthouse.** 123 Seale Ln.; 337-457-3753
Restored century-old home in the countryside two miles south of Eunice. Large wraparound porch with rockers beneath tall pines. Continental breakfast; hot boudin on the weekends.

✕ **Mathilda's Country Kitchen.** 611 St. Mary Rd.; 337-546-0329 $
Immaculate, informal little place where plate lunches, barbecue, and daily specials are served cafeteria style on trays. Barbecued ribs, pork steaks, chicken and hot links, pork stew, shrimp stew, fried catfish, fried shrimp, and sweet dough pies are some of the standbys.

✕ **Ruby's Cafe.** 221 W. Walnut; 337-457-2583 $
Conveniently located downtown near the Liberty Theatre and the Acadian Prairie Cultural Center, featuring plate lunches (baked chicken, pork roast) with vegetables.

Grand Coteau/ Sunset Area *map page 120, B-1*

⛏ **La Caboose.** 145 S. Budd St., Sunset; 337-662-5401 $-$$
Railroad buffs will particularly appreciate these accommodations in original railroad cars and a restored train depot. Continental breakfast, including the proprietor's homemade preserves.

LA CABOOSE

⛏ **Chretien Point Plantation.** 665 Chretien Point Rd., Sunset; 337-662-5876 or 800-880-7050 $$-$$$$
Grand 1831 plantation home with staircase that was the model for Tara in *Gone With the Wind*. Situated on 20 acres with pool, tennis court and pond. Overnight guests enjoy cocktails and hors d'oeuvres in the evening, a full breakfast in the morning, and a guided tour of the home.

✕ **Catahoula's.** 234 King Dr., Grand Coteau; 337-662-2275 $$
Innovative and creative south Louisiana cooking in a handsome restaurant named after Louisiana's state dog. Specialties include oysters Ignatius, lemon fish and seafood napoleon, roasted smoked duckling, and savory crabmeat cheesecake.

Lafayette Area
map page 120, B-2

☰ **Aaah! T'Frere's House & Garconniere.** 1905 Verot School Rd., Lafayette; 337-984-9347 or 800-984-9347 $$
Proprietors Pat and Maugie Pastor used to operate a restaurant in Lafayette, and their charm and flair for promotion shines through in this small operation. Welcome hors d'oeuvres and cocktails, after-dinner drinks, and full breakfast.

☰ **Best Western Hotel Acadiana.** 1801 West Pinhook Rd., Lafayette; 337-233-8120 or 800-826-8386 $-$$

BOIS DES CHENES

☰ **Bois des Chenes.** 338 N. Sterling St., Lafayette; 337-233-7816 $$
Five rooms, each decorated in a different period style, are located in the Charles Mouton plantation house and in a carriage house behind the main home. Breakfast is served in a light and airy solarium. The proprietor's boat tours of the

Atchafalaya Basin and Lake Martin are particularly favored by birders and photographers.

☰ **Cajun Country Home.** 1601 LaNeuville Rd., Lafayette; 337-856-5271 $
Broussard family home dating from circa 1830 is located on 120 acres (formerly a dairy farm) at the edge of Lafayette. Full breakfast includes Mrs. Broussard's homemade preserves.

☰ **Hilton Lafayette & Towers.** 1521 West Pinhook Rd., Lafayette; 337-235-6111 or 800-33-CAJUN. $-$$$

☰ **La Maison de Campagne.** 825 Kidder Rd., Carencro; 337-896-6529 or 800-895-0235 $$-$$$
An 1871 Victorian home and cottage with pool in the countryside north of Lafayette. Includes full breakfast.

✕ **Cafe Vermilionville.** 1304 W. Pinhook Rd., Lafayette; 337-237-0100 $$-$$$$
Splendid south Louisiana cooking, both traditional and innovative, in an historic building that once served as an inn. Specialties include turtle soup, Kahlua grilled shrimp, bananas Foster. The bar is a popular meeting place for locals, the herb garden a nice spot for a stroll.

✕ **Charley G's Seafood Grill.** 3809 Ambassador Caffery Pkwy., Lafayette; 337-981-0108 $$-$$$
Stylish and popular seafood grill and bar with a very urban atmosphere. Specialties from the open kitchen include duck and andouille gumbo, grilled fish, crab cakes, and softshell crabs.

✕ **Don's Seafood & Steakhouse.** 301 E. Vermilion, Lafayette; 337-235-3551 $-$$$
Landmark downtown restaurant featuring a wide variety of seafood preparations. Particularly recommended: gumbos, crabmeat dishes, crawfish etouffée, crawfish bisque, broiled fish.

✕ **Poor Boy's Riverside Inn.** 240 Tubing Rd., Broussard; 337-837-4011 $-$$
Popular casual restaurant featuring a large number of seafood dishes. Particularly known for its crab dishes, mammoth broiled or stuffed flounder, and various preparations of alligator.

✕ **Prejean's.** 3480 Interstate 49 North, Lafayette; 337-896-3247 $$-$$$
Extensive menu with a variety of gumbos and bisques, alligator, seafood and game dishes, both traditional and innovative. Fried or grilled seafood platter, sauteed red snapper, grilled flounder, crawfish etouffée, crawfish enchilada. Desserts are a specialty, so save room. Cajun music and dancing nightly.

PREJEAN'S

✕ **Randol's.** 2320 Kaliste Saloom Rd., Lafayette; 337-981-7080 or 800-YO-CAJUN $-$$
Very casual seafood restaurant with live Cajun music and dancing nightly. Boiled crabs, crawfish, and shrimp are best bets.

Lake Fausse Pointe
map page 120, D-3

⌂ **Lake Fausse Pointe State Park.** 5400 Levee Rd.; 337-229-4764 or 877-226-7652 $
About 18 miles southeast of St. Martinville, this 6100-acre wilderness park has 18 waterfront cabins, each with a screened porch, kitchen, air conditioning, and a pier. Rates include linens and cooking equipment; all you need to bring are towels and groceries.

New Iberia Area
map page 120, C-3/4

⌂ **Alice Plantation.** 9217 Old Jeanerette Rd., Jeanerette; 337-276-3187 or 800-330-8393 $$
Two guest cottages and one suite in the 1796 plantation home. Situated on Bayou Teche, the grounds include gardens, swimming pool, and tennis court. Rates include full breakfast and a guided tour of the home.

⌂ **Best Western.** 2714 LA 14, New Iberia; 337-364-3030 $-$$

⌂ **Holiday Inn.** 2915 LA 14, New Iberia; 337-367-1201; 800-465-4329 $

RIP VAN WINKLE GARDENS B&B

🛏 **Rip Van Winkle Gardens Bed & Breakfast.** 5505 Rip Van Winkle Rd., Jefferson Island; 337-365-3332 or 800-375-3332 $$-$$$
Three cottages with kitchens on the grounds of Jefferson Island. Rates include continental breakfast, access to the gardens, and a tour of the Joseph Jefferson home.

LE ROSIER COUNTRY INN

🛏 **Le Rosier Country Inn.** 314 E. Main St., New Iberia; 337-367-5306 or 888-804-ROSE $$
Six well equipped and comfortable guest rooms in a lovely inn across the street

from Shadows-on-the-Teche. Le Rosier offers breakfast and dinner on Friday and Saturday night. The inn is well known for the creative south Louisiana food served in its dining room.

✗ **Cafe Jefferson.** 5505 Rip Van Winkle Rd., Jefferson Island; 337-364-5111 or 800-375-3332 $$-$$$
Lovely view of Lake Peigneur with seasonal menus that feature fried, grilled, and sauteed seafood, crabcakes, aged ribeye steaks, and sassafras pork chop.

✗ **Clementine.** 113 East Main St.; 337-560-1007 $$-$$$
Stylish downtown restaurant and bar featuring seasonal menus with fresh seafood, steaks, chops, and poultry, in a variety of preparations. Stuffed, fried soft-shell crabs a speciality.

✗ **Guiding Star.** 4404 Highway 90 W., New Iberia; 337-365-9113 $$
Quintessential boiled seafood house, with newspapers on the tables and a sink in the dining room for washing your hands after eating boiled crabs, crawfish, or shrimp. The seafood is cooked with Tabasco pepper mash from Avery Island, which gives it an incomparable flavor. Pool room in the back.

✗ **Lagniappe Too.** 204 E. Main St., New Iberia; 337-365-9419 $-$$
A downtown cafe and restaurant popular for weekday lunch and weekend dinner. Offerings range from homemade soups, gumbos, and salads to steaks, chicken, and seafood.

Opelousas

map page 120, B-1

THE ESTORGE HOUSE

The Estorge House. 417 N. Market St.; 337-942-8151 or 888-655-9539 $$
An 1827 townhouse, centrally located. Rates include wine or tea service in the afternoon, a bedtime snack, full breakfast, and a guided tour of the home.

THE PALACE CAFE

The Palace Cafe. 135 W. Landry; 337-942-2142 $
Situated across the street from the courthouse, the cafe (around since 1927) serves breakfast, plate lunches, sandwiches. Patrons come for crawfish etouffée, fried chicken salad, and pecan baklava.

St. Martinville

map page 120, C-3

Bienvenue House. 421 N. Main St.; 337-394-9100 or 888-394-9100 $$
Four rooms in columned 1830 home located in downtown St. Martinville. Rates include full breakfast and amenities basket with souvenirs.

OLD CASTILLO HOTEL

Old Castillo Hotel. 220 Evangeline Blvd; 337-394-4010 or 800-621-3017 $-$$
Historic building dating from the early 1800s adjacent to the Evangeline Oak on Bayou Teche. Once a small hotel, then a Catholic high school for girls, now a B&B with five rooms. Rates include a full breakfast in La Place d'Evangeline, a restaurant located on the premises.

Maison de Ville. 100 N. Main St.; 337-394-5700 $$
Located on the church square, this rambling restaurant and bar features a selection of both traditional and creative south Louisiana cooking, including gumbos, etouffées, crabcakes, softshell crabs, grilled or fried seafood, steaks, and chops.

CANE RIVER RAMBLES

by Stanley Dry

■ HIGHLIGHTS *page*

Food & Lodging, page 190
Maps, pages 170, 171, 174

■ TRAVEL OVERVIEW

The historic town of Natchitoches ("NAK-a-tish"), founded in 1714 by French settlers, was the first permanent settlement in the entire Louisiana Territory; its French heritage is visible to this day. This charming, historic town makes an excellent base for exploring the surrounding area. The rich soil of the Cane River region south of Natchitoches gave rise to large plantations, including one founded by a freed slave.

The Cane River is not a river, but a long, narrow, meandering lake set in a swath of lush green farmlands six miles wide and 35 miles long, stretching from Cloutierville to Natchitoches. A sophisticated French colonial culture flourished here in the 1700s, its legacy reflected in the French Creole style of architecture still to be found in the region's plantation houses. This is a veritable cultural treasure trove.

Most of this area, and that further north, has more in common with neighboring Mississippi and east Texas than it does to the Cajun country south of Alexandria or the Creole settlements in the Cane River. The area outside the Cane River was settled by Protestant yeoman farmers of Scotch-Irish descent and wealthy Anglo planters from other Southern states. Apart from the principal cities—Shreveport, Monroe, and Alexandria—this area is sparsely settled. Most of the land is devoted to agriculture and forestry. Cotton, soybeans, and in the northeast section of the region, sweet potatoes are principal crops. Fat cows grazing in golden fields of wildflowers, gently rolling hills, thick pine forests, and pecan groves provide most of the scenery, and it is especially nice in March and April.

Travel: Natchitoches is a four-hour drive northwest of New Orleans and four hours southeast of Dallas, Texas. Both drives are on Interstates. During harvest time, the pace of traffic can be glacial as trucks overladen with cotton or cane poke along the back roads. Long trucks can be a menace year round. US 84, which is notorious for speed traps, loosely follows Nolan's Trace—a late-18th-century cattle trail extending from Natchez to Texas. (Nolan, a notorious horse-trader, was later shot by the Spanish.)

Climate: Beyond the reach of the moderating Gulf winds, the northern part of the state experiences greater extremes of temperature than does the coast. Summer temperatures range from lows in the 70s to highs in the 90s or above. Winter temperatures frequently dip below freezing at night and rise into the 50s or above during the day. Spring and fall temperatures range between a high of 75 and a low of 45.

Two features characterize the climate throughout the Gulf South: high humidity and a brief but perfect spring and fall. March, April, May, September, and October are generally good months. Bring rain gear and a sweater for air conditioning that can make a place colder than a meat locker.

Nightlife: Natchitoches does have something of a music scene since it is a college town. Others travel to the Indian-run casino in Clarenton. Check the local papers for current listings.

Food & Lodging: Although the Natchitoches area offers some Cajun and Creole cooking, food in central and north Louisiana is more akin to the mainline Deep South cooking. Barbecue and fried catfish are both staples. A notable exception is the breakfast the Tante Huppé Inn, where owner Bobby DeBlieux serves a candlelight breakfast straight from the pages of an 18th-century Cane River cookbook. Meat pies are a specialty of Natchitoches and the Cane River region, and tamales reflect the early presence of the Indians and Spanish in the area. Lodgings include the chains and many charming B&B inns. **See page 190 for listings; see page 333 for price designations and toll-free numbers for chain accommodations. For a chart of listings by region, see page 334.**

■ CULTURE AND HISTORY

In 1714, Frenchman Louis Juche-reau de St. Denis traveled up the Mississippi River from New Orleans and continued north on the Red River to set up a trading post at its farthest navigable point—site of present-day Natchitoches. St. Denis traded with the agricultural Natchitoches Indians and with the few explorers and settlers who came drifting into the area.

For most of the 18th century, the area remained remote: some traders came by, some settlers moved in. This region's remoteness made it a natural haven for escaped slaves from New Orleans.

Some French planters took slave mistresses whom they freed and

Granddaughter of the famous Marie Thérèze Coincoin, this elegantly dressed woman is Marie Thérèze Carmelite Anty, a Cane River Free Person of Color. (Courtesy of the Cammie G. Research Center, Northwestern State Univ. of Louisiana)

CANE RIVER

cared for, the most famous being the Cane River's Marie Thérèze Coincoin *(see page 173).* Isle Brevelle, an area lying to the south of Natchitoches between Cane River and the Old River, is still home to Cane River's Creoles of color, a close-knit community. Even today the name Metoyer, which belongs to Coincoin's descendants, fills the local phone book.

Following the acquisition of this area by the United States with the Louisiana Purchase in 1803, the population grew to 3,500 people. In 1818, the massive log-jam north of Natchitoches, which had closed the Red River to navigation, was broken. The area opened to trade, and ambitious, well-financed planters came to grow short-staple cotton on vast plantations worked by thousands of slaves.

In the 1830s, however, the Red River changed its course, cutting off the town of Natchitoches from river commerce and leaving a placid lake in its wake. After the Civil War, northern Louisiana remained a backwater, poor and racially divided, fertile ground for the populist politics of its native sons, brothers Huey and Earl Long of Winnfield, who became governors in the 20th century.

(opposite) The Cane River meanders through the lovely town of Natchitoches. (Syndey Byrd)

CENTRAL LOUISIANA

0   5   10 Miles
0   5   10   15 Kilometers

0   5   10   15 Kilometers

■ NATCHITOCHES

Once a prosperous Red River trading town, in the 1830s Natchitoches became isolated after the river changed its course. The isolation that followed undoubtedly contributed to the preservation of the town's charm. Today, it's home to 17,000 people, with 38,000 in Natchitoches Parish. (Don't be disheartened by the concrete outskirts lined with Jiffy Lubes and Walmarts—the old town remains intact.) In more recent times, Natchitoches gained fame as the setting for the 1988 movie *Steel Magnolias,* written by native Robert Harling. Tours focusing on sites that appeared in the movie are available.

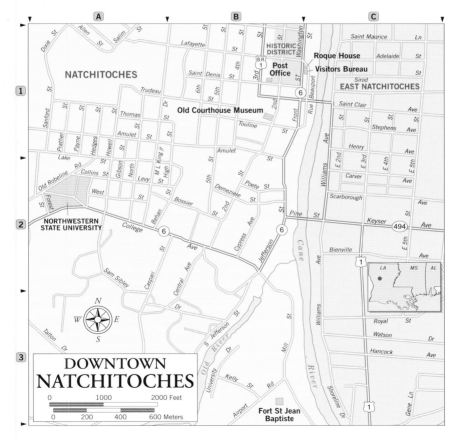

DOWNTOWN
NATCHITOCHES

Natchitoches (pronounced "NAK-a-tish") has a picturesque 33-block National Landmark Historic District reminiscent of the New Orleans French Quarter. Its brick streets have been worn smooth over the years, and lacy ironwork adorns the galleries that overlook Cane River Lake. A fine collection of historic residential and commercial buildings give the town a special old colonial charm. Most historic sites are in the vicinity of Second, Front, Washington, and Jefferson Streets. A number of historic homes are now inns *(see page 190-191)*. If you dine here, you'll find Natchitoches meat pies are a local specialty. They are made of ground beef, pork, and onions liberally spiced and cooked in a roux, then encased in pastry and fried. They used to be sold by street vendors; today they're available in a number of local restaurants.

Below is a list of some of the area's more interesting sights. Maps that give a self-guided tour of the Historic District are available at the Natchitoches Parish Visitors Bureau. Even without a map or a brochure, it's hard to find a local who doesn't have an encyclopedic knowledge of the history. They'll let you know right off the bat that Natchitoches is older than New Orleans.

Natchitoches Visitors Bureau
Maps and information. *781 Front St., 800-259-1714 or 318-352-8072.*

Fort St. Jean Baptiste
This is the site of a French trading post. The fort, commandant's house, chapel, and huts you see today on this five-acre compound were painstakingly recreated from the original drawings. *130 Moreau St. on Cane River Lake; 318-357-3101.*

Old Courthouse Museum
This 1896 building features changing exhibits on Louisiana history, and has included displays of quilts and exhibits explaining the history of the Louisiana Purchase. *600 Second St., Mon–Sat 9–5; 318-357-2270.*

Roque House
Beside the Cane River lakefront is the Roque House, the outbuilding of an 18th-

century French colonial cottage, containing many photographs of Cane River Creole buildings. Operated by the Creole Heritage Commission. *Just below Front St. on Rue Beauport; 318-356-5555.*

Williamson Museum
For those interested in local Native American history, this museum on the Northwestern State University campus is worth a visit. *210 Keyser Hall; for information on hours call 318-357-6195.*

Festivals
The town's most famous event, Christmas Festival of Lights, draws throngs in December. In July, the Natchitoches/NSU Folklife Festival is the state's largest celebration of Louisiana's rich folk traditions. *Prather Coliseum, NSU campus; 800-259-1714 or 318-3357-4332.*

The Christmas Festival in Natchitoches lights the historic district, with its wrought-iron balconies overlooking the Cane River. (Syndey Byrd)

■ CANE RIVER REGION   *see map page 174-175*

To drive between Natchitoches and Cloutierville is to meander country roads along the lovely Cane River: it is a trip of exceptional beauty at any time of the year. The rich farmland is bordered in brilliant wildflowers in the spring; during pecan season (October to January) you can stock up on freshly shelled pecans, sugared pecans, or delectably nutty pecan syrups. Plan to wander for the day and eat lunch at Ms. Ruby's *(see page 191)*, or have a picnic of meat pies on the banks of the lovely river.

◆ MELROSE PLANTATION   *see map page 174-175*

The most historic of the plantations on Cane River is Melrose, founded in 1786 by Marie Thérèze Coincoin, a freed slave whose alliance with a wealthy Frenchman produced several children. When the alliance ended in 1786, her lover and former master gave her 68 acres of land. From this, she and her children built a large and successful plantation, becoming slave owners themselves, and achieving

Map labels

Natchitoches 6

Fort St Jean Baptiste

1

1

494

Cane

494

2

Cherokee Plantation ●

Natchez 119

Beau Fort Plantation ●

3

Oakland Plantation ●   **Bermuda**

1

494

119

River

494

119

4

To Shreveport

Cypress

120

49

484

Melrose ○
Melrose Plantation ●

5

493

St Augustine Church ■   484

Montrose

119

Magnolia Plantation ●

493

1

Kate Chopin House & Bayou Folk Museum ■

491

6

Cloutierville ■

N W E S

CANE RIVER

| 0 | 5 | 10 Miles |
| 0 | 5 | 10 | 15 Kilometers |

● Plantation

49

119

Derry

To Alexandria

Inset map
LA   MS   AL
New Orleans

A   B

CANE RIVER SITES

BEAU FORT

Beau Fort 1790

On the site of old Fort Charles, Beau Fort is an early Creole–style home with an 84-foot gallery, hand-hewn cypress beams, period memorabilia; open to the public daily. *4078 Hwy. 494/119.*

CHEROKEE

Cherokee 1839

A perfect example of a raised Creole cottage and the site of the famous Bossier-Gaiennie duel fought on the savannah out back. Named for the Cherokee roses in front yard. *Private; Hwy. 494.*

OAKLAND

Magnolia *1835*
Since 1835, the main house has been owned by the same family; the grounds, meanwhile, have been given to the National Park Service.

MAGNOLIA

Rangers give tours of the brick slave quarters and tell stories of slaves' lives there. *5487 Hwy. 119; 318-379-2221.*

Oakland *1821*
The most complete Creole plantation in the South. The first cotton in Louisiana was planted here and the 17 original outbuildings are considered the finest examples of Creole architecture in the state. *Hwy. 494; private.*

St. Augustine Catholic Church *1827*
The first Catholic Church in the nation to be founded and financed by Free People of Color. Site of the wedding scene in *Steel Magnolias* and the Creole Heritage Festival each January 22. *2262 Hwy. 484; 318-379-2521.*

ST. AUGUSTINE CHURCH

Kate Chopin House & Bayou Folk Museum
Home of noted 19th-century writer Kate Chopin (1851-1904). *At Derry turn east off Hwy. 1 onto Hwy. 491. In town of Cloutierville; 318-379-2233.*

Melrose Plantation *1786*
Founded by Marie Thérèze Coincoin, a freed slave whose alliance with a wealthy Frenchman had produced several children. *17.8 miles south of Natchitoches at 3533 Hwy. 119 at the junction of Rte. 493 (two miles east of LA Rte 1); 318-379-0055.*

MELROSE

KATE CHOPIN HOUSE

(All photos by Syndey Byrd)

An 18th-century Congo-style house at Melrose Plantation. Murals by noted artist Clementine Hunter decorates its interior walls. (Syndey Byrd)

high social status in the process. By the time of her death in 1816, Coincoin and her children owned some hundred slaves and 1,200 acres of prime farm land.

The eldest of Marie Thérèze Coincoin's sons, Augustin Metoyer, became the patriarch of Cane River's Free People of Color and founder of the St. Augustine Church. The prominent Metoyers socialized with white planters who worshiped with them at the Metoyers' church. They also served as private bankers at a time when the area had no banking institution. (Ironically, the Metoyers lost the plantation in 1847 after Augustin co-signed on a loan for a white friend, who then defaulted.)

Melrose went through several owners until John Hampton and Cammie Garrett Henry inherited it in 1898. Miss Cammie, as she was known, was fascinated by local history and culture. She began an active program of restoration and turned Melrose into a cultural center where visiting

Augustin Metoyer, eldest son of Marie Coincoin, who lived at Melrose and built St. Augustine Church. (Courtesy St. Augustine Catholic Church, Natchitoches)

artists and writers came—sometimes for long periods—to work. These included William Faulkner, John Steinbeck, Frances Parkinson Keyes, Erskine Caldwell, and Lyle Saxon.

It was here at Melrose that noted painter Clementine Hunter grew into adulthood working as a field hand, domestic servant, and cook. At the age of 54, she began painting, eventually achieving worldwide acclaim. The 50-foot mural of her life covers the walls of the upper story of African House. This is one of the few 18th-century Congo-style structures remaining in the United States.

The Melrose Arts and Crafts Festival is held on site the second weekend in June. *Melrose is a private residence, but it can be toured from 1–4 P.M. as part of a guided one-and-a-half hour tour. Melrose location: 17.8 miles south of Natchitoches at 3533 Hwy. 119 at the junction of Rte. 493 (two miles east of Hwy. 1); 318-379-0055.*

HOT HEART OF LOUISIANA

Sidda is a girl again in the hot heart of Louisiana, the bayou world of Catholic saints and voodoo queens. It is Labor Day, 1959, at Pecan Grove Plantation, on the day of her daddy's annual dove hunt. While the men sweat and shoot, Sidda's gorgeous mother, Vivi, and her gang of girlfriends, the Ya-Yas, play *bourrée,* a cut-throat Louisiana poker, inside the air-conditioned house. On the kitchen blackboard is scrawled: SMOKE, DRINK, NEVER THINK—borrowed from Billie Holiday. When the ladies take a break, they feed the Petites Ya-Yas (as Ya-Ya offspring are called) sickly sweet maraschino cherries from the fridge in the wet bar.

She walks barefoot into the humid night, moonlight on her freckled shoulders. Near a huge, live oak tree on the edge of her father's cotton fields, Sidda looks up into the sky. In the crook of the crescent moon sits the Holy Lady, with strong muscles and a merciful heart. She kicks her splendid legs like the moon is her swing and the sky, her front porch. She waves down at Sidda like she has just spotted an old buddy.

Sidda stands in the moonlight and lets the Blessed Mother love every hair on her six-year-old head. Tenderness flows down from the moon and up from the earth. For one fleeting, luminous moment, Sidda Walker knows there has never been a time when she has not been loved.

—Rebecca Wells, *Divine Secrets of the Ya-Ya Sisterhood,* 1996

◆ CLOUTIERVILLE'S KATE CHOPIN HOUSE &
BAYOU FOLK MUSEUM   *map pages 174-175*

Cloutierville was home to noted 19th-century writer Kate Chopin (1851-1904), who lived here with her husband and children for several years. Chopin, who had previously lived in New Orleans, shocked locals because she sat with her legs crossed (ladies didn't) and smoked. Her collection of stories, *Bayou Folk,* an affectionate depiction of the quiet, impoverished life she saw all around her, displeased her neighbors even more.

Chopin moved to Cloutierville with her husband after he suffered financial reverses in New Orleans. Together they ran a store and lived in the still extant Creole cottage, now part of the Bayou Folk Museum. The museum's Chopin collection contains everything from first editions to her sidesaddle. Visiting is a delight. Those at the museum seem genuinely delighted to see the few people who drop by. Inside the house are homey furnishings; outside the house, life looks as if it might have been socially claustrophobic.

After Kate Chopin's husband died, she moved to St. Louis. Her novel *The Awakening,* published in 1889, reveals the desperate inner life of a mother and wife who yearns to escape. Such sentiments were considered deeply shocking at the time the book was published. *Cloutierville is off Hwy. 119 on Hwy. 491; follow museum sign east; 318-379-2233.*

❖

A nearby plantation, closed to the public, is **Little Eva Plantation,** one of the oldest and largest pecan producers in the country. The Chopin family owned this property at the time that Kate Chopin lived in Cloutierville. Supposedly, it was once owned by a distant relative of Harriet Beecher Stowe, who came to visit her cousin here and used him as the model for Simon Legree.

After the Chopin family sold this farm, subsequent owners named it Little Eva Plantation and offered visitors a glimpse of a cabin out back they called "Uncle Tom's cabin." The owners who followed discontinued the practice.

Author Kate Chopin looked down this road when she came to live in Cloutierville. Later she wrote The Awakening, *a novel about a lonely wife going mad. (Kit Duane)*

CANE RIVER

■ KISATCHIE NATIONAL FOREST *map page 170, A/C-2/3*

The Kisatchie National Forest is a sportsman's and naturalist's paradise that covers 600,000 acres in seven central and northern Louisiana parishes. The forest is divided into six ranger districts, each with its own special scenic attractions.

Kisatchie means "long cane," and is thought to be of Caddoan Indian origin. The forest was established in 1930 as the result of a crusade by naturalist Caroline Dorman to save some of Louisiana's wilderness areas. It is the only national forest in the state. Elevations range from 80 feet to 400 feet above sea level, which is almost a mountain in Louisiana.

Some of the highlights of the forest include the **Wild Azalea Trail** for hiking, the **Caroline Dorman Trail** for hiking or horseback riding, **Saline Bayou Scenic River** and **Kisatchie Bayou** for boating or canoeing, and the **Longleaf Trail Scenic Byway** for driving. Camping, swimming, and cycling, as well as hunting and fishing are also permitted in sections of the forest. *Check for areas burned in the 2000 fire. Forest roads maps are available at the Kisatchie National Forest office, 2500 Shreveport Hwy. (Hwy. 71) in Pineville. For information call 318-473-7160.*

Wildflowers in Kisatchie National Forest. (Syndey Byrd)

CANE RIVER

JULIA SANDERS' FLORA GUIDE: KISATCHIE NATIONAL FOREST

Wild Azalea
Rhododendron conescens
A large shrub with fragrant flowers. Blooms March into April. Found along creeks and lakes in hilly pine forest such as Kisatchie.

Bird's Foot Violet
Viola pedata
The queen of violets. Leaf shape is similar to a bird's foot. Blooms March until April. A jewel along Kisatchie's walking trails and forest roads.

CANE RIVER

■ WEST OF NATCHITOCHES

It's a pretty ramble through the rolling hills to the **Rebel State Commemorative Area** near Marthaville, about 25 miles west of Natchitoches. The dense piney woods are interspersed with lush green fields and little ponds down in the low spots. The Rebel SCA takes its name from the grave of the Unknown Confederate Soldier, which is on the site. When the nameless soldier was killed, the Barnhill family gave him a Christian burial and then tended his grave for a hundred years. In 1962, a marker was finally placed on the grave.

A tour of the **Louisiana Country Music Museum** (on the grounds of the RSCA) begins with a video that gives a good overview of the history of country and gospel music in Louisiana. The exhibits, which include photographs, memorabilia, explanatory panels, and snatches of recorded music, are fascinating and enlightening. There is a large exhibit on the Louisiana Hayride *(see page 183),* the weekly country music show held in Shreveport's Municipal Auditorium, beginning in 1948. *Located 25 miles west of Natchitoches on LA 1221 North; 318-472-6255.*

This being Louisiana, country and gospel music have figured prominently in politics. Jimmie Davis was elected governor in 1944 and again in 1960 on his fame as a musician and author of "You Are My Sunshine." Earl Long used hillbilly bands to gather crowds for his stump speeches; and governors McKeithen, Edwards, and Treen also campaigned with country bands and gospel quartets.

For those who wish to spend additional time at the museum, there is a listening room and library. Concerts, as well as the Louisiana State Fiddling Championship, are held in the amphitheater outside the museum.

❖

The town of **Many** was founded as a trading post by Belgians in 1843. Nowadays its claim to fame is **Hodges Gardens,** with a 4,700-acre arboretum and 60 acres of formal terraced gardens on a 255-acre bass fishing lake. It features miles of hiking trails, waterfalls, babbling brooks for boating and fishing, and ethereal campsites.

CANE RIVER

Elvis Presley first performed on the Louisiana Hayride *radio show in October of 1954 in response to a recommendation from legendary music promoter Sam Phillips of Sun Records. The Hayride enjoyed its greatest success between 1948 and 1960, at which point television began to compete for the loyalty of country music fans.*

Stories of the Hayride glory years may be enjoyed in two books by historian Robert Gentry, Johnny Horton: From New Orleans to Alaska. *and* I Was There When it Happened, *about Tillman Franks, host of the radio show. (photo courtesy Robert Gentry)*

COUNTRY RADIO AND *THE LOUISIANA HAYRIDE*

From 1948 to 1960 the live, cutting-edge music show, *The Louisiana Hayride* was broadcast to the Gulf South with 50,000 watts of power from Shreveport over KWKH. CBS Radio carried music that could make a girl squeal the polish off her toenails from coast to coast, and Armed Forces Radio beamed it oversees. At a time when the Grand Ole Opry in Nashville held to traditional values by forbidding drums, horns, and rockabilly on their stage, each and every Saturday night a musical fireball was generated from the stage of the Shreveport Municipal Auditorium.

Shreveport became known as the "cradle of the stars," for it was here that Arkansas native **Johnny Cash** played to his first national audiences in 1955 and **George "Possum" Jones** made his name. It was on this stage that the immortal words were uttered, "**Elvis** has left the building" by producer Horace Logan at the end of The King's 18-month run as a regular. (Elvis earned $18 a week and lived across the river at the Al-Ida Motel in Bossier City.)

"**The Singing Governor**" **Jimmie Davis's** hit "You Are My Sunshine" was a favorite with people the world over. Jimmie was raised in a three-room home in Beech Springs, one of 11 God-fearin' children. At the age of 100, and at the end of the last century, Davis continued to tour.

Another *Hayride* regular, **Slim Whitman**, worked as a Shreveport postman between his *Hayride* performances. Whitman's 1953 recording of "Indian Love Call" made him the first "Hayrider" to earn a gold record. Then on October 16, 1954, **Elvis Presley** was brought on stage as the "Lucky Strike special guest" just after 9 P.M. Presley was soon being called "The King of Western Pop" and the "Memphis Flash."

Hank Williams first performed for the *Hayride* in August of 1948. By fall, Hank was known as the "Ol' Syrup Sopper," because the show was sponsored by Johnny Fair Syrup. In late 1949, "Lovesick Blues" propelled the yodeling Hank into worldwide stardom and sent him from Shreveport to Nashville.

On "Slim Whitman Appreciation Night" on September 13, 1952, Hank made a surprise visit. Hank's boozing and missed shows had gotten him fired from the Opry in Nashville. Hank thrilled the Louisiana audience when he announced that he'd "come home to *The Hayride* for good," and sang his "Jambalaya."

By the early 1960s, the advent of television and a decline in the popularity of this genre spelled the end of *The Louisiana Hayride*. In 1969, the show ended. A second incarnation ran from 1973 to 1987. A 50th Anniversary Show on April 3, 1999, featured old regulars Willie Nelson, Jimmie Davis, and Hank Williams's daughter Jett.

—Bethany Ewald Bultman

There is an Easter Sunrise Service, a Christmas Lights Festival, and a Fourth of July Crafts Festival.

After the timber companies had clear-cut the area, conservationist A. J. Hodges planted thousands of trees in the 1940s. Today, this is one of the largest privately operated gardens in the nation. The old-fashioned rose garden is gorgeous in the warm months, and the petrified tree near the entrance is thousands of years old.

■ EAST TOWARD THE MISSISSIPPI RIVER

Highway 6 (also 84) passes through rolling green pastures and forest on its way to the Mississippi River bridge and Natchez. **Winnfield** *(map page 170, B-1&2)*, 36 miles east of Natchitoches is the birthplace of Huey and Earl Long, the two most fascinating politicians the South has produced. You don't have to be a partisan of either "The Kingfish" or "Uncle Earl" to appreciate their importance in modern Southern history, but whether you "love them, hate them, or don't have an opinion," a visit to Winnfield (pop. 7,000) will be an enlightening experience.

For a Louisiana political junkie, a trip to the **Louisiana Political Museum & Hall of Fame** takes on the same importance as a pilgrimage to the Shreveport Municipal Auditorium does for diehard Elvis fans. The museum is housed in the town's old train depot; *499 E. Main St.; 318-628-5928.*

Huey and Earl are the dominant figures in the museum as they are in Louisiana political history, but they are joined by many former cronies and adversaries who once strode across the Louisiana political stage. Jimmie Davis ("The Singing Governor") is there, as is Cajun governor Edwin Edwards, Dudley J. LeBlanc, New Orleans mayor De Lesseps Chet Morrison (whom Earl mimicked for his citified Creole ways, calling him "Della-soups"),

Mannequin of Gov. Huey Long at the Louisiana Political Museum. (Syndey Byrd)

HUEY AND EARL LONG: REBELS WITHOUT A PAUSE

Winn Parish, where two of Louisiana's most famous politicians were born, has a history of going its own way. When Louisiana first seceded from the Union in 1861, the parish initially refused to go along with this idea, and for a brief period formed the Free State of Winn. During the first years of the 20th century, populist sentiment was strong in this poor hard-scrabble land, and in the election of 1912, Winn Parish voted Socialist. It was in this climate that Huey Long (1893-1935), one time patent medicine and shortening salesman, rose to power, becoming governor in 1928 and U.S. senator in 1932. (Long's career was cut short by an assassin's bullet in September of 1935.)

In the depths of the Depression, Long advocated redistribution of the wealth, a position that pleased his poor constituents. Affluent Louisianans described Huey's ideas as "Marxism with a redneck accent."

Huey's younger brother, Earl (1895-1960), was a three-time governor of Louisiana. "The Last of the Red-Hot Papas," as he called himself, Earl was a master of the stump speech, blending the fervor of an evangelist with down-home humor and earthy language. He was easily the most entertaining and eccentric politician Louisiana has ever seen, and that's high praise in this state. The Baptists long ago disapproved of Earl's wanton ways: drinking and carousing with a stripper named Blaze Starr (subject of the 1989 Ron Shelton film *Blaze).*

To this day, feelings in Louisiana run deep about the Longs. Huey Long has been called a demagogue, described as the closest thing to a dictator this country has produced. Earl Long's detractors referred to him as a "demented hillbilly," and that's when they were being charitable. But those who benefited from the Longs' social programs esteemed the brothers mightily.

Historians tend to vacillate in their assessments. Huey was, without question, a man who ran roughshod over fundamental liberties. Yet there is no denying that he delivered material benefits to a very backward state long, governed by a planter class indifferent to the poor. One historian figures that there were 300 miles of paved road in the state when Huey was elected governor. At the end of his term, 1,583 miles were paved.

Huey Long took great pride in his program to provide free textbooks in the schools. Earl Long counted old-age pensions and his school hot-lunch program his proudest achievements. Neither Long engaged in race-baiting. In the charged racial climate of the late 1950s, Earl Long proved his worth by standing up against the racial harangues of fire-eating white supremacists.

—Stanley Dry

Former Louisiana governor Jimmie Davis performing his hit song, "You Are My Sunshine." (Syndey Byrd)

Camille Gravel (attorney and political confidante to many Louisiana politicians), labor leader Victor Bussie, St. Landry Parish sheriff Cat Doucet, pioneer civil rights attorney Louis Berry, and Huey Long biographer T. Harry Williams.

A statue of Huey P. Long stands on the courthouse square and a statue of his brother Earl in Earl K. Long Memorial Park, the site of the Long home, where the two men were born. Huey is buried at the state capitol in Baton Rouge and Earl is buried beneath his statue in Winnfield.

Huey Long's golf clubs are on display in the museum as are several wild hogs shot by Earl. In honor of Earl's sport, Winnfield hosts Uncle Earl's Hog Dog Trials in late March. (Contestants are a native Louisiana breed, the catahoula hound.)

Just off US 84 West is the 1.5-mile **Winn Parish Dogwood Trail.** It's a glorious hike, especially around Easter when the dogwood is in bloom. If you drive along the main road to Natchez from Winnfield, you'll pass acres of commercial pulpwood pine forest, rusty, pumping oil wells, and power lines.

❖

Frogmore, in Concordia Parish *(map page 170, F-3),* is no more than a wide spot on US 84 in the Delta cotton country. The town was named by surveyors from the railroad who said they saw more frogs here than they'd ever seen before. Rich alluvial deposits from floodings of the Mississippi to the east and other rivers to the west created fertile ground for the growing of cotton, and Natchez planters had established large plantations in this area by 1793.

Frogmore Plantation is an 1,800-acre working cotton plantation. The current owners have relocated to the site 18 antebellum structures, including an overseer's dogtrot house, a plantation commissary, and slave cabins. Owners Buddy and Lynette Tanner offer a tour that begins with a video and proceeds to a rare 1884 Munger steam cotton gin and some of the plantation buildings. According to the Tanner tour, the slaves who once worked the cotton fields here were "well cared for and content."

Following the tour, Mr. Tanner offers a visit to his nearby modern cotton gin and farm. Cotton is in the fields from May to September. During the cotton harvest in September, visitors can see the operation at work; during the off-season, a video details the highly mechanized cotton farming and the computerized, automated gin of today. Following the video, Mr. Tanner will share with you his concern that foreign competition threatens farmers—and that government needs to protect the latter from the former. A display features various byproducts of cotton production, including Crisco, which is an acronym for "crystallized cottonseed oil." *Frogmore is located 71 miles east of Winnfield, LA, and 19 miles west of Natchez, MS; 11054 Hwy. 84; 318-757-2453.*

Aside from a few pecan groves, the seven-mile stretch between Frogmore and Ferriday (pop. 4,000) is pockmarked with power lines, rusted trailer homes, gravel pits, auto graveyards, and flea markets filled with crocheted acrylic handicrafts. There are about as many Holiness and Assembly of God churches as there are road-killed dogs and run-over turtles, and that's a lot. At Ferriday, the scenery doesn't improve, but there is a greater concentration of fast food joints, nursing homes, and abandoned gas stations.

Ferriday is the little town that gave the world rock 'n roller Jerry Lee "Killer" Lewis, TV evangelist Jimmy Lee Swaggart, and country music's Mickey Gilley, cousins all, whose characters were formed by an upbringing in the local Assembly of God Church.

❖

CANE RIVER

At the corner of US 84 and Louisiana Avenue in **Ferriday** *(map page 170, F-3)*, next to the family's Pik-Quick Drive Thru, is the **Lewis Family Museum,** a bizarre shrine to the famous rock 'n' roller Jerry Lee Lewis that is maintained by his sister Frankie "Killerette" Lewis and her tobacco-chewing husband.

Avid fans from around the world make the pilgrimage to see memorabilia including whiskey bottles, clothes, cigarette lighters, and autographed pictures of George and Lurleen Wallace. There is a mountain of Lewis artifacts piled to the ceiling, so much that Lewis's brother-in-law admits he and his wife had to stop living there. Compared to this, Elvis's Graceland looks like Monticello.

As a youth, Jerry Lee Lewis thought he would become a preacher, but he lost the opportunity to distinguish himself in the ministry when he was kicked out of a Texas Bible college for livening up hymns with a boogie-woogie beat. Some of the sermons he wrote when he was young are on display in the museum, as are religious records and books by cousin Rev. Jimmy Swaggart, the fire-and-brimstone preacher who fell from grace when caught visiting a prostitute in Room 7 of the

The memory of rock 'n' roller Jerry Lee Lewis of Ferriday is kept alive by his sister Frankie Jean Lewis at the Lewis Family Museum, described above. (Syndey Byrd)

Travel Inn Motel on Airline Highway in New Orleans.

Jerry Lee Lewis, who won fame for the hits "Whole Lotta Shakin' Goin On" and "Great Balls of Fire" and who faced his own moral censure when he married his 13-year-old cousin, summed it up this way: "I should have been a Christian, but I'm too weak for that. I'm a rock 'n' roll cat." *Corner of US 84 and Louisiana Ave. next to Pik-Quick Drive Thru.*

■ DETOUR TO POVERTY POINT   *map page 2, top, right*

Outside Epps in the northeastern corner of Louisiana, in the vicinity of the towns of Transylvania and Lake Providence (a three-hour drive from New Orleans), is the site of one of North America's earliest and largest Native communities. Be forewarned, no matter what road you take, the trip is endless and dreary enough to make you wonder if it's all worth it. It is! Despite its name, by which a more modern farmer described the infertile soil, Poverty Point is one of those places that many will think back on often, forgetting just how loathsome the journey to get there was.

Poverty Point is but one of several prehistoric Indian sites in the immediate area, some dating back 6,000 years. It was erected by a culture that is estimated to have existed between 3,700 and 2,700 years ago at the beginning of the American Neolithic Age, when it was home to some 5,000 people. The site is dominated by a mammoth eagle-shaped mound, 640 by 710 feet long and 70 feet high, the second tallest Indian mound in North America, and 35 times the cubic volume of the Great Pyramid in Egypt. Archaeologists marvel at the fact that the Indians had to dig the earth with sticks and transport over a half a million tons of dirt in baskets.

Close by the Eagle Mound is another mound, this one 600 feet long and 55 feet high. In all there are six earthen mounds scattered around the 1,500-acre site. A 2.6-mile trail connects the points of interest. From Easter to Labor Day a tram also makes the loop. The extensive earthworks took an estimated five million man-hours to build.

The site includes a museum with an explanatory video, as well as artifacts from the site. A brochure is available for those who wish to take a self-guided tour. Bring your own food, as there isn't even fast food in this part of the state. *The site is on LA 577 right off Hwy. 134; 318-926-5492.*

CANE RIVER

■ CANE RIVER FOOD & LODGING

☎   For chain lodgings see toll-free numbers on page 333

$$ For room (☎) and restaurant (✕) price designations see page 333.

Natchitoches & Cane River Area *map pages 170, 171*

☎ **Breazeale House.** 926 Washington St.; 318-352-5630 or 800-352-5631 $-$$ Victorian home (ca. 1898) in Historic District. Rates include full breakfast.

☎ **Days Inn.** 1000 College Ave.; 318-352-4426 or 800-329-7466. $

☎ **Fleur de Lis Inn.** 336 Second St.; 318-352-6621 or 800-489-6621 $-$$ A 1903 Victorian home in the Historic District with five guest rooms and a private cottage. Rates include drinks and full breakfast.

☎ **Judge Porter House.** 321 Second St.; 318-352-9206 or 800-441-8343 $$-$$$ Rambling 1912 home with two-story wraparound gallery located in Historic District. Four rooms in the main home plus a guesthouse. Rates include drinks and full breakfast.

JUDGE PORTER HOUSE

☎ **Levy-East House.** 358 Jefferson St.; 318-352-0662 or 800-840-0662 $$-$$$ Greek Revival home (c. 1838) in the Historic District. Rates include full breakfast, plus wine and champagne for couples celebrating special occasions.

LEVY-EAST HOUSE

☎ **Magnolia Plantation.** 5487 Hwy. 119, near Cloutierville; 318-379-2221 $$ Located 22 miles south of Natchitoches this is a working plantation that has been in the same family since 1753. The big house was built in the early 1830s, burned during the Civil War, and rebuilt in the 1890s. Three inn rooms; rates include breakfast and tour of the home.

☎ **The Queen Anne Inn.** 125 Pine St.; 318-352-0989 or 888-685-1585 $$ Queen Anne home (1905) in the Historic District. Rates include full breakfast, wine, and beverages.

☎ **Tante Huppe Inn.** 424 Jefferson St.; 318-352-5342 or 800-482-4276 $$

An 1830 French Creole home in the Historic District, with its original furnishings. Three suites with private entrance and kitchen. Includes full breakfast in the dining room and a tour of the home. Delightful; highly recommended.

TANTE HUPPE INN

✕ **Grayson's Barbecue.** US 71N, Clarence; 318-357-0166 $
About five miles outside Natchitoches. Real barbecue beef, pork ribs, and ham with all the fixin's. Homemade buns for the sandwiches are a special touch.

✕ **Just Friends.** 750 Front St.; 318-352-3836 $
Popular luncheon spot for soups, sandwiches, salads, desserts, and almond tea.

✕ **The Landing Restaurant.** 530 Front St.; 318-352-1579 $$
Stylish restaurant overlooking Cane River, with a wide-ranging menu including Natchitoches meat pies, fried green tomatoes, alligator, a variety of seafood and steaks, as well as pastas and salads.

✕ **Lasyone's Meat Pie Kitchen & Restaurant.** 622 Second St.; 318-352-3353 $
Local institution known for its Natchitoches meat pies and photographs of

celebrities who have eaten there. Open for breakfast, lunch, and dinner.

✕ **Mariner's Seafood & Steakhouse.** Hwy. 1 bypass; 318-357-1220 $$
Located on Sibley Lake, just minutes from downtown. Specialties include broiled and fried seafood, steaks, chops, chicken, and quail.

✕ **Merci Beaucoup.** 127 Church St.; 318-352-6634 $
Offers courtyard dining in the Historic District. Open for lunch only, specialties include crabcakes with crawfish etouffée.

✕ **Mrs. Ruby's Cafe.** Hwy. 1 above Cloutierville
No more than a funky roadhouse, but noted for crawfish pies and meat pies. Breakfast and lunch; closes at 2 P.M.

✕ **Papa's Bar and Grill.** 604 Front St.; 318-356-5850 $-$$$
The menu, served all day, includes sandwiches, cold beer, and steaks.

Winnfield Area
map page 170, B-1

✕ **Dodson Fish Market.** 202 N. Third St., Dodson; 318-628-5568 $
Located about 12 miles north of Winnfield, this fish market and restaurant specializes in catfish and buffalo ribs (from the buffalo fish, not the animal).

✕ **A Little Bit of Heaven.** 7855 Hwy. 167 S.; 318-648-2080 $-$$
Gospel music supper club with live gospel music on Friday and Saturday nights. Catfish and seafood are the principal items on the menu. No alcoholic beverages or smoking.

CANE RIVER
FOOD & LODGING

M I S S I S S I P P I
P L A N T A T I O N   C O U N T R Y
by Malia Boyd

■ HIGHLIGHTS   *page*

Food & Lodging, page 237
Maps, pages 194, 205, 232

■ TRAVEL OVERVIEW

Along the lower Natchez Trace in Mississippi, the "Old South" of the 18th and 19th centuries survives among the dogwoods and oaks, azaleas and gardenias. Natchez is undoubtedly the belle of this ball, with historic collonaded mansions at nearly every corner, and its famous garden and home tours during Spring Pilgrimage in March and April. Small towns also reveal the culture—the eerie ruins of Windsor, the giant golden finger pointing to heaven atop a church steeple in Port Gibson. Vicksburg straddles past and present, with its Civil War cemetery and its neon riverboat casinos.

Your near-constant companion during this drive will be the Mississippi River. The wide, brown, fast-flowing Mississippi has served as a commerical artery through the centuries—but such an unpredictable and ornery one that few roads or homes are built along its edges. Unless you take a trip up the Mississippi on the *Delta Queen*, you'll merely catch glimpses of it. Recreational boating is not available and would be dangerous if it were; there are few marked parks and trails along the loess bluffs above the river.

Climate: Weatherwise, the best times to visit this area is March through May and October through December. During these months you'll find the humidity fairly low

(left margin, vertical text) MISSISSIPPI PLANTATION COUNTRY

and temperatures (Fahrenheit) ranging between the 70s in the day and the 50s at night. Summers are hot and fairly humid in the 80s and 90s, but luckily there's air-conditioning. Winters are usually mild (50s and 60s), though you can expect several freezes during the coldest months.

Food & Lodging: Accommodations in gracious mansions are the ticket in this part of the world, many of them oozing charm right off their rocking chair–furnished porches. There are always the mid-scale chains if you're in the mood for a more reasonable price.

Local cuisine is served in small places with homestyle food, while large-scale opulent dining experiences are few and far between. But who says homey is bad? If you choose right, you're bound to eat some of the best comfort food—cheese grits, fried chicken, fruit pies—this region has to offer. At least one restaurant in Natchez offers first-class cuisine.

Sidewalks are rolled up by 9 P.M., so don't expect late nights of merriment.

For restaurant and lodging listings, see page 237; see page 333 for price designations and toll-free numbers for chain accommodations. For a chart of listings by region, see page 334.

The gardens at Monmouth Plantation. (Brian Gauvin)

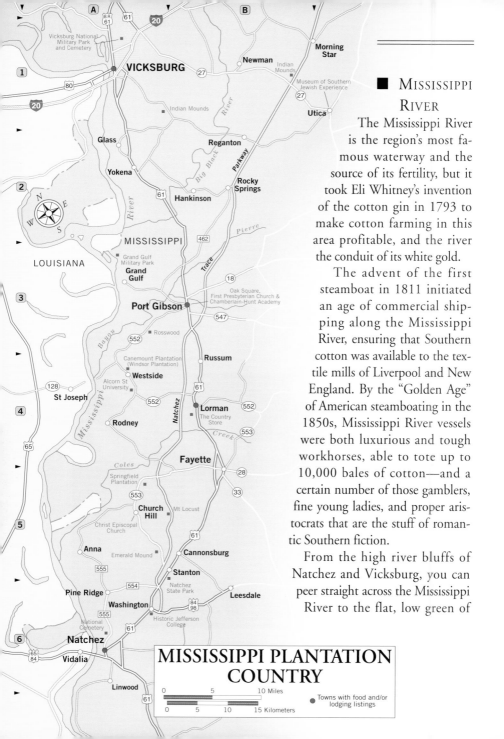

■ MISSISSIPPI RIVER

The Mississippi River is the region's most famous waterway and the source of its fertility, but it took Eli Whitney's invention of the cotton gin in 1793 to make cotton farming in this area profitable, and the river the conduit of its white gold.

The advent of the first steamboat in 1811 initiated an age of commercial shipping along the Mississippi River, ensuring that Southern cotton was available to the textile mills of Liverpool and New England. By the "Golden Age" of American steamboating in the 1850s, Mississippi River vessels were both luxurious and tough workhorses, able to tote up to 10,000 bales of cotton—and a certain number of those gamblers, fine young ladies, and proper aristocrats that are the stuff of romantic Southern fiction.

From the high river bluffs of Natchez and Vicksburg, you can peer straight across the Mississippi River to the flat, low green of

MISSISSIPPI PLANTATION COUNTRY

0	5	10 Miles

| 0 | 5 | 10 | 15 Kilometers |

● Towns with food and/or lodging listings

Louisiana. Pleasure boats that take overnight travelers up and down the river compete for river space with barges that haul produce and dry goods along the waterway. The casino river boats—painted facades plopped on top of barges—never take to the eddies, because they're just not built for it.

Mississippi Travel:

River Barge Excursions offers a delightful combination of the comfort of a motel and the experience of cruising the river. Information: *504-365-0022 or 888-462-2743; www.riverbarge.com.*

Delta Queen Steamboat Co. has three elegant cruise ships. Information: *800-543-1949; www. deltaqueen.com.*

This drawing of the interior of the steamboat Princess, *done by Marie Adrien Persac in 1861, reveals the opulence of antebellum steamboats. Note the lavish dinner setting, special tables for top hats, gentlemen's bar, and spittoons. (Louisiana State University Art Museum)*

Natchez Indian chief (center) with Choctaw warriors and children,
by A. DeBatz, an early visitor.

■ NATCHEZ: DEEP IN HISTORY AND CULTURE

In 1716, French colonists decided to construct a fort high atop the banks of the Mississippi River in the present day city of Natchez. An agricultural community of approximately 3,500 Native people lived nearby, but it was soon destroyed *(see page 220)*. Between 1727 and 1800, the Natchez area was the most successful farming community in the entire Louisiana Territory. By 1727, 6,000 acres of fine tobacco, rice, cotton, and indigo were under cultivation. But as the French Empire dwindled, so did its commitment to invest in the protection needed to sustain far-away colonies.

After the area was transferred to British control in 1763, English-speaking Anglicans began to outnumber French-speaking Catholics. A diplomatic error transferred Natchez into Spain's hands, where it remained between 1779 and 1798, but Natchez greatly benefitted from management by the Spanish. Taxes remained low, and generous land grants were handed out to English Protestants. By the late 18th century, the population of Natchez included a total of 4,500 people, half of whom were slaves.

Spain peacefully ceded Natchez to the United States in April 1798, giving it a permanent home within the U.S. Mississippi Territory. Between 1798 and 1802 it served as the capital of the new American territory. Several buildings remaining from this era are described on the pages that follow.

◆ BELLE EPOQUE

The highlight of 19th-century cultural life came in 1851, when Jenny Lind, "the Swedish Nightingale" was paid $5,000 by her patron P. T. Barnum to sing five songs for the Natchez elite—who paid up to $12 a ticket. The finest piano in Adams County was brought to the Methodist Church by mule-drawn wagon from Richmond Plantation for the momentous occasion.

At the pinnacle of the Natchez cotton empire in 1860, the total population was a mere 6,600 people, of whom 2,000 were slaves. Yet tiny, isolated Natchez had more millionaires per capita than any city in America. At a time when 75 percent of Southerners owned no slaves, 63 percent of Adams County plantations claimed more than 20.

Natchez grandees, (called the "Nabobs" or "4,000-bale Planters" for the size of their cotton crop) bought their wines in Le Havre and their frills in New Orleans, educated their sons at Harvard and Yale, and enjoyed grand tours of Europe. Adam Hodgson wrote from Natchez in 1820, "During the day many of the party amused themselves by shooting alligators."

Cotton—the source of the Natchez Nabobs' great wealth—is loaded onto a steamboat.

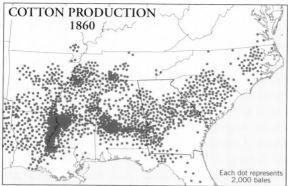

COTTON PRODUCTION 1860

Each dot represents 2,000 bales

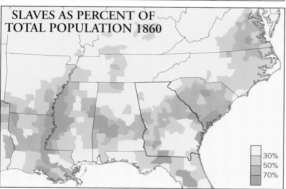

SLAVES AS PERCENT OF TOTAL POPULATION 1860

30%
50%
70%

Cotton and slavery went hand in hand, as these maps demonstrate. Note the high concentration of both along the southern Mississippi River—especially between Natchez and Vicksburg.

A disastrous tornado in 1840 destroyed many downtown buildings and all of the china trees that had lined the main streets. A new Natchez arose from the rubble, with gravel sidewalks and wide streets. Natchez boasted several schools and Masonic lodges, and two thriving newspapers. Horse races, dueling (across the river in Louisiana), and balls were regular events for Natchez Nabobery.

◆ CIVIL WAR (1861-1865)

During the Civil War, nearly half the city's white male population joined the Confederate army; 300 of them died in war. **Linden** *(see map page 205, C-3),* a Natchez plantation, became known as the home of "the Little War Mother" because its owner sent seven sons and five sons-in-law off to fight for the Confederacy. Not all the Nabobs joined the Confederate ranks, however. Many of them were English- or Yankee-born, and their livelihoods were dependent on "cotton diplomacy" with the industrial Northeast and England. The 4,000-balers argued that a bloody, prolonged "unpleasantness" would not serve their interests. Those who could "baled" out to safer territory to await the inevitable outcome.

Frank Surget, one of the wealthiest of the 4,000-bale planters, hedged his bets by trading and fraternizing with both the Confederates and the Union forces. Somehow Surget managed to offend one of his Yankee buddies by not inviting him to dinner. The officer retaliated by demolishing Surget's mansion, Clifton, in order to construct Fort McPherson. Years later Surget made it clear that he had not offended the Union officer intentionally. "I would have dined with the devil himself if it would have saved Clifton."

Ironically, the only real war violence in Natchez was brought on entirely by the foolhardy actions of its own citizens. When the USS *Essex,* a Union gunboat, pulled into the city dock in September of 1862 to load supplies, several of the 200-man home guard—made up of men too old or infirm to go to war—fired on the crew, killing one and wounding six. The heretofore quiet gunboat let loose a two-and-a-half hour barrage of shells on the city and killed a seven-year-old girl in the process.

After Vicksburg fell to the Union on July 4, 1863, Natchez was occupied by the Federals. The Blues took revenge on some of the staunchest Confederate supporters by stabling horses in their fine homes—Monteigne, home of Confederate General William T. Martin, and Choctaw among them.

Portraits of Jefferson Davis and Varina Howell, who were married in the front parlor of her parents' Natchez home, The Briars, in 1845. Varina, the oldest of 10 children, was 18 at the time, and Jefferson was a 38-year-old widower. Jefferson Davis distinguished himself in the American war with Mexico, became a U.S. Senator, and went on to become President of the Confederacy. Raised near Woodville, Mississippi, he lived his last days at Beauvoir, on the Mississippi Gulf Coast. (courtesy Bob Cannon, The Briars)

◆ AFTER THE WAR: RECONSTRUCTION TO THE GAY '90S

During Reconstruction, the former Nabobs didn't stay home weeping into their silver julep cups. Many moved on to New Orleans or cities on the East Coast. Those who remained in Natchez, rehired or replaced their slaves with black tenant farmers. The year 1875 saw the elite of Natchez throw the first Mardi Gras celebration in Mississippi since French explorer Pierre le Moyne, Sieur d'Iberville, landed on the Mississippi Gulf Coast in 1699. By the 1890s, the citizens of Natchez were looking toward the 20th century with optimism. They were enjoying the benefits of indoor plumbing, one of the state's first

At the end of the 19th century, Natchez society was enjoying itself. Here Mary Britton dons the crown of the Queen of the Kirmess in 1887. (Collection of Thomas H. Gandy and Joan W. Gandy)

public libraries, electricity, a mule-drawn trolley system, a baseball team (the Natchez Indians, part of the Cotton States League), and a fancy five-story hotel complete with an elevator. In 1909, President Taft toured the streets of the town in a chauffeur-driven motorcar.

◆ 20TH-CENTURY WHITE GOLD AND BLACK GOLD

In 1892, *Anthonomous grandis,* the boll weevil, crawled across the Rio Grande River from Mexico. By 1903, it was eating its way across Louisiana; in 1907 it claimed Mississippi. In Natchez, planters let their fields lie fallow and their work force headed north in search of employment. By the time the Depression hit in 1929, the granddaughters of Nabobs of Natchez had become too poor to paint, too proud to whitewash. Then in 1945 an oil well was drilled on the LaGrange Plantation in Adams County (near Cranfield, the birthplace of author Richard

Wright, just as his novels were gaining international acclaim). Suddenly sleepy little Natchez awoke as a wildcatter's dream. All those tracts of useless land began to pay off with buckets of black gold. Between the lucrative tourist dollars brought by a popular new event, "Pilgrimage," and the oil money, antebellum Natchez got a facelift.

■ VISITING NATCHEZ   *maps pages 194 and 205*

One legacy of Natchez society's rapid glide from vast mid-19th-century prosperity to intense early 20th-century poverty is that its architectural treasures were sealed away like Sleeping Beauty beneath the kudzu in rural Mississippi. Today more than 500 antebellum structures remain, and thanks to the tourist and oil booms, the homes where Marquis de Lafayette, Stephen Foster, and Jenny Lind dined amidst Sèvres and Waterford are lovingly restored. Unlike Williamsburg, most of the 500 restored treasures are not museums but homes where kids have watermelonseed spitting contests in the front hall, and family doggies drool on the priceless rugs. Some architectural treasures were the homes of generals and governors—Monteigne, Monmouth, Melrose, Gloucester, and Dunlieth. A few of the mansions on display were working plantations—Edgewood, Elgin, Landsdowne, and Routhland. Most of the antebellum houses were the town residences of those whose vast cotton plantations spread across the river in Concordia Parish, Louisiana (over 81 percent of its land was owned by absentee landowners from Natchez) and up north into Arkansas.

Downtown Natchez is eminently walkable—if the weather's agreeable. Otherwise the best tactic is to drive, park, then walk around, getting back in your air-conditioned car for a short drive to another part of town, where you will again park and walk. There are also scads of antebellum splendor outside the downtown district. Most mansions are within a few minutes' drive of the center of town.

Spring Pilgrimage: Held every year between the first week in March and the first week in April, Pilgrimage, as it is simply called, has become the biggest annual event in Natchez. The Pilgrimage format packages eight different tours of four historic homes each that can be taken by coach or carriage. Tours are led by trained guides who illuminate the history and architecture of the homes. For more information contact Pilgrimage Headquarters at the Natchez Visitors Reception Center, *640 S. Canal St. 800-647-6742 or 601-446-6631.*

(continues page 205)

Natchez and its Famous Pilgrimage

To be born and raised in Natchez, Mississippi, is to be a social unicorn. No matter how hard you try, your origins in a mythical kingdom cannot be erased. Natchez even has its own accent, a softness like the swishing of a long skirt across a finely polished floor. Natchez may be the oldest city on the Mississippi River, and at times served as the territorial capital, but in truth, it dominates nothing except the high loess bluffs atop which it teeters. And, of the 60-family elite of antebellum Natchez, called the Nabobs or 4,000-bale Planters, few could claim their status on grounds of birth, political power, or cultural status. By all accounts these 4,000-balers had about as much social awareness as the Ptolemies.

So why then do we natives think Natchez is the center of the galaxy? Perhaps it is because equality of the sexes has yet to be visited upon our hometown. For you see, in Natchez the thousand ladies of the three Garden Clubs are large and in charge. Men, even if they own historic homes, are merely allowed to be "honorary" Garden Clubbers. Until recently they weren't allowed to attend meetings, having to send their assistants or housekeepers in their stead.

Don't come to Natchez expecting to find Scarlett O'Hara. (Had Scarlett been a Natchez belle, she'd have frightened Melanie away and married Ashley. When faced with losing Tara she'd have mixed up a pitcher of bourbon-laced milk punch, had a bunch of neighborhood gals over to help cook, and invited the Yankees for brunch as paying guests. All the while Ashley would be out in the front yard raking leaves.)

Natchez is a "high cotton" state of mind, where the myth of the Old South is not gone with the wind. In order to understand it, one must look not to the 1850s, but to the 1920s. The boll weevil, World War I, the Depression, and the migration of many to better lives in far-off cities left the granddaughters of the antebellum Natchez stranded. These young women, while freed from the yoke of bustles, corsets, and hoopskirts, were nevertheless stuck on the wrong side of history. Their only tangible legacies were drafty rooms full of threadbare, unfashionable furniture in unsalable, decaying mansions, with snakes in the attic and massive tax bills stacked atop their marble parlor tables. In order to put ham and grits upon their Dresden plates, many of these belles were reduced to milking cows and selling eggs, or taking jobs in shops. When these resourceful gals couldn't afford electricity, they'd bathe their shabby parlors with the shimmer from homemade candles. When ice was too expensive, they'd place cheesecloth bags filled with broken Coca-Cola bottles in their silver pitchers to create the illusion of ice. And if poverty couldn't stop them, Prohibition certainly couldn't. Ever agile at dodging the arrow of despair, these ladies would throw house parties where the price of admission was bathtub gin made by the medical students at Tulane University.

One elderly granddame used to tell me about her life in the 1930s. She recalled it in a voice like cold, sweet butter on a hot biscuit:

My architectural relic may have its original Belter furniture and been in our family since the 1830s, but it was five miles down a dirt road.

In those days, coming into Natchez you had a choice—riding with your windows closed and being saturated in perspiration or letting the breeze cake you with a thick layer of dust. That's how I came up with a solution of how to drive with the windows down: I'd poke eye holes in a grocery sack and stick the bag over my head to protect my hair and makeup. Then I'd wear my housecoat over my slip. Once I got to the blacktop road outside of town, I'd duck behind a large azalea bush to get all gussied-up.

In the early 20th century, many of Natchez's architectural treasures were falling to ruin until Spring Pilgrimage began to save the day. (Collection of Thomas H. Gandy and Joan W. Gandy)

"THE PILGRIMAGE":
HOW IT CAME TO BE

The harsh reality was that these young women were the weight-bearing wall holding up Natchez. They realized that either they would become bitter and brittle or they had to make things better. So these spunky belles got the inspiration to dust off their hoopskirts. Furthermore, they'd invite the Yankees back as paying guests! The ringleader of the scheme was Katherine Grafton Miller, a cross between P. T. Barnum and Talullah Bankhead. (She encouraged local favorites to call her "Play Mama.") Miller convinced her lady friends in the Garden Club to raise a public relations budget of $7.00 (yes, $7.00) so she and her hoopskirt could take a cross-country bus trip to spread the word in more than 75 American cities, "Come to Natchez where the Old South still lives and where shadowed highways and antebellum homes greet old and new friends."

By 1932, 22 of their antebellum homes were put on display for two days. The ladies of Natchez drove the "'pilgrims" around from mansion to mansion, where their hoop-skirted friends awaited to regale them with tales of how they wished the Old South had been. Soon the buzz prompted a visit from First Lady Eleanor Roosevelt. And thus was launched the city's most profitable endeavor.

THE GARDEN CLUB GOES TO WORK

Members of the Garden Club—dominated by Southern belles, fondly nicknamed the Dragon Ladies—donate hundreds of hours to make paper flowers to decorate the Pageant. At events they officiate properly attired in gowns based on 19th-century patterns (hoopskirts can cost from $300-$1,000 each), and they drive hours of carpools to get their children to Tableaux rehearsals. The homeowners divvy up all the proceeds, which they invest in the upkeep of their homes. And what do we other Garden Club ladies get out of it? We get the privilege of preserving the legacy of our beloved Natchez.

For information on Spring Pilgrimage call the Natchez Visitors Reception Center, 800-647-6724.

—*Bethany Ewald Bultman*

The Pilgrimage Garden Club meets in front of its headquarters, Stanton Hall, in Natchez.

MISSISSIPPI
PLANTATION COUNTRY

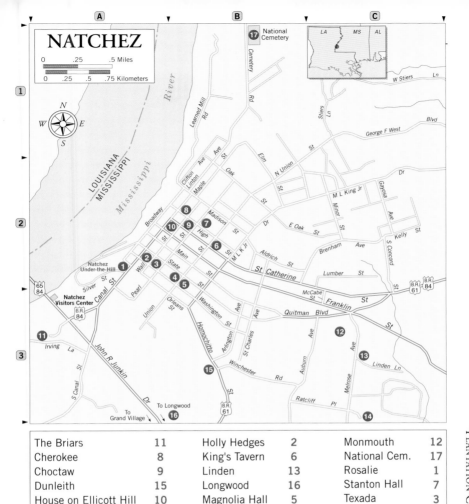

NATCHEZ

0   .25   .5 Miles

0   .25   .5   .75 Kilometers

The Briars	11	Holly Hedges	2	Monmouth	12
Cherokee	8	King's Tavern	6	National Cem.	17
Choctaw	9	Linden	13	Rosalie	1
Dunleith	15	Longwood	16	Stanton Hall	7
House on Ellicott Hill	10	Magnolia Hall	5	Texada	3
Gov. Holmes House	4	Melrose	14		

Natchez Visitors Reception Center

The hands-down best way to get acquainted with Natchez is to proceed directly to the visitors center where the 20-minute film "The Natchez Story" gives you a brief historic overview of the city and its people. Grab some brochures and maps, and then amble up the sky-ramp for an excellent view of the Mississippi River to get your bearings. *640 S. Canal St. at the intersection of Highway 84; 800-647-6724 or 601-446-6345; www.natchez.ms.us.*

From the visitors center take Canal Street toward the downtown **Historic District.** Every house in Natchez has a story and on the following pages, we will single out but a few, and include some other edifices and areas of note.

Rosalie, built circa 1820, is one of the finest homes in Natchez. (Brian Gauvin)

◆ HISTORIC DISTRICT HOUSES
map page 205

1 Rosalie *A-2*

Rosalie was built in 1820 in the Georgian style near the original location of Fort Rosalie by Peter Little, the town's first sawmill owner. Little literally inherited his 13-year-old bride, Eliza Low, when she was left to his care. He sent her away to school in Bal-

Rosalie is known for its rosewood furniture made by John Henry Belter. (Brian Gauvin)

timore, only to have her return as a Bible-thumping Methodist. (Little built his wife The Parsonage in 1840 in his front yard so she could entertain her preacher friends.) *Open daily 9–4:30 except during Pilgrimage. Canal St. at Broadway; 601-445-4555, or Pilgrimage Tours (page 201).*

2 Holly Hedges

Formerly known as Carson Cottage, this house was built in 1796. Gov. Gayoso de Lemos granted the land to Dr. John Scott in 1795, on the condition that Scott promise not to hold bullfights in the side yard. When the house changed hands for the third time in 1832, the new owners, John and Mary McMurran, added many of the Greek Revival touches that grace the house still. *Private home open only during Pilgrimage (page 201); 214 Washington St.*

MISSISSIPPI
PLANTATION COUNTRY

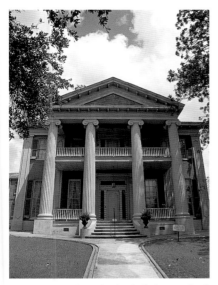

Magnolia Hall was hit by shells from Federal gunboats during the Civil War. (Brian Gauvin)

3 Texada

This simple, largely unadorned red-brick edifice is one of the longest surviving members of the city's old Spanish Quarter. Named after the original owner, Don Manuel Texada, who built it in 1792, it has alternately served as a home, a tavern, and, for a short while, the designated meeting place of the territorial legislature. Now a charming B&B *(601-455-4283). 222 S. Wall St.; Call Pilgrimage Tours (page 201).*

4 Gov. Holmes House

The biggest claim to fame here is that the house once belonged to Jefferson Davis, the Confederacy's President. Before that, though, it was the home of David Holmes, the last territorial governor of the state. Today, it's a B&B *(page 239). 207 S. Wall St.; Call Pilgrimage Tours (page 201).*

5 Magnolia Hall *map page 205, B-2*

Magnolia Hall was built by a native Natchezian, Thomas Henderson, son of John Henderson, who published the first book in the Natchez territory. Constructed in 1858, it was one of the homes hit by shells from a Union gunboat during the Civil War. *215 S. Pearl St., at Washington St.; 601-442-6672, or Pilgrimage Tours (page 201).*

◆ TEMPLES AND CHURCHES

The First Presbyterian Church was completed in the late 1820s in the Federal style with seating for 700. Inside, the trompe l'oeil niche is the only surviving area of the elaborate decorative interior painting, most of which was wiped out in renovations near the turn of the last century. The clear glass

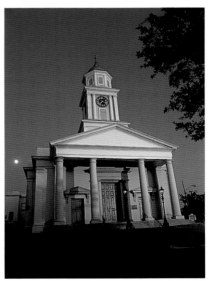

First Presbyterian Church was completed in 1820. (Brian Gauvin)

windows, pews, columns, and rear slave gallery are original to the building. *S. Pearl and State Sts.; 601-442-2581.*

Trinity Episcopal Church, dating from 1823, is the oldest remaining church building in Natchez, and the oldest existing Episcopal church building in the state. Originally in the Federal style, the church was turned into a copy of the Doric Temple of Thesion at the foot of the Acropolis in 1838, during the Greek Revival craze. The Aldrich and Koontz family stained-glass windows were made by Tiffany. *305 S. Commerce at Washington; 601-445-8432.*

The original building of **Temple B'nai Israel** was constructed between 1870 and 1872, and became the first synagogue in the state. The current building was built in 1905, after fire destroyed the original structure. Done in the Beaux-Arts style, it was built to accommodate the prosperous Jewish community, which was also responsible for commissioning many of the finest examples of late 19th-century architecture in the city. Ironically, the temple faces the George Armstrong Library, built in honor of a man who once offered a local college one million dollars to refuse admission to blacks and Jews. *Washington and Commerce Sts. For more information call the Museum of Southern Jewish Experience; 601-362-6357.*

St. Mary's Basilica started in 1842 and completed in 1859, this Gothic-style basilica stands in lovely contrast to the various styles of nearby houses of worship. It was the first Catholic cathedral in Mississippi. (It gained its distinction as a basilica in the 20th century.) The 1880s were a pivotal decade for the church: installation of its German stained glass began, the painting of the Crucifixion that hangs above the main altar was commissioned, and it was finally officially consecrated. *107 S. Union at Main St.; 601-445-5616.*

6 King's Tavern

Built circa 1789, King's Tavern is the oldest building to be untouched by Victorian embellishment or destroyed by neglect in the Natchez territory. Way back then, in addition to being a tavern, it was also the place where Indian runners delivered U.S. mail. Today it's a restaurant featuring hickory-smoked steaks *(page 241). 619 Jefferson St.*

King's Tavern, built 1789. (Brian Gauvin.)

7 Stanton Hall

Commissioned in 1851, Stanton Hall took six years to build. Before the Civil War, Frederick Stanton owned 444 slaves and six plantations, together encompassing more than 15,000 acres. Stanton, a native of Belfast, Ireland, sent his builder to select sterling silver doorknobs and Sheffield hinges from England and gold-leaf mirrors from France. Stanton paid $83,000 to

Stanton Hall. (Brian Gauvin)

build his dream dwelling, only to die three months after he moved in.

With ceilings soaring more than 16 feet and a parlor 70 feet long, it was the last and grandest of the great Natchez mansions to be completed before hard times descended on the city's aristocracy.

The Pilgrimage Garden Club purchased the home for the staggering sum of $25,000 in the early days of Pilgrimage.

Since that time its windows and upholstery have been the site of endless skirmishes waged between the Pretty and the Purist factions of the Pilgrimage Garden Club ladies. Notice "Play Mama's" portrait on the stairs. *401 High St.; Open daily except during Pilgrimage; Call Pilgrimage Tours (page 201).*

8 Cherokee *map page 205*

When Cherokee was being built in the 1790s, Spanish provincial officials were possessed of the belief that yellow fever was lurking in the soil under this lot. So original owner Jesse Greenfield chose the highest point on the land for the house, presumably the farthest away from the nasty disease that "lived" underground. Its white-columned facade was added in 1810. Frederick Stanton lived here before moving into his palatial, eponymous Stanton Hall. *Corner of North Wall and High Sts. Open only on Spring Tour—call Pilgrimage Tours (page 201).*

9 Choctaw *map page 205*

Built in 1836, this is one of two houses right across the street from each other with Indian names. With Choctaw the name is probably more deserved, as it has baluster decorations knows as "Indian cross sticks of war." Many remark that the house, with its double entrance-steps looks straight out of downtown Charleston. Architect James Hardie built the house for Joseph Neibert, and it remains one of Natchez's grander town houses with its massive portico and white columns topped with Ionic capitals. *Corner of North Wall and High Sts.*

10 House on Ellicott Hill *map page 205*

Looking more like a grand manse than a tavern, this building was actually both. Built in 1795 as Connelly's Tavern, it played host for a few decades to organ grinders, frontiersmen, and Spanish colonial dandies, as well as to more famous patrons such as the Duc d'Orleans (who later became Louis Phillippe, King of France) and Aaron Burr—before the treason trial. After 1816, the house served as a primary residence to many local muckety-mucks including the founder of the first Natchez hospital. *211 N. Canal St. at Jefferson; 601-442-2011, or Pilgrimage Tours (page 201).*

MISSISSIPPI
PLANTATION COUNTRY

♦ OUTER RING MANSIONS
map page 205

11 The Briars

This charming 1814 cottage (i.e. a large but comfortably proportioned home) surrounded by 19 acres of gardens sits atop the bluffs of Natchez overlooking the Mississippi River. Once home to the Howell family and their 10 children, it was here their eldest daughter, Varina, became the wife of 38-year-old Jefferson Davis, marrying him in the parlor. Varina was a young belle of 18 at the time, and when Davis became President of the Confederacy 16 years later, she became its first lady. Briars is now a 14-room inn with lovely sitting rooms, and breakfast at separate tables for guests. Two adorable St. Bernards can be seen lolling about playfully at the edge of the property. Reached via the road at the back of the parking lot for the Ramada Inn *(page 257). 31 Irving Ln.; 601-446-9654 or 800-634-1818, or Pilgrimage Tours (see page 201).*

The Briars. (Brian Gauvin)

12 Monmouth

Monmouth (circa 1818), while formidable in design, is all the more intriguing when you hear the dramatic history of one of its

Monmouth Plantation. (Brian Gauvin.)

former owners, John Quitman. A Mexican War hero, he returned to Natchez to become governor of Mississippi, only to die a lingering death of poisoning at a banquet for President James Buchanan in 1859. It is now a 30-room inn *(page 239). 36 Melrose Ave.; Daily tours 9:30–4:15; 800-828-4531 or call Pilgrimage Tours (see page 201).*

13 Linden *map page 205*
See page 198 for description. 1 Linden St.

14 Melrose

Now part of the National Park System, Melrose is nestled in a park-like setting with ponds rimmed by cypress knees. It is particularly unique because there have been no major structural changes since its completion in the mid-1840s. Even its original furnishings and slave cabins remain intact. *Daily tours 9–4; 1 Melrose Montebello Parkway; 601-446-5790, or Pilgrimage Tours (see page 201).*

15 Dunleith

Surrounded on four sides by 26 sparkling white Tuscan columns, this circa-1856 mansion is a photo op for every tourist who passes it. The daughter of the original

Dunleith dining room.

owners, Sarah Dahlgreen Dorsey, is noted as the one who loaned her Gulf Coast home, "Beauvoir," to Jefferson Davis. *84 Homochitto St.; 601-446-8500, 800-433-2444 or Pilgrimage Tours (see page 201).*

16 Longwood

Probably the most beautiful unfinished building you'll ever tour. Just four months from completion when the Civil War broke out. Owner Haller Nutt, a staunch Union sympathizer, died before war's end. To this day the house remains a shell of his grand octagonal plan. A short walk through the woods leads to the family graveyard. *Open daily 9–4:30; 140 Lower Woodville Rd.; Call Pilgrimage Tours (see page 201).*

Longwood. (Syndey Byrd)

Houses on Natchez bluff overlook the Mississippi River. (Brian Gauvin)

Natchez Demi-Belles

Girls growing up in Natchez are in demi-belle Nirvana. As tots we worshiped a bevy of white-gloved grande dames with impeccable manners, instinctive hospitality, finely honed feminine wiles, and wicked senses of humor, who could drink any Yankee under a Hepplewhite table. By the age of three, we made stage debuts in the Little Maypole, a Confederate Pageant tableau. Stage fright takes no prisoners among ranks of little girls who know by heart the order of Pilgrimage tableaux they will participate in. We adored antebellum costumes, learning as toddlers to swish hoopskirts winsomely as lacy pantalettes peaked from under frothy costumes, to ride in Volkswagens without denting hoops and to eat chili dogs at the Dairy Queen without dripping on organdy ruffles. Little boys had to be brave. While little girls skip instinctively, little boys, bless their hearts, don't—unless their mamas are Garden Club members, in which case it was their duty. The pitiful boys dashed from football practice to Pilgrimage rehearsals to be trained to respond to our curtsies with sweeping bows. Adding insult to injury, we little belles-from-hell teased them for wearing required lipstick and rouge and tromped on their ballet-slippered toes.

For residents, Natchez lifestyle is a state of mind, a shared identity. But author Bethany Ewald Bultman and I learned that exploiting heritage for personal gain is verboten. One long, hot summer Sunday afternoon, we donned hoopskirts, flounced out to Highway 61 to sell Spanish moss to passing tourists in order to earn some money to buy Barbie doll clothes. We did fine, thank you, 'til vigilant grande dames reported our enterprise to our mothers. They defrocked us, taking our hoops away. Our stint as juvenile entrepreneurs in belles' clothing, selling bug-infested moss to innocent tourists was considered tawdry, tacky, and traitorous to the communal cause.

Bethany Bultman, the author of this book, as a Natchez demi-belle. Escorts were required to wear lipstick.

—*Lucille Hume*

◆ NATCHEZ UNDER-THE-HILL

map page 205, A-2

On Silver Street, right next to the Mississippi River, you'll find the historic underbelly of Natchez society. Today, the area has sprung to new life with fine restaurants, shops, and bars-and even the Lady Luck Riverboat Casino nearby. But, oh, how times have changed. *The Majesty of Natchez,* by Reid Smith and John Owens, refers to the Under-the-Hill of the early 1800s as "a malignant scab with no peers."

During its heyday hundreds of boats docked daily, their crews greeted by "half-naked sporting ladies" and the lure of hard drinking and hard brawling. The bargeman landed their rafts,

To the west of Natchez-Under-the-Hill lies the wide Mississippi River and the bridge to Louisiana.(Brian Gauvin)

running ashore with a Bible in one hand and a jug of whiskey in the other.

The Reverend Ingraham's early 19th-century diary provides an eyewitness account: "Indians in gay blankets lounged about; trappers and hunters in fur caps; shopkeepers in bright smocks; gentlemen wearing gay velvet coats; and soldiers in flamboyant uniforms and tricolors made for an endless pageant of nations." The Rev. Ingraham goes on to complain of dancing and of tippling; of the incessant lewd language and of houses both of gambling and of ill-repute.

Only one sedate street remains of the former "Sodom of the South," because in the 1930s the Army Corps of Engineers rerouted the river and flooded most of the fun away. By the 1940s, Under-the-Hill was deserted, only to be reborn in the late

(continues page 216)

AFRICAN AMERICANS IN NATCHEZ

Since the 1850s, when "The Black Swan," **Elizabeth Taylor Greenfield**, a former Natchez slave, sang for the crowned heads of Europe, Natchez has had its own African-American aristocracy. During Reconstruction, former slaves resolved through education and religion to rise above their circumstances. By 1870 there were black attorneys and doctors, 18 black Baptist and African Methodist Episcopal congregations, and a dozen schools. In 1894, Mississippi's first African American Catholic church, the Holy Family Church, was founded. Many former slaves also entered the trades, making livings as master plasterers, painters, masons and carpenters, cobblers, tailors, and blacksmiths.

By the beginning of the 20th century, Natchez boasted a number of success stories: **Hiram Revels**, the first African American to serve in either house of the U.S. Senate (who took the seat of Jefferson Davis), and **John Roy Lynch** who became Speaker of the Mississippi House of Representatives when he was 24 and in 1872 was elected to the U.S. Congress. Ex-slaves **August and Sarah Mazique** were prosperous enough to purchase the plantation of their former owner, and within 30 years their descendants had amassed thousands of acres and a dozen plantations.

William Johnson (1809-1851), a Free Person of Color, kept a diary which later became a book entitled *William Johnson's Natchez: The Ante-Bellum Diary of a Free Negro* (Louisiana State University Press, 1951), an illuminating account of the African-American experience in the pre-War South. Free blacks such as Johnson could own property, operate a business (he was a barber), be legally married, and own slaves. They could not, however, vote, serve on a jury, or testify in court against a white man. When Johnson was murdered by a white man in 1851, the only witnesses to his murder were black, thus spelling a fast, certain acquittal for the killer.

Natchez's most celebrated literary native son, **Richard Wright**, was born in 1908 on a plantation a few miles east of Natchez. His father deserted the family, and soon afterwards, Wright's mother suffered a debilitating stroke. By the time Wright was six he was hanging about in Natchez

Evans-Bontura-Smith House, built in 1851, is a historic African-American home in Natchez. (Brian Gauvin)

saloons where the patrons gave the boy liquor and paid him to spew profanity for their amusement. The only stability in Wright's troubled young life came from his grandparents, former slaves, who lived in a neat white home in downtown Natchez.

In adulthood, Wright drifted from Mississippi to Chicago, New York, and the Communist Party. By 1947 he had found a home in Paris among the intelligentsia —Jean-Paul Sartre, Albert Camus, and Gertrude Stein. Wright published 15 books, the most acclaimed being *Black Boy,* his autobiography published in 1937, and *Native Son* in 1940. His compelling voice and biting visceral descriptions forever changed the literary landscape of the 20th century. Richard Wright died in France in 1960. The Natchez Literary Celebration honors his legacy each year with an award presented to writers.

For an overview of the lives of slaves and former slaves of Natchez, the **African-American Experience Tour** is a must. *Call 601-442-5448 or 601-445-8309.* Also of interest is the **Mostly African Marke**t in the historic Angelety House. *St. Catherine St. at McCabe; Open Wed–Sat, 1–5; 601-442-5448.*

John R. Lynch, a prominent black citizen of Natchez, was born a slave at Taconey Plantation near Vidalia. He later became a house servant at Dunleith (see page 210).

After the Civil War, Lynch became Speaker of the House in the state legislature and later was elected to the U.S. Congress. He poses here in the 1870s.

(Collection of Thomas H. Gandy and Joan W. Gandy)

The Mississippi River divides western Mississippi from eastern Louisiana. This bridge spans the crossing to Natchez, Mississippi. (Brian Gauvin)

1970s as a tourist hub. But even today, habitués of the area have a penchant for tawdry trouble.

The most recent event to scandalize locals was the arrest of one of the Under-the-Hillers for sexual relations with a horse—he still wears a gold horseshoe around his neck in commemoration of the event.

■ WASHINGTON *map page 194, A-6*

Well worth an hour's stop is Washington, five miles northeast of Natchez on Highway 61. Washington served as the capital of the Mississippi Territory from 1802 to 1817 and hosted the state's first constitutional convention in 1817 at Jefferson College (16 Old North Street). Named for Thomas Jefferson, the school was incorporated in 1802, but due to financial difficulties, it didn't actually start teaching pupils until 1811.

Jefferson College became the first chartered institution of higher learning in the Mississippi Territory and one of the first in the country to offer soil chemistry and land management as courses of study. It was here that Aaron Burr, Jefferson's Vice

President, was arrested for treason in 1807. General Andrew Jackson camped on the grounds in 1815 after his victory at the battle of New Orleans. John James Audubon taught here and Confederate President Jefferson Davis was a pupil. Today Jefferson College is a Mississippi historic site where several early 19th-century buildings designed by Levi Weeks are open to the public. There are nature trails, the historic cemetery, the original swimming hole, and shaded picnic areas. *16 Old North St.*

■ LOWER NATCHEZ TRACE PARKWAY

The Natchez Trace was well beaten by bison and Indian traders long before Spanish explorer Hernando de Soto and his band of 600 armor-clad men wandered along it in 1541. By the 18th century, herds of tobacco-spitting bargemen known as "Kaintocks" were making the 600-mile trek from Natchez back north to Nashville, having rafted their produce down the Mississippi River and sold everything, including the raft wood, in Natchez or New Orleans. In 1800, the Trace became an official U.S. mail route and was widened so it could serve as a strategic military artery.

MISSISSIPPI
PLANTATION COUNTRY

The first institution of higher learning in the Mississippi Territory, Jefferson College counted among its students Confederate President Jefferson Davis. (Brian Gauvin)

With the end of the steamboat era (1830s) and the railroad (1850s), the famed trail fell into disuse and became overrun with weeds until the Mississippi Chapter of the Daughters of the American Revolution saw to it that the Trace was resurrected in 1909. Once called the Devil's Backbone for its rough terrain and cutpurse lawlessness, today it's smooth and shady—a little slice of heaven. Cole's Creek provides a wonderful opportunity to wade, and the parkway is an ideal biking and picnic area.

❖

Getting on the Trace is a breeze, no more than 12 miles from the heart of Natchez. From the center of town, take Franklin Street until it veers left to join D'Evereux Drive. From there you'll link up with Highway 61 North, and you'll

JULIA SANDERS' FLORA GUIDE: NATCHEZ TRACE

Dogwood	**Redbud**
Cornus florida	*Cercis canadensis*
Four white "petals" are modified leaves with tiny yellow flowers in the center. Blooms March into April. Abundant under the canopy of larger trees in hilly, wooded areas.	The flowers of this small tree appear in profusion before the leaves and make an early show of spring color. Blooms February into March. Abundant in hilly wooded areas and cultivated landscapes.

Along the Natchez Trace Parkway between Natchez and Vicksburg. (Brian Gauvin)

soon see a clearly marked right exit to the beginning of the Natchez Trace Parkway. We'll follow this first stretch of the Trace for approximately 30 miles to Port Gibson, where we will veer off towards Vicksburg on Highway 61.

Signs point to an ancient Indian site, **Emerald Mound,** which dates from A.D. 1400. It is the second largest Indian mound in the United States and is located at the Route 553 turnoff at the south end of the Trace. A sign on the site tells what little is known about the people who built this earthen hill as a temple site, then disappeared before historic Indian tribes came on the scene. It's a nice place to take a short walk, look out over the hills and forest, and ponder the mysteries of lost peoples.

Mount Locust, about 16 miles from Natchez, is thought to have been built by a British naval officer shortly after Natchez was ceded by England to Spain in the late 18th century. The house has been restored to the way it looked in the 1820s when it was an inn. Bicyclists may want to begin a 20-mile loop from here, north to Highway 533, west toward Christ Church and back along the Natchez Trace to Mount Locust.

NATCHEZ INDIANS

At the time of the first French settlement in this area, the Natchez numbered approximately 3,500 and were a successful agricultural community, though culturally different from other tribes in the region. Descended from an early community now called the Mississippian culture, the Natchez practiced human sacrifice. When their absolute monarch, "the great sun king" died, his wives and retainers were strangled and buried alongside to accompany him into the next life.

The Natchez had a stringent four-class social structure: the sun class, the nobles, the honored people, and the common folk, known by the French word that translates into English as "stinkards." A matrilineal society, status in Natchez society derived from the female line. The young women of the tribe were allowed to trade sexual favors for items of value.

When it came to captives, the Natchez liked to tie their victims to a frame, scalp them alive, and artfully poke them with burning canes, keeping them alive for as long as possible. Other times they would tie a grapevine leash around a prisoner's neck, letting the women and children torture him. The scalp of the victim was then presented to the dead man's family so they could use it to wipe their tears.

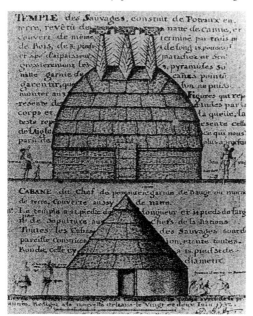

By 1729 appropriation of Indian land by French settlers had infuriated this fairly sophisticated and well organized Indian society. The Natchez stormed the French Fort Rosalie and massacred

A Natchez Indian Temple and chief's house as depicted in an early French manuscript.

Emerald Mound, constructed between 1300 and 1600 by the pre-historic Mississippian culture, is one of the largest Indian temple mounds in the United States. (Brian Gauvin)

its residents. After the massacre the Natchez attacked Fort St. Jean Baptiste at Natchitoches, Louisiana; the entire tribe was killed seven miles south at Bayou Natchez. The few Indians remaining alive were chased down the Cane River to a place in the hills now called "Sang pour Sang" (Blood for Blood).

There are two sites worth visiting, related to the Natchez tribe and its predecessors.

The temple mound in the Grand Village was used for funeral rites and contains the bones of kings or "suns." *Open 9–5 Mon–Sat and Sun 1:30–5; 400 Jefferson Davis Boulevard; 601-446-6502.*

Emerald Mound is another important Native site, which may or may not have been built by ancestors of the Natchez. Located on the Natchez Trace, it is maintained by the National Park Service *(see map page 194, A-5).*

◆ CHURCH HILL *map page 194, A-5*

Once on the Trace, you'll go only a mile or so before you come to the Route 553 junction on the left. Following this will take you off the Trace for a quick diversion to Church Hill.

The Church Hill community, also known as the Old Maryland Settlement, is packed with fabulous old manses, most of which, unfortunately, are not visible from the road and are closed to the public.

The area was first settled in the early 1800s, by a Marylander named Gen. James G. Wood. Others soon followed and eventually set up still-standing grand houses. In the 1980s, scandal rocked the community, when The Cedars (built by General Wood for his daughter in 1830) was purchased by a group of Hare Krishnas from California. After a few years of quiet ownership, the house was seized from the Krishnas by federal agents because its occupants were using it as home-base for manufacturing and selling drug paraphernalia. Word is, the local postmaster, never a fan of the melon-robed worshippers in the first place, became suspicious of the huge volume of packages the Krishnas constantly received.

Church Hill was named after **Christ Episcopal Church** (1858), built in the Gothic Revival style for the first Episcopal congregation in Mississippi. (The church was brought back to life by author Bethany Bultman for her wedding in 1976.) It's like a slice of Olde England in the countryside, and it is regarded as the cradle of Episcopacy in the state. The gravestones in its little cemetery give a poignant portrait of the lives and deaths of the settlers.

The first Episcopal clergyman in Church Hill was the Rev. Adam Cloud, who arrived in the Natchez area in 1790 when it was under Spanish rule. Non-Catholic worship was forbidden, though Cloud conducted baptisms, marriages, and burials until 1795, when he was arrested and expelled from the colony.

He returned to the Maryland Settlement in 1815 to found Christ Church in 1820. Today, the church is open once a month—usually on the second Sunday—for 3 P.M. services.

◆ ALCORN STATE UNIVERSITY   *map page 194, A-4*

Established in 1871, Alcorn State University was one of several educational institutions set up for African Americans near Natchez during Reconstruction. Hiram
Revels, the first president of the school, was also the first African American to
serve in either house of the U.S. Legislature, filling Confederate President Jefferson Davis's spot in the U.S. Senate. Rather than seek a second term in Washington, Revels returned to run Alcorn, one of the earliest African-American colleges
in the Americas and the first land grant college in the United States. *West of US
61, on Highway 552, 1000 ASU Dr.; 601-877-6130.*

◆ WINDSOR (CANEMONT) PLANTATION   *map page 194, A-4*

Near Alcorn State University, off Highway 552, lies a sort of antebellum Stone-
henge. In a lonely wooded area, cleared only enough for you to drive your car up
to it, are 23 Corinthian columns, all that is left of the grand house of Windsor,
finished in 1861 at a cost of $175,000.

Mississippi author Bern Keating in *The Mighty Mississippi* recounts meeting the
grandson of Windsor's builder, Smith C. Daniell IV, and quotes him as follows:

> Grandfather had just finished building on his 2,000-acre plantation
> when the Civil War broke out…When Grant landed his troops near Bru-
> insburg, he mistook the furniture on the third-floor veranda for soldiers.
> It took all of my grandmother's considerable persuasive power to keep the
> General from burning the house. But it did burn 27 years later, in 1890.
> When I was about five we had a house party for a number of young
> ladies, and naturally all the eligible bachelors in the countryside came to
> call. Some were smoking cigarettes, a new fad at the time, and one of
> them, I am told, carelessly tossed aside a stub. The place was in flames
> and the roof falling in minutes.

For years, historians have spun myths and hypotheses about how Windsor, now
listed on the National Register of Historic Places, must have looked, for it was
thought that no sketches of the house survived. Until 1992, that is. It was then
that a freelance writer doing research at the Ohio State Archives, found a sketch in
the diary of a Union officer marked: "May 1st, 1863. Residence Near Bruinsburg,
Miss." Windsor is in fact near the former town of Bruinsburg, where Union
troops passed on their way to fight in Port Gibson. The discovery set off a furor

among architectural historians and refuted the conventional wisdom regarding Windsor's appearance. Not at all a perfect model of Greek Revival style, as was previously thought, the house is in fact an amalgam of Gothic, Italianate—as well as Greek—Revival.

Windsor's ruins are on the grounds of **Canemount Plantation**, a privately owned 10,000-acre area with a grand house of its own. The splendid Italianate Revival main house is considered to be the best example of its kind in the county. Owners Ray and Rachel Forrest operate Canemount as a nine-room B&B and game preserve. A stay there includes dinner, breakfast, and an evening Jeep safari through the preserve where you can ogle white tail deer, Russian boar, and wild turkey. And if you're so inclined, you can shoot 'em too, as the Forrests are happy to arrange a hunt for guests. Only guests are allowed to tour the house and property, though, so if you come to visit, you should plan to stay. *Highway 552 W., 601-877-3784.*

◆ Rosswood *map page 255, A-3*

The only other documented house built by the architect of Windsor, David Shroder, is **Rosswood**, further up the road on Highway 552. Unlike Windsor, Rosswood is no mystery. Its original owner, Dr. Walter Wade, kept detailed records of its commission and construction. *Open daily 9–5; Highway 552 W.; 601-437-4215.*

(right) This gravestone from the Natchez cemetery is one among many that testify to the large and prosperous Jewish population in this area. (Brian Gauvin)

MISSISSIPPI PLANTATION COUNTRY

(opposite) Ruins of the Windsor Plantation. (Brian Gauvin)

■ PORT GIBSON AREA *map page 194, B-3*

By 1788 this township in Claiborne county (40 miles north of Natchez, 28 miles south of Vicksburg, and eight miles southeast of the Grand Gulf Military State Park), bore the name of Samuel Gibson. Gibson obtained an 820-acre Spanish land grant on the south fork of Bayou Pierre, an area that had once been a principal stronghold of the Choctaw nation. It was incorporated in 1811, thus becoming the third oldest town in the state.

By 1818, Port Gibson boasted the first library in Mississippi. It rates a footnote in literary history as the birthplace of Irwin Russell, the heavy-drinking author of *Christmas Night in the Quarters,* the first published work to contain slave dialect. Largely spared during the Civil War—some say because General Grant thought Port Gibson, with its wide, magnolia-tree-lined avenues and deep lawns, was "too beautiful to burn"—the picturesque town of 1,800 still has several historic homes along with well-preserved houses of worship, parks, and even a university.

Spring Pilgrimage

Port Gibson (pop. 1,800) hosts a Spring Pilgrimage every year, usually the next-to-last weekend in March. Though the four-to-six homes that are open vary from year to year, there are some that are easily seen from outside whether they're on the schedule or not: Englesing House (1817), Gage House (1830), and Idlewild (1833). And Gibson's Landing (formerly called Disharoon, circa 1832), another beauty, is now open as a B&B. For more information on Pilgrimage, call the Chamber of Commerce; *601-437-4351.*

Oak Square

Oak Square is a B&B operated in the town's largest mansion (circa 1850) and presided over by Martha Lum, the granddaughter of a Confederate soldier. Her great grandmother grew up at Linden in Natchez. Her husband's people were Tories who settled in Natchez in 1772.

The historic house is homey; a sign over the door reads, "Christ is the Lord in the House." The chilly swish of air conditioners can be heard throughout. It is worthy of a visit for a tour or an overnight, just for the pleasure of Martha Lum's lilting voice and her passion for the past. She might even confide the scandalous tale of the Lum belle who fell in love with Grant's surgeon. *1207 Church St; 601-437-4350.*

First Presbyterian Church

As you explore the town, the First Presbyterian Church will swiftly grab your attention. Actually it's the steeple that will make you look: it's topped with a 12-foot-high golden hand, index finger pointing skyward 165 feet from earth. Originally, the hand was crafted of wood by a 17-year-old in 1859. But years of wear and tear eventually saw it replaced with a metal one. Driving through this tiny town, you may stop short at the sight of this wonderful and bizarre steeple, and perhaps contemplate the power of the divine. *Church and Walnut Sts.*

Chamberlain-Hunt Academy

This idyllic 19th-century campus was established in 1830 as a Presbyterian bastion of higher learning called Oakland College. When Oakland closed some years later, the determined Presbyterians established Chamberlain-Hunt (named after founder of Oakland Dr. Jeremiah Chamberlain and big-time donor David Hunt) in 1879 to educate a slightly younger crop of men. Today it's a Christian military prep school, which went co-educational in 1970. *124 McComb Ave.; 601-437-4291.*

If you are really ambitious, you can follow the Natchez Trace 400 more miles to Nashville, Tennessee—but not by using this book! Stay on the Natchez Trace just a short ways toward Jackson and you will pass the ghost town of Rocky Springs and the Owen Creek Waterfall. A little further on, off Highway 18 in Utica, is **The Museum of the Southern Jewish Experience** where you can pick up a brochure for their Cultural Corridor Tour, a fascinating road trip through Jewish history in Mississippi, Louisiana, and Tennessee. *601-362-6357.*

Ten miles northwest of Port Gibson and across the Bayou Pierre Bridge, you'll find **Grand Gulf Military Monument Park,** home to a museum, hiking trails, a cemetery, and two old Confederate forts. The spot marks the site of shelling by Union gunboats during the Civil War. Whether for another dose of Civil War history, or just a stroll through the woods, it's a worthwhile stop. *Open daily, 8 A.M.– 5 P.M.; www.grandgulf.state.ms.us; Grand Gulf Rd.; 601-437-5911.*

■ VICKSBURG *maps pages 194, A-1, and 232*

In the Mississippi vernacular, Vicksburg (pop. 27,500) is a pretty good-sized city. It is 215 miles north of New Orleans, and it might as well be in another universe. North of town on US Highway 61 there is a red, white, and blue sign, "All is welcome—Here at Margaret's Gro and Mkt and Bible class," marking the roadside temple, a local landmark, Margaret's Grocery: "Home of the Double Headed Eagle, Rev. H. D. Dennis presiding." Church is held next door in a silver school bus. Reverend Dennis is always ready to preach God's glory as long as he has willing ears.

Vicksburg is a nice overnight destination. The historic sites are located off I-20, Clay Street/Exit 4B.

◆ VICKSBURG'S HISTORY

Vicksburg, "the Gibraltar of the Confederacy," began in 1719 as part of the French colony on a high bluff (177 feet) overlooking the Mississippi River. It became a Spanish Territory in 1791, before finally landing comfortably in 1798 in Americans hands. For the first few years it was an obscure U.S. military outpost. Then in 1814, the Rev. Newitt Vick moved his Methodist flock from Virginia to this Warren County town giving it both a name and a mission—literally. Vicksburg soon began a steady period of growth attracting merchants from as far away as Syria, those engaged in river transport, and men seeking God.

Vicksburg had both a thriving port and—from the 1850s on— railroad access, propelling it past agrarian-based Natchez, which had a port but no railroad, as the dominant commercial presence on that stretch of river. (The railroad remains an important part of Vicksburg. The sound of heavy freight rattles the walls of homes near the train yard.) That turn of fate would haunt both cities in the years to come. As the Civil War commenced, the Confederacy chose to fortify the commercially significant, well-linked Vicksburg instead of Natchez. This left Natchez

A re-enactment of the siege of Vicksburg, during which gunners fire a 12-pound Napoleon cannon in the National Military Park of Vicksburg. (Brian Gauvin)

MISSISSIPPI
PLANTATION COUNTRY

vulnerable to Union invasion, while making Vicksburg a far more strategically important trophy for the Union. In effect the very thing that attracted the Grays to fortify Vicksburg—the railroad and port—was the same thing that drew the Blues to lay siege to it.

Union General Ulysses S. Grant pushed through the South, fighting battles in Port Gibson, Raymond, Champion Hill, Big Black River Bridge, and Jackson throughout the spring of 1863, as he made his way to take Vicksburg. Once there, he came to a dead stop. Grant tried various ways to break into the fortified city, losing more than 4,000 men in several unsuccessful attempts. In late May, Grant realized the only way to breach Vicksburg was to starve out its defenders. Throughout June, Union troops shelled the city. During the 47-day siege, the Union attempted to subvert the Confederate fortifications from the outside. Inside the walls, soldiers and citizens alike were succumbing to wounds, disease, and lack of nourishment.

By the time a relief force was gathered in Jackson to reinforce the Grays in Vicksburg, it was too late. Casualities from the days leading up to the siege, and the siege itself were as follows:

Union: 1,581 soldiers killed; 7,554 wounded; 1,007 missing.

Confederates: 1,413 killed; 3,878 wounded; 3,800 missing.

Civilians: 12 killed.

These numbers don't reveal the number of men who were maimed for life nor do they tell of the thousands of civilians who hid, starving in caves in the loess bluffs. As one veteran wrote, "a cat couldn't have snuck in and out of his place it was sealed so tight."

One soldier who fought with the 95th Illinois Regiment, Albert D. J. Cashier was actually a Miss Jennie Hodgers. The name Cashier appears inside the Illinois monument in the military park.

On the Fourth of July, the Confederates surrendered Vicksburg. (Up until the 1960s, Independence Day was not officially celebrated in this part of Mississippi.) While these events were unfolding in Vicksburg, Confederate General Robert E. Lee, was admitting defeat in Pennsylvania after the Battle of Gettysburg, which was fought on July 1–3. These two defeats marked the turn of the tide in favor of the Union. After the War, Vicksburg never forgot that Natchez had given in to the Yankees without a fight. To visit the site of the battle, see "Vicksburg National Military Park," following.

◆ VICKSBURG NATIONAL MILITARY PARK *map 232, B/C-1*

The best way to get a sense of the magnitude of the events that took place in Vicksburg in 1863 is to visit the Vicksburg National Military Park. The 1,740-acre park is set on a rolling green bluff. You can drive your car, walk, or bike, along the park's 16-mile driving tour which is strewn with a total of 1,324 monuments, interpretive markers, obelisks, heroic military statuary of ragged fighting men, temples, grass-covered trench remnants, and other relics of this pivotal battle. There is something poignantly eerie here, as if you can almost hear the blasts of cannons and heart-stopping screams of pain. Every major roadway anywhere near the park has signs pointing you in its direction, so whether you're coming straight in off the interstate, or from somewhere else locally, you cannot miss this mammoth outdoor shrine. Rows of unmarked graves of the 17,000 Union soldiers and 13,000 unknown soldiers (the Confederate dead are buried in the city's Cedar Hill Cemetery) may lead you to ponder why the war was called "civil."

Excellent licensed guides are available to ride in your car for a two-hour detailed tour at a cost of $20. Inexpensive cassette tapes and CDs can be purchased for

Most of the 3,000 Confederate and Union soldiers who died during the battle for Vicksburg are buried here at Vicksburg National Military Park Cemetery. (Brian Gauvin)

*Mac Elmor, Chris Withrow, Rachel Patten, and Pete Scott perform
Civil War rifle and artillery demonstrations. (Brian Gauvin)*

do-it-yourself tours. Whatever you do, don't wander without the step-by-step map that provides good background information about all the sites.

The gift shop is excellent. There are reprints of Civil War diaries, copies of *Harper's Weekly* from the period, a detailed book about the battle strategies, uniform buttons, and a computer game called "Civil War Explosion."

Civil War buffs could probably spend the better part of a day rapt in the park's stories and stones. Others may prefer a brisker pace. But everyone should stop at the USS *Cairo* Museum, which is right next to the Fort Hill Drive exit. The *Cairo* is an ironclad Union gunboat that was sunk just north of Vicksburg on the Yazoo River by an electrically detonated Confederate mine, giving it the distinction of being the first boat in the world to be sunk this way. The ship was salvaged in the 1960s and has been reassembled outside the museum, along with the heart-rending personal effects of the dead soldiers, which line the walls, along with plaques retelling the mesmerizing story of the resurrection of the *Cairo*.

Vicksburg National Military Park, open daily; information: 601-636-0583.

USS *Cairo information: 601-636-2199.*

◆ HISTORIC VICKSBURG SIGHTS

Navigating the City: Vicksburg is arranged with commendable logic, making it easy to navigate. There are signs all over Vicksburg pointing to sights of interest.

Vicksburg Convention and Visitors Bureau, *www.vicksburgcvb.org; Clay St. at Old Highway 27, across from the Military Park; 800-221-3536 or 601-636-9421.*

Mississippi Welcome Center, *I-20 and Washington St.; 601-638-4269.*

Old Courthouse Museum *map A/B-2*

This imposing building, set atop a terraced hill can be reached by following Connecting Avenue to the Fort Hill Drive exit and then follow the drive (it eventually turns into Cherry Street) for about a mile.

The old courthouse was constructed in

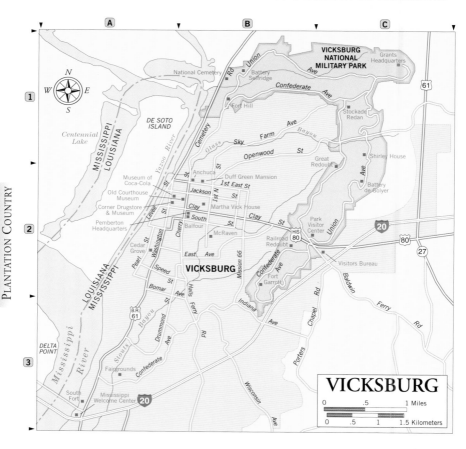

MISSISSIPPI PLANTATION COUNTRY

Old Courthouse Museum (Brian Gauvin.)

1858 only to become the site chosen by U.S. General Grant to raise the Union flag after the Confederate defeat on July 4 of 1863. Listed on the National Register of Historic Places, it is a must-see for any visitor to Vicksburg.

Opened in the late 1940s, it's one of the largest, most instructive, and quirkiest small-town museums ever built. Each of the named rooms is crammed with artifacts bequeathed by residents: a picture of the Blue-Gray sisters, who had the same mother but had different fathers from each side of the conflict; an entire case full of early versions of the hand grenade; a Ku Klux Klan hood with a disturbingly benign interpretation of the Klan's role in the South. Every single artifact has a little white typed card that explains the item in detail. And every room has an attraction, whether it's the Indian beads and arrowheads in the Pioneer Room, or the amazing period get-ups in the Costume Room.

The gift shop itself is worth the trip, especially if you are in need of Rebel flag kitchen magnets, Jefferson Davis dish cloths, or a Vicksburg sno-globe. There is plenty of Union stuff too, because as the curator concedes, if it hadn't been for them, there'd be no museum. *Open Mon–Sat 8:30–4:30, Sun 1:30–4:30; 1008 Cherry St.; 601-636-0741.*

Offbeat Museums

Vicksburg is noted as the first place in the world where Coca-Cola was bottled. **The Biedenharn Candy Company and Museum of Coca-Cola Memorabilia** houses artifacts in the original 1890s building where soft-drink history was made. It's still a soda fountain for ice cream floats and candy treats. *1107 Washington St.; 601-638-6514.*

A few doors down Washington Street is the **Attic Gallery**, an eclectic collection of regional outsider art, yard sculpture, and contemporary art. This is the real thing, no cutesy paintings of magnolias or blue geese with gingham bows around their necks. *1101 Washington St.; 601-638-9221.*

The Corner Drugstore and Museum at 1123 Washington Street, on the corner of China Street (601-636-2756), has an extensive collection of moonshine jugs. (Brian Gauvin.)

◆ ANTEBELLUM HOMES

While Vicksburg is no Natchez, it nonetheless has a collection of formidable historic homes in its Garden District (Clay/Oak Streets) and in the residential area around Clay and First Street East. Following Natchez's lead, Vicksburg has an annual Spring Pilgrimage that runs from late March to early April and another fall pilgrimage in mid-October. For information call the Vicksburg Convention & Visitors Bureau, *800-221-3536 or 601-636-9421.*

Vicksburg is known for fine antebellum homes such as Balfour House. (Brian Gauvin.)

A drive through the old section—especially up Crawford Street—will provide a glimpse of many of the nicest antebellum homes. Several cobblestone blocks of Washington Street provide lovely overlooks of the river.

Anchuca   *map page 232, B-2*

One of the oldest (1830) homes in the city available to tour. It's listed on the National Register perhaps due to the fact that it became the home of Confederate President Jefferson Davis's older brother, Joseph

Emory Davis. President Davis once addressed the townspeople from the balcony. Of interest are the former slave quarters adjacent to the formal gardens. *Open Wed–Sat 11–3; 1010 First East St.; 601-661-0111 or 888-686-0111.*

Balfour House   *map page 232, B-2*

Built in 1835, this is a Federal-style home listed on the National Register of Historic Places. It is considered by many architectural historians to be the finest pre–Civil War house in town. The house was used as Union Headquarters during the occupation of Vicksburg and is curiously close to Pemberton Headquarters, which was the Confederate Headquarters before and during the siege.

There is an annual re-enactment of the Christmas Ball interrupted by the arrival of Federal troops in the city. Some years there are as many as five balls held in order to accommodate all who want to attend (*second Saturday in December*). *Open Mon–Sat 10–5, closed Jan–Feb; 1002 Crawford St.; 601-638-7113 or 800-294-7113.*

Interior of Balfour House. (Brian Gauvin)

Pemberton Headquarters
map page 232, B-2
Until a few years ago the home, built during the architectural transition between Federal and Greek Revival, had a natural brick facade. The new paint job caused consternation amongst purists and preservationists. The decision to surrender Vicksburg was made in the parlor. Today the home is a B&B *(page 244). Open Mon-Sat 9–5, Sun 1–5; 1018 Crawford St.; 601-636-9581 or 877-636-9581.*

Martha Vick House *map page 232, B-2*
This cozy home was built in 1830 for the spinster daughter of the town's founder, Rev. Newitt Vick. *1300 Grove St.; 601-638-7036.*

Duff Green Mansion *map page 232, B-2*
This three-story Palladian-style mansion, festooned with cast iron, dates from 1856 and served as a Union and Confederate hospital during the War. During the siege, Mary Green gave birth to a son in a nearby shelter and named him Siege Green. The home is now a B&B *(page 244). Open daily 10–5; 1114 First East St.; 601-636-6968 or 800-992-0037.*

Cedar Grove *map page 232, A-2*
A 1840–1858 Greek Revival home built by the Klein family, the home still has a cannonball lodged in its parlor wall, compliments of a Union gunboat. It's now an inn complete with gas-lit chandeliers and surrounded by four acres of lovely gardens with gazebos and fountains *(page 243). Open daily for tours from 9–4; 2200 Oak St.; 601-636-1000 or 800-862-1300.*

McRaven *map page 232, B-2*
The house began life as an early 1800s Colonial frontier cottage. The more gentrified Creole mid-section was added in 1836. The final sophistication was completed in 1849 with Greek Revival moldings made of molasses, horsehair, and marble dust. Serving as home of Union General McPherson, it served as the Union headquarters and sits within the military park. In the 1990s an Episcopal minister attempted to exorcise the General's ghost. By some accounts, it didn't work. The three-acre gardens, once a Confederate campsite, are the site of annual battle re-enactments in May, on the July 4 weekend, and Labor Day. *1445 Harrison St.; 601-636-1663*

◆ THE MISSISSIPPI RIVER AT VICKSBURG

Thirteen years to the day after Grant's siege on Vicksburg and on the centennial of the founding of the nation, the Mississippi cut across the very loop from which the Union gunboats bombarded the city. Suddenly the city sat closed-off, cornered on an oxbow lake. After years of pleading to their former enemy—the federal government—for assistance, inhabitants of Vicksburg got their wish. The Army

Corps of Engineers dug a nine-mile canal north from Vicksburg to the Yazoo River, whose name means "river of death," thus giving the city the superb harbor you'll see today.

The Mississippi River remains an important factor in the economics of Vicksburg, but not as a tourist attraction or a big commercial port. Today, the largest of Vicksburg's gambling havens—the Ameristar Casino—is located on the river's banks near Washington Street. In fact, Vicksburg has become more or less a gambling mecca in this region with three other casinos scattered around the smallish city. As new jobs, gamblers, and their money flow into the city—along with all the attendant problems gambling can bring to a town—Vicksburgers are still contemplating whether this is a new opportunity or a new siege.

At the foot of Clay Street **Mississippi River Adventures** offers river cruises during peak tourist times (from March to November). They include lectures describing 500 years of Mississippi River history, the natural environment, and details about the siege of Vicksburg. *800-521-4363 or 601-638-5443.*

The Reverend Denis, 83 years old, sermonizes in front of the church he built north of Vicksburg along the river. (Brian Gauvin)

■ MISSISSIPPI PLANTATION COUNTRY FOOD & LODGING

by Lucille Bayon Hume

⛿ For chain lodgings see toll-free numbers on page 334.

$$ For room (⛿) and restaurant (✗) price designations see page 333.

Natchez *map page 205*

⛿ **Hotel/Motel Chains:**
Comfort Inn;
800-228-5150 or 601-446-5500
Days Inn;
800-329-7466 or 601-445-8291
Executive Inn;
601-442-1691
Isle of Capri Casino & Hotel;
800-722-5825 or 601-445-0605
Ramada Inn;
800-2-RAMADA or 601-446-6311

⛿ **Guest House Historic Inn.** 201 N. Pearl St.; 601-442-1054 $$
Seventeen spacious rooms, individually decorated in elegantly understated luxury. The Guest House has a European small luxury-hotel atmosphere. Coffee/sandwich shop on premises. Good downtown location close to Antiques Row.

⛿ **Radisson Natchez Eola Hotel.** 110 N. Pearl St.; 800-888-9140 or 800-333-3333 or 601-445-6000 $$-$$$
Built in 1927, when downtown hotels were cultural/social centers possessing distinct personalities, the Eola, decorated with crystal chandeliers and marble, is a reminder of bygone days. Least expensive rooms are small, but still attractive. All are equipped with amenities expected in Radisson properties.

Natchez Bed & Breakfasts

The increasingly popular Bed and Breakfast industry has found a natural niche in Natchez, offering travelers a taste of life in the slow lane in town or country Natchez homes, where hospitality is as much a part of the home as antique furnishings and classic architecture. Some operate independently, while many are handled by Pilgrimage Tour Headquarters; 800-647-6742. Visitors calling Headquarters are encouraged to express preferences concerning interaction with homeowners, which ranges from complete independence to being taken into the bosom of the family.

⛿ **Aunt Pitty Pat's.** 306 S. Rankin St.; 601-446-6111 or 800-748-748-9728 $$-$$$
If Tara-esque plantations seem too formal, this homey, eclectic Victorian cottage will appeal. Stay in downstairs guest rooms with private parlor or in separate flat. Relaxing porch and courtyard. Convenient location.

⛿ **The Briars.** 31 Irving Ln.; 800-634-1818 or 601-446-9654 $$$$
Site of Jefferson Davis's wedding, this architectural gem is perched high on river bluffs nestled in acres of meticulously landscaped gardens and gentle woods. More a discreet inn than a standard B&B, it offers 14 luxurious room choices. Pool and dining pavilion on grounds. *(See picture next page.)*

THE BRIARS

⊡ **The Burn.** 7121 N. Union St.; 800-647-6742 $$$-$$$$

First Natchez Greek Revival home. The Burn is furnished with period antiques and art, many from original furnishings. The courtyard shelters the oldest working fountain in Mississippi. Carefully renovated for modern convenience while maintaining the house's historical integrity. In downtown area.

THE BURN

⊡ **Dunleith.** 84 Homochito St.; 800-647-6742 or 601-446-8500 $$$-$$$$

Greek Revival mansion enclosed by statuesque Doric columns and surrounding galleries, Dunleith rests on 40 acres of park-like grounds within city limits, "country comes to town." Guest rooms in main house and courtyard wing.

DUNLEITH

⊡ **Elgin.** 1 Elgin Plantation Rd.; 800-647-6742 $$-$$$

Old experimental gardens of a pioneer horticulturalist metamorphosized into informal naturalized grounds contribute sweetness to this country plantation home furnished with family heirlooms. Inviting front gallery. Four-poster beds in comfortable guest house.

ELGIN

⌑ **Governor Holmes House.** 207 S. Wall St.; 888-442-0166, or 800-647-6742, or 601-442-2366 $$$
Built in the old Spanish Quarter in 1794 and decorated in period furnishings, this is a welcoming B&B.

⌑ **Hope Farm.** 147 Homochitto St.; 800-647-6742 or 601-445-4848 $$-$$$.
Two houses (1794 and 1789) were joined, resulting in a 14-room home. Restored in the 1920s by J. Balfour Miller and his wife, Katherine, mastermind of the Natchez Pilgrimage, Hope Farm was a B&B before the concept was widespread. Intriguing heirlooms.

⌑ **Linden.** 1 Linden Pl.; 800-647-6742 or 601-445-5472 $$-$$$.
A Federal plantation house with long, irresistible galleries, Linden continues a six-generations-long tradition of hospitality and grace. Furnished in Federal period antiques, including a cypress punkah above the banquet table in the dining room. Seven guest rooms.

LINDEN

⌑ **Monmouth Plantation.** 36 Melrose Ave.; 800-828-4531, or 800-647-6742, or 601-442-5852 $$$$
If Scarlett O'Hara were alive and well, she'd live here. Ranked among the most romantic places in America, Monmouth allows guests to enjoy results of the owners' dreams of restoring the magnificent 30-bedroom mansion and gardens to original glory.

MONMOUTH

⌑ **Oakland Plantation.** 1124 Lower Woodville Rd.; 601-445-5101 $
Refreshingly simple, no frou-frou restored early planter's cottage provides fulfilling country living on a wooded game refuge with stocked ponds, canoeing, and a tennis court. Wake to cooing mourning doves. Separate two-story brick guest house.

⌑ **Ravenna.** 8 Ravenna St.; 800-647-6742 or 601-445-8516 $$$
Known for its dramatic elliptical stairway, hallway arch and ancient gardens, Ravenna is located in the downtown Garden District in a secluded location, close to downtown activity yet shielded from hustle and bustle.

⊞ **Shields Town House.** 701 N. Union St.; 800-647-6742 or 601-442-7680 $$$ Completed just before the Civil War, the Shields Town House has two exquisitely furnished spacious guest houses hidden behind it. "Private" is the key word here: private suites, private phone lines, private courtyard.

⊞ **Wensel House.** 206 Washington St.; 888-775-8577, or 800-647-6742, or 601-445-8577 $$ A good downtown location and reasonable prices. Comfortable and relaxed. Furnished with century-old family antiques, second-story guest rooms are spacious and stocked with conveniences like hair dryers and irons. Parlor and dining room are at guests' disposal.

✕ **Biscuits and Blues.** 315 Main St.; 601-446-9922 $-$$ This link in a tiny chain would be more appetizing with lights lowered. Nonetheless, it serves up literally finger-lickin' smoked ribs and chicken, grilled catfish and steaks, and po' boys. Live blues most weekends makes the food go down easy. Lunch/dinner. Closed Monday.

✕ **The Carriage House.** 401 High St.; 601-445-5151 $-$$ On Stanton Hall's grounds, the Carriage House is locals' traditional choice for luncheons and Sunday brunch. Tiny featherweight biscuits, tomato aspic, Southern fried chicken, and pecan pie are valid reasons to leave the diet at home. Dinner only during Pilgrimage.

✕ **Clara Nell's Downtown Delicatessen.** 408 Main St.; 601-445-7799 $ Although the converted cafeteria lacks ambiance, Clara Nell's has a bevy of faithful patrons who welcome inexpensive and lighter lunch options of soup, sandwiches, and a well-stocked salad bar. Sinful desserts often undo benefits of the light lunch. Closed Sunday.

✕ **Cock of the Walk.** 200 N. Broadway; 601-446-8920 $$ Choose the specialty, fried catfish fillets, with a pot o' greens. Named for 19th-century swaggering rivermen, the restaurant maintains the theme as boatman reincarnations serve patrons drinks in rustic tin cups and flip hot cornbread from skillets to plates.

✕ **The Fare—A Little Cafe.** 109 N. Pearl St.; 601-442-5299 $ Good things come in small packages if you're not claustrophobic. This tiny cafe offers tasty breakfasts (omelets, muffins, croissants) and lunches (soups, sandwiches) on weekdays. Best bet may be boxed lunches taken to the riverfront gazebo.

✕ **John Martin's Restaurant.** 21 Silver St.; 601-445-0605 $$$-$$$$ This relatively new kid on the Natchez-Under-the-Hill block presents a sophisticated dinner and Sunday brunch fusing traditional Southern dishes with a nouvelle twist. One of the best local dining experiences. Sit by the windows overlooking the river. Reservations suggested.

*JOHN MARTIN'S RESTAURANT
(BRIAN GAUVIN)*

✕ **Julep's.** 110 N. Pearl St.; 601-445-6000 or 800-888-9140 $

Inside the Radisson Natchez Eola hotel, this attractive-casual space provides low-key comfort and a glorified mini-cafeteria buffet breakfast and lunch. Vegetable choices often include Southern favorites like okra and tomatoes.

✕ **King's Tavern.** 619 Jefferson St.; 601-446-8845 $$-$$$

One of the oldest buildings from territorial days, King's Tavern provided lodging and meals for weary Natchez Trace and river travelers. Authentically rustic, it still serves hearty dishes like hickory smoked prime rib, plus shrimp and catfish.

KING'S TAVERN (BRIAN GAUVIN)

✕ **The Malt Shop.** 4 Homochitto St.; 601-445-4843 $

Hungry tourists would be foolish to scoff at this tin-roofed, revamped 1950s Dairy Queen. The drive-through shoves through its windows some of the best plate lunches and hamburgers in town. Icy sno-cones and slushes derail potential heatstrokes. Call ahead for take-outs.

✕ **Mammy's Cupboard Restaurant and Gift Shop.** 555 Hwy. 61 South.; 601-445-8957 $

You can't miss the gigantic Mammy figure beaming benignly as diners enter a doorway in her red brick skirt. Mammy's serves luncheon specials like almond chicken salad, blueberry lemonade and homemade pies, blending simple with imaginative. Closed Sunday, Monday.

✕ **Monmouth Plantation.** 36 Melrose Ave.; 601-442-5852 or 800-828-4531 $$$$

For the quintessence of Old South moonlight-and-magnolias mystique, treat yourself to a sumptuous five course dining experience in the lap of luxury, complete with trappings of ornate silver and candlelight. Call ahead.

✕ **Pearl Street Pasta.** 105 S. Pearl St.; 601-442-9284 $$

Recently expanded to accommodate growing patronage, Pearl Street Pasta now has a big-city slick feel combined with down-home friendliness. Options like shrimp or crawfish over a choice of pasta, and traditional pasta dishes seldom fail to please. Lunch and dinner.

PLANTATION COUNTRY
FOOD & LODGING

✕**The Wharf Master's House.** 33 Silver St.; 601-445-6025 $-$$
Sallie Ballard's unpretentious restaurant draws so many foreign tourists she has a German translation of her menu. Enjoy spectacular sunsets over the river while dining on perfectly seasoned selections ranging from the gumbo combo to barbecued chicken to stuffed filet mignon.

Port Gibson
map page 194, B-3

☓**Canemount.** Hwy. 552 W. in Lorman; 800-423-0684 or 601-877-3784 $$$$
Escape down a road less traveled off the Natchez Trace to Canemount. Stay in the luxuriously renovated carriage house or slave quarters and enjoy a jeep safari tour to see Russian wild boar, deer, turkeys, and the haunting "Ruins of Windsor." Price includes dinner.

☓**Oak Square Plantation.** 1207 Church St.; 601-437-5300 $$$
Enjoy small-town atmosphere and the quiet beauty of Port Gibson here at Oak Square. Choose opulent rooms in the main house or take over the guest house with its central sitting room.

OAK SQUARE PLANTATION

✕**The Depot Restaurant and Lounge.** 1202 Market St.; 601-437-4711 $-$$
In business 24 years with little competition, the nostalgic Depot's friendly waitresses, who know all the local customers, dish up shrimp, catfish, and steak. Open Mon–Weds for lunch, and Thurs–Sat for dinner. Dependable and simple.

✕**JB Davis Grocery and Restaurant.** 313 Market St.; 601-437-3429 $
Feed stomach and soul and follow prominent signs marked with a big arrow to J.B.'s Place. Jessie Davis grows the vegetables and Bernice Davis serves them up with pork, beef, or chicken. Chitterlings on Saturday.

Vicksburg
maps pages 194, A-1, and 233

☓**Hotel/Motel Chains:**
Ameristar Casino Hotels;
800-700-7770 or 601-638-1000
Best Western;
800-528-1234 or 601-636-5800
Comfort Inn;
800-228-5150 or 601-634-8438
Days Inn;
800-329-7466 or 601-634-1622
Fairfield Inn (Marriott);
888-424-1811 or 601-636-1811
Hampton Inn;
888-568-4044 or 636-6100
Harrah's Casino Hotels;
800-843-2343 or 601-636-3423
Holiday Inn;
800-847-0372 or 601-636-4551
Isle of Capri;
800-WIN-ISLE or 601-636-5700

Jameson Inn;
800-526-3766 or 601-619-7799
Quality Inn;
800-221-2222 or 601-634-8607
Rainbow Casino Hotels;
800-667-4657 or 601-638-7111
Ramada;
800-2 RAMADA

AN OVERVIEW OF VICKSBURG.
(BRIAN GAUVIN)

Battlefield Inn. 4137 Frontage Rd.; 800-359-9363 or 601-638-5811 $
Next to the National Military Park, locally owned Battlefield Inn maintains its individual personality while working hard to please. Senior-citizen discounts, free breakfast, free shuttles, free evening cocktails in the lobby where caged parrots contribute freely to the conversation. Good restaurant.

Anchuca. 1010 First East St.; 888-686-0111 or 601-661-0111 $$-$$$
A large 1830 Greek Revival house, Anchuca combines nostalgic elegance with modern conveniences and luxuries like a swimming pool. Six individually decorated guest rooms with baths.

Annabelle. 501 Speed St.; 800-791-2000 or 601-638-2000 $$-$$$
Victorian-Italianate 1868 home containing fine art and heirlooms, Annabelle is an appealing 1880s guest house with gallery looking over the river to the Louisiana delta. Peaceful brick courtyard with fountain, pool. Relax and be pampered. Host fluent in German.

Balfour House. 1002 Crawford St.; 800-844-2308 or 601-638-7113 $-$$$
Home of Emma Balfour, Civil War diarist, the Balfour House was the site of a lavish Christmas ball that ended when Union troops crashed the party. Furnished with period antiques and graced by a swirling elliptical staircase. Three guest suites.

Cedar Grove Mansion Inn. 2200 Oak St.; 800-862-1300 or 601-636-1000 $$-$$$$.
Original gas-lit chandeliers glow softly. Trees outside are decorated with tiny lights. Emphasis: romance. Take cocktails to the roof for sensuous sunset river viewing. Grounds include gazebos, fountains, courtyards, gardens, and pool. Thirty rooms of varying sizes, fitness room, restaurant, bar.

Cherry Street Cottages–Schlenker House. 2212 Cherry St.; 800-636-7086 or 601-636-7086 $-$$$
This century-old, prairie-style house with three cottages, all with fully equipped kitchens. Washer/dryer available, pets welcomed. A good resting spot for self-sufficient travelers valuing comfort, independence, privacy.

The Corners. 601 Klein St.; 800-444-7421 or 601-636-7421 $-$$$

A wedding present from Cedar Grove owners to their daughter, the house was built in 1873. Fifteen rooms, one suite in-house, and separate cottage with parlor and kitchen with options including private porches, fireplaces, whirlpools, rooms with a view.

THE CORNERS (BRIAN GAUVIN.)

The Duff Green Mansion. 1114 First East St.; 800-992-0037 or 601-636-6968 $$-$$$$

A Civil War hospital for Union soldiers (some reputed to remain in ghostly form), the three-story mansion is embraced by oak trees. Beautifully restored and maintained. Five luxurious guest rooms, two of which are VIP suites.

Pemberton Headquarters B&B Inn. 1018 Crawford St.; 877-636-9581 or 601-636-9581 $$-$$$$

The decision to surrender Vicksburg, ultimately resulting in surrender of the Confederacy, was made in the parlor of this imposing Greek Revival/Federal mansion—a history buff's nirvana. Five guest suites fuse modernity and antiquity.

Andre's at Cedar Grove Mansion Inn. 2200 Oak St.; 601-636-1000 $-$$$

Carl Flowers, a.k.a. Chef Andre, prepares appealing-to-the-eye-and-palate meals presented in the aesthetic Old Courtyard room or Garden Room. Seafood dishes are always good. Service is slow despite a plethora of servers, so just relax and savor the food.

Beechwood Restaurant and Lounge. 4451 E. Clay St.; 601-636-3761. $-$$

With no pretense of trendy gourmet dining, the Beechwood, where waitresses call you "Honey," has been patronized forever for shrimp, steaks, oysters in season, and an enigmatic salad dressing called Kumbak sauce—and diners do Kumbak for the food, but not for the atmosphere.

The Biscuit Company Cafe. Entrance on Grove St. down the hill from Washington St.; 601-631-0099 $-$$

The Biscuit Company (look for fading letters on building's exterior from a past life: U Need A Biscuit) is often jam-packed on weekends but low-key during the week. Consistently good, lots of options. Pecan-encrusted catfish is a treat.

Duff's Tavern and Grille. 1306 Washington St.; 601-638-0169 $$-$$$

In the heart of downtown Vicksburg, Duff's is one of the most attractive spots for lunch and dinner, but it does have high turnover rate for chefs. The gumbo remains reliably good. Choose uncomplicated entrees. Closed Sunday.

✕ **El Sombrero Mexican Restaurant.** 1820 S. Frontage Rd.; 601-638-1388 $-$$

Unimpressive from outside, the interior of this small restaurant with a large menu is a pleasant surprise, allowing diners to imagine they have slipped farther south than Mississippi. Pleasantly spicy—but not fiery—Mexican favorites.

✕ **Goldie's Trail Bar-B-Q.** 4127 S. Washington St.; 601-636-9839 $

In business since 1960 and featured in numerous magazines, homely little Goldie's has served up the best true-pit barbecued pork and beef for so long that most Vicksburgers have Goldie's barbecue sauce in their circulatory systems. Closed Sunday.

✕ **Jacques Cafe in the Park.** 4137 I-20 Frontage Rd.; 601-661-0019 $$

Jacque's Cafe, unintentionally retro in atmosphere, is tucked away in the Battlefield Inn, but is far superior to standard hotel/motel restaurants. Specials with crawfish or crabmeat toppings have lured locals for years.

✕ **Maxwell's Restaurant.** 4207 E.Clay St.; 601-636-1344 $-$$$.

Lunch buffet offers soup, salad, fish or meat, and homestyle vegetables. Dinner choices include excellent crabmeat dishes and other seafood along with steaks, veal, chicken, and Maxwell's special prime rib. Closed Sunday.

✕ **Rowdy's Family Restaurant.** Int. of Hwy. 27-Hwy. 80; 601-638-2375 $-$$

Mississippi pond catfish fried (choose either "thin fish" or "thick fish"), grilled, or blackened. No atmosphere, but you can satisfy a whole family with a bucket of fried catfish, hush puppies, and coleslaw.

✕ **Walnut Hills.** 1214 Adams St.; 601-638-4910 $-$$

No nouvelle spoken here. Choose round tables with big lazy susans allowing selections from entire menu, or standard tables. Fried chicken, vegetable, and dessert recipes are bona fide Southern classics. To find Tipsy Pudding on the menu is to be gastronomically blessed.

WALNUT HILLS (BRIAN GAUVIN)

COASTAL MISSISSIPPI

by Bethany Ewald Bultman

■ **HIGHLIGHTS** *page*

Food & Lodging, page 280
Map, page 255

■ **TRAVEL OVERVIEW**

The 88 miles of Mississippi Gulf Coast shoreline gives the first impression of being the love-child of Florida and California, tucked away where they thought no one could find it. A look at any of its technicolor brochures will convince you the foundling had been reared by Atlantic City! But beneath all of that neon makeup is one of the most congenial and seductive regions in the entire Gulf South. A few days dawdling under the oaks of Bay St. Louis or Ocean Springs is guaranteed to capture the heart of even the most jaded traveller. Locals are friendly; you'll make friends as you wander through Old Biloxi just by smiling and asking for directions.

Getting There: Scenic Highway 90 follows the water's edge for most of the journey along the Mississippi Gulf Coast. It also serves as the main drag for most of the coastal towns, so traffic can slow to a crawl during the summer months when every-one over 16 gets into a automobile to cruise the strip. If you're driving from New Or-leans toward the coast, the quickest way is to take Interstate 10 to Slidell. Be certain not to depart during rush hour because the high rise bridge in New Orleans East will be clogged with traffic moving at a glacial pace. Also note that in New Orleans Friday rush hour begins at 3 P.M. (They don't call it "the Big Easy" for nothing!) Take the Bay St. Louis/Waveland exit.

Scenic Routes: There are scenic routes (Highway 90 to Highway 11 or Highway 190) that allow you to mosey through the funky fishing camps along the Rigolets (RIG-O-LEES). One of the camps even looks like an ersatz medieval castle. The road winds through the Rigolets, a narrow channel between Lake Pontchartrain and Lake Borgne and the Mississippi Channel. You may recall that it was in this area on a foggy pre-dawn morn that starlet Jayne Mansfield was killed in the 1960s when the car in which she was riding hit the Rigolets' Bridge on her way to New Orleans after her performance at the Gus Stevens, a nightclub on Highway 90 in Biloxi. (No, Mansfield wasn't decapitated; that was her wig on the hood.)

Climate: Annual rainfall is 64.5 inches. It can sometimes rain as much as 11 inches in two hours, then within minutes the sun is shining again. Rain down here means enough water to dent lawn furniture. Temperatures drop into the 50s in January and February, and climb into the high 90s in July and August. October is the driest and prettiest month. The Gulf is a big weathermaker, which accounts for the rain and also the nice breezes.

Nightlife: One blissful outgrowth of the casino boom is the number of venues for live music and places to dance, drink, and generally club-hop the night away. Check the local papers for up-to-the-minute listings.

Food: To drive anywhere in the original French colony of the Gulf South is to immerse oneself in one of many rich culinary traditions—Creole, Cajun, French, West African, Caribbean, you name it. Creole favorites include crawfish etouffée and jambalaya. Cajun cooks add fire to the mix with dishes like blackened redfish and peppery gumbo. Breakfast is pure down-home Southern: grits (a corn mush seasoned like mashed potatoes), biscuits, and a rich assortment of pork products. **Restaurant listings begin on page 280.**

Lodging: Can vary from elegant bed and breakfasts in restored 18th-century homes to funky beachfront motels. Due to the plethora of casino hotels, there are always rooms to be had, though prices do fluctuate like the stock market. As a matter of fact, there are more than 15,000 hotel rooms along the coast. **For lodging listings see page 280; see page 333 for price designations and toll-free numbers for chain accommodations. For a chart of listings by region, see page 334.**

COASTAL
MISSISSIPPI

■ ABOUT THE GULF COAST

Don't be put off by the fact that Gulfport and Biloxi beach is manmade—26 miles of glistening, sugar-soft white sand. And you'll want to ignore the fact that the water in the Mississippi Sound is the color of sipping whiskey—silt from the Mississippi, the Pascagoula/Singing, and the Pearl Rivers disgorge into it. The barrier islands trap the fertile sludge on the coastal side, but on their other side shimmers the grey-green Gulf of Mexico. There is a significant, unspoiled coastal wilderness just a crab's crawl from the new casinos and putt-putt courses. The area is scalloped with 9,786 acres of oyster reefs and 9,727,000 acres of barrier islands.

Some fanciful soul in the late 19th century coined the term "American Mediterranean" for the Mississippi shore. Nowadays tourist brochures refer to it as the "Playground of the South," making old-time residents cringe. The coastal views

Mississippi Panorama *by Robert Bramme (1850) reveals a dreamy waterscape with ships in the distance. (Roger Houston Ogden Collection, New Orleans).*

(opposite) Sunset over the Gulf. (Brian Gauvin)

they cherished—pink sunrises illuminating offshore shrimp-fishing trawlers, the sea gulls and pelicans circling the fishing boats, and the graceful sailboats chasing the gulf breezes—are still there, but the land along the coast itself is being paved over as a massive RV park for the 50,000 visitors per day who flock to the coast to gamble. But look on the positive side: as long-time residents will remind you, obliging hurricanes will continue to obliterate the latest of mankind's follies.

Those who have loved the coast for generations know the unspoiled beaches on Ship Island and Horn Island to be the most beautiful in the Gulf South, and that the coldest beer and the hottest lore can be found in most any convivial bait shop.

No doubt about it, the residents of the Mississippi Gulf Coast are more welcoming than those of any other surrounding state. Truth be told, however, the snooty plantation class of the north Mississippi Delta still doesn't claim the Mississippi Gulf coast as part of the state. They wouldn't be caught dead on a beach where radio playing, beer drinking, volleyball, jet skis, and para-sailors compete for attention with ferocious (flying-ant like) no-see-ums.

The Mississippi Sound is way too warm and jellyfishy for much swimming, even if you hike the 100 yards out to where it is over knee-deep. The beach is

Commercial strips like those above have changed the landscape of the Mississippi Gulf Coast in recent decades. (Brian Gauvin)

Playing volleyball on the white sands of West Ship Island. (Brian Gauvin)

more of a backdrop for anglers eager to pit their skills against the world's largest variety of fish and those who enjoy strolling along the miles of soft, flat beach. Snow birds—those from cold, northern states or from way up in Canada—rent condos here for less than their winter heating bill back home. They keep coming back for the friendly locals and the area's 20 or so golf courses.

Tip: Locals swear that "no-see-ums" (pesky biting flies of the family *Ceratopogonidae*) will not come near you if you douse yourself with imitation vanilla extract, undiluted, and applied with a spray bottle. You'll smell like a wedding cake, but the no-see-ums won't bug you.

■ THE GULF STORY

La Page Du Pratz, overseer of the plantations for the Companie des Indies in Louisiana 1718-1734, wrote disparagingly of the French colonial settlement at New Biloxi on the Gulf Coast, "The land is the most barren of any to be found thereabouts; being nothing but a fine sand, as white and shining as snow… There was nothing in plenty but fish (and oysters)." By the 1840s, these were viewed as great attributes, especially by New Orleans cotton brokers, pleased to trade sweltering heat and yellow fever for the soothing breezes of the Mississippi Sound. Bay St. Louis, Pass Christian, and Biloxi soon saw gracious summer cottages, boarding houses, and hotels constructed amidst the shacks of boat builders and fishermen. Daily steam packets brought hundreds of eager visitors to the charming antebellum resort communities.

During Prohibition, the piney woods near the coast were noted for producing fine bootleg hootch. The fishermen on the coast carried the moonshine through the bayous and bays to the "rum runners," gangster Al Capone's liquor ships anchored off the barrier islands in the Mississippi Sound. To combat the illegal liquor industry, the U. S. Coast Guard established a Biloxi substation in 1927 with as many as 80 patrol boats operating at its peak.

In 1960s the Mississippi shoreline had no beach, merely a seawall. From 1951-1954 the Army Corps of Engineers dredged an offshore channel and dumped six million cubic yards of muddy ooze on the coastal resort's front porch from the Biloxi Lighthouse to Henderson Point. Resort owners and beach-goers screeched. Then a miracle happened: the tide leeched out the mud, leaving a 26-mile beach as white as confectioner's sugar.

In 1969 Hurricane Camille obliterated the scenic coastal road, along with gracious homes, fishing boats, stately churches, and venerable live oaks. After the road and houses were rebuilt, a hurricane of a different sort arrived: gambling. In a 46-mile area there are more than 12,000 casino-related hotel rooms, and many more planned.

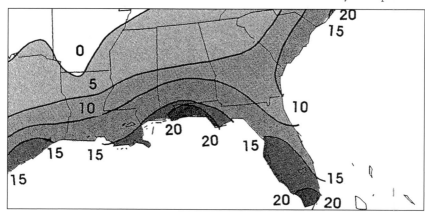

This graphic clearly illustrates the vulnerability of the Mississippi and Alabama Gulf Coast to hurricane strikes. The numbers refer to the number of damaging hurricanes to strike the coast in a given area between 1901 and 1955. (NOAA)

MISSISSIPPI BOOZE

Since the Civil War, Mississippi's drinking life has been an ongoing, sometimes violent and often laughable tug-of-war between bootleggers, teetotalers, "trippers," tax collectors, moonshiners, "revenooers," criminals, politicians, police,

Driving home after a Sunday baptism, 1912.
(Mississippi Department of Archives and History)

preachers, and the average citizen who just wants his little nip of John Barleycorn.

Nowhere was the "wet" vs. "dry" drama onstage longer than in Mississippi, a stubbornly independent state that jumped the gun on Prohibition in 1908, prompted by hardshell religious fundamentalists. By the time the 18th Amendment became law in 1919—Mississippi rushed to be the first state to ratify—moonshiners and bootleggers had long been in place, with corn liquor stills hidden in the woods and "trippers" racing jacked-up Ford two-seaters along back roads dodging "revenooers." The banned booze business was so lucrative that it was not until 1966 (33 years after the nation repealed Prohibition) that Mississippi finally passed local-option liquor legislation, in the process breaching the historic bonds between bootleggers, preachers, and bribe-happy sheriffs.

For a girl like me, growing up in Prohibition's last stronghold was an education in irony. Not only did I take my handbag out for dinner and dancing, I took my brown bag—a paper sack hiding a bottle of illegal liquor or wine. Dispersed in various ingenious ways, demon rum came to our house via a white Cadillac and a bootlegger in a white linen suit. Even the smallest town had its ramshackle bootleg joint; some straddled the county line, so when police staged a raid, crates quickly could be shifted from one jurisdiction to the other. Shoe stores handed off intoxicants in Buster Brown shoe boxes; gas stations dispensed booze along with gasoline; grocery stores had a hidden cubbyhole behind the meat counter; drugstores sold alcohol for medicinal purposes. Nobody went thirsty, and the state made millions from 20 years of collecting "black-market tax" on illicit liquor, 95 percent of which was purchased legally from Louisiana liquor wholesalers.

Today in 49 of the state's 82 counties it is legal to buy booze legally from more than a thousand state-owned liquor stores. The rest are still "dry." Come to think of it, Mississippi has never repealed Prohibition, just adapted to it.

—Marda Burton

■ FROM NEW ORLEANS TO THE MISSISSIPPI GULF

◆ SLIDELL, LOUISIANA   *map A-3*

If you drive toward the Mississippi Gulf from New Orleans, you'll cross Lake Pontchartrain on I-10 as you go, passing **Slidell**, Louisiana, the industrial hub of St. Tammany Parish. Old Slidell is loaded with charming antique shops. Check the listings for their frequent festivals. To get a nice feel for the area stay at **The Garden Guest House B&B** on Highway 433 *(page 283)*. It is surrounded by ancient live oaks, palms, and 10 acres of lush foliage. (From here you may want to linger a few days to explore many of the charming North Shore communities of Lake Pontchartrain such as Abita Springs.)

◆ NATURAL AREAS   *map A-3*

Slidell is the home port for several worthwhile nature tours. It is situated on numerous secluded bayous along the eastern shore of Lake Pontchartrain, and near the Pearl River and its basin. Two interesting natural areas are situated in the basin.

Bogue Chitto National Wildlife Refuge

This tupelo and cypress swamp, and hardwood forest is criss-crossed with hiking trails. For maps and information contact the U.S. Fish and Wildlife Service in Slidell, *504-646-7555,* or the St. Tammany Parish Tourist and Convention Commission, *800-634-9443.*

White Kitchen Nature Preserve

Within the 55-acre **Pearl River Wildlife Management Area** is the Nature Conservancy's White Kitchen Nature Preserve. Named after a restaurant formerly on the site, the preserve has attracted eagle watchers for a half-century. A 300-foot boardwalk over the swamp complete with picnic tables makes bird-watching both comfortable and dry. *Intersection of Highway 190 and Highway 90. Louiaiana Nature Concervancy; 225-338-1040.*

Honey Island Swamp

Adjoining the White Kitchen Nature Preserve is one of the Gulf South's pristine wilderness areas, the Honey Island Swamp, named by early settlers because it attracted swarms of honeybees. It has its own legendary monster, Wookie, covered in short hair, standing over seven feet tall, and leaving four-toed prints. Whether or not you see Wookie, you should see ibis, hawks, herons, wild turkeys, owls, and bald eagles.

It is possible to rent 10-foot pontoon boats, kayaks, and canoes. If canoeing or kayaking is of interest, check the water levels in the daily *Times-Picayune* in New Orleans.

UNTAMED AND DEADLY, she ruled the swamp with a BLAZING GUN and a LUSCIOUS SMILE.

'GATOR BAIT

HALF ANIMAL.. ALL WOMAN

A poster for the cult film Gator Bait *(1976) shows the movie's heroine— played by Claudia Jennings—on the rampage. Referred to as the "swamp rat" in the film by the evil deputy and his pals, the character is named Desirée—a classic, stereotypical Cajun name.*

Interesting to note that there was actually a sequel made to this movie —14 years later. Its name? Gator Bait II: Cajun Revenge.

Honey Island Swamp Tours

This is a two-hour scientific flatboat tour of the wetland area. Ecologist Dr. Paul Wagner and his staff are extremely knowledgeable about the habitat and the natural history. The trips depart from Crawford Landing and meander through one of the country's least-altered river swamps. *504-641-1769.*

Gator Swamp Tours

Now if it is "yee-haw" folksiness you hanker for, Gator Swamp Tours are just the ticket. Boats are boarded through a yard of free-range chickens, and the tours pass the shacks of the people who still live deep in the swamps—and as their ancestors did, for that matter. *Off I-10 Exit 263, Hwy. 433 to US 90; 800-875-4287.*

Swamp Monster Tours

Aboard the *Swamp Monster,* Captain Roy McManus, a native of the area, regales you with the lore of the deep swamp. You'll pass an Acolapissa Indian village, and you're likely to see a profusion of animals from alligators and turtles to otters, beavers, raccoons, and wild boars. *108 Indian Village Rd., Off I-10 Exit 263 East on Highway 433; 800-245-1132 or 504-641-5106.*

◆ PICAYUNE   *map page 255, A-2*

Between New Orleans and the coast you will pass through the heart of the Mississippi timber country. In 1904 this sawmill town of 10,600 was incorporated and named by the wife of the publisher of the New Orleans paper, *The Picayune*. A picayune was a half dime, the cost of the paper.

The nature lover will be wise to make a half-day detour at the **Crosby Arboretum**. Billed as a "civilized walk in the woods," it is a 64-acre native plant center featuring more than 300 species. Boardwalks and paths take you winding through a pine forest, hammocks, bogs, a grassy savannah, and woodlands. The gorgeous

JULIA SANDERS' FLORA GUIDE: MISSISSIPPI COASTAL AREA

BRIAN GAUVIN

Parrot's Pitcher Plant
Sarracenia psittacina
One of several insectivorous plants growing along the coastal plain. Pitcher-shaped leaves have enzymes that digest insects. Blooms May through June. Found in open bogs and pine-cypress woods between US 90 and I-10.

Southern Magnolia
Magnolia grandiflora
This large evergreen tree is often planted along roadsides. Mississippi state flower. Blooms April to June with some flowers in fall. Grows naturally in wooded areas along stream banks.

Pinecote Pavilion, designed by Fay Jones, a student of Frank Lloyd Wright, overlooks a pond surrounded by native plants. The visitors center offers an informative 12-minute orientation video. *Wed–Sun, 9–4:40; 370 Ridge Rd.; 601-799-2311.*

Picnicking is not allowed, so plan to eat a few miles away in Kiln. To get to Kiln from I-10 take Exit 13, the Kiln/Bay St. Louis Exit.

◆ KILN   *map page 255, B-2*

At first glance there doesn't seem to be much to this old paper-mill town. Kiln got its name from the giant kilns the colonial French erected in the town to burn charcoal for sale in New Orleans and Natchez. In 1870 Samuel L. Favre established a prosperous sawmill. Yes, all you athletic supporters, he is an ancestor of Brett Favre, Kiln native son, the famed quarterback for the Green Bay Packers who made a cameo appearance in the film *There's Something About Mary.*

When the W. W. Carre Lumber Company bought the mill in 1908, they set about creating one of the largest mills in the south and moved all the old homes from the river bank. By the Depression, it was almost a ghost town. Almost, not literally, because Kiln made its reputation during Prohibition. Kiln whiskey was considered premium hooch up north, and the moonshine families were great fans of the notorious Chicago gangster, Al Capone whose men guarded the Kiln/Delise Road.

The town is just 13 miles north of Bay St. Louis and is a popular area for New Orleanians, who have country homes along the many majestic bayous and streams that feed the Jourdan River. **McCloud Park** has camping, a great swimming hole, and wonderful bird-watching. Horses can be rented at Papa Lee's or Moran's Stable. The downtown has several excellent family hometown diners of the 1960s vintage, groaning with Southern food. **Rooster's** has such killer country food that people drive up to Kiln from the coast to eat here *(page 280).*

The center of local culture is a hole-in-the-wall honky-tonk called **The Broke Spoke**. It's a great place for a cold one or to hear endless Brett Favre tales; *6358 Kiln/Picayune Rd.; 228-255-7793.*

Overnight accommodations can be found at the clean, modest motel adjacent to the Conoco Gas station/ D and K truck stop, off I-10 at MS 603.

◆ JOHN C. STENNIS SPACE CENTER   *map page 255, A-3*

One of those strange juxtapositions of the old rural South and the 21st century techno-coast sits 14 miles west of Bay St. Louis. The installation is named for John Stennis, Mississippi's 20th-century Congressional titan who funneled billions in federal dollars to his home state during his 40-year career in in the Senate. It includes NASA's space shuttle test facilities, as well as environmental, oceanographic, and space studies. The tour begins at the center's 90-foot-tall observation tower from which Wernher von Braun watched test launches in the 1950s and '60s. The Center is surrounded by a 126,000-acre acoustical buffer zone. The first Saturn 5 rocket booster was tested here for the Apollo lunar landing in 1966. The Apollo 4 command module, a 78-foot-tall Jupiter-C rocket, and a moon rock are also on display. More than 100,000 visitors visit annually, so allow half a day, as the center may be crowded. *I-10, Exit 2, Highway 607. On I-59 at Exit 1; 228-688-2370 or 800-237-1821.*

■ BAY ST. LOUIS   *map page 255, B-3*

Bay St. Louis (pop. 8,100), where you pick-up Scenic US 90, rests on a promontory with Mississippi Sound on the front and St. Louis Bay at the back. Bay St. Louis is one of the loveliest sections of the Mississippi coast, worth a few hours of browsing or even an overnight stay. With 56 shops, bars, and places to eat there is plenty to do and see. Downtown maintains much of its moonlight-and-magnolias charm, and the wide, flat white beach that runs along North Beach Boulevard provides an ideal stretch to walk for miles and miles. The water, however, is only about three inches deep so no swimming, and the Dupont plant has so polluted Bay St. Louis that it's better to gaze at the water than fish in it.

Dock of the Bay

Jerry Fisher, former lead singer of Blood, Sweat and Tears, retired here, and he and his wife, Melba, serve up terrific fried seafood. (Jerry cooks a mean burger). The tables on the porch are the perfect place to dine at twilight on a long summer night. *119 North Beach Blvd.; 228-467-9940.*

Scenic Drive

Hurricanes and fires have ravaged the once-elegant hotels, but many of the gracious antebellum cottages remain. For one of the nicest drives, take a short detour off Highway 90 and turn on to North Beach Boulevard. If you come to Casino Magic, you have gone too far.

Small, Interesting Places

Alice Moseley is a noted Primitive artist who documents her long-ago life in paintings and limited-edition prints. Ninety-year-old Moseley, described as a cross between Grandma Moses and Phyllis Diller, welcomes visitors to her studio, located in her royal blue cottage. *214 Bookter St.; 228-467-9223.*

Another gallery, **Serenity,** was transplanted from the French Quarter in New Orleans more than 25 years ago. It contains a mind-boggling mix of work. Of note is local artist Mary Perrin. *126 Main St.*

Bookends is housed in a charming four-room cottage with a screened-in porch that invites reading. The cottage is crammed with antique cabinets containing top-notch books, including first editions and books on the region. *111 US 90; 228-467-9623.*

Across from the courthouse is the Hancock County Historical Society housed in the **Kate Lobrano House.** Hours are erratic, so call first. *108 Cue St.; 228 -67-4090.*

St. Rose De Lima Church

Founded in 1926, this church is noted for its mural of an African Christ. Today the church features a wonderful enthnically mixed gospel choir. *301 Necase Ave.; (from Highway 90 take Main St. to Necase Ave.); 228-466-7347.*

Fishing and strolling along wharves and walkways are popular pastimes along the Gulf, where water is often too shallow for swimming. (above) Dock of the Bay in Bay St. Louis; and (opposite) wharves at Waveland. (Brian Gauvin)

■ HARRISON COUNTY

Harrison County was named after William Henry Harrison, who died one month into his presidential term in 1841, the year the county was established. The county extends from Bay St. Louis to Biloxi Bay. Time in this county is still measured in B.C. and A.C., before Hurricane Camille and after Camille, the category five hurricane that leveled the region on August 18, 1969. Even today you will see vacant lots and concrete steps leading to nowhere, monuments to the devastation.

The shoreline stretches 26 miles. On one side of the road is the Mississippi Sound, the back porch of the Gulf of Mexico, a generally waveless pool, the temperature of bath water. The road takes you by deep lawns, majestic oaks and lovely homes interspersed with strip malls, pawn shops, and cheap motels. You'll see a series of islands about 10 miles offshore, part of the Gulf Islands National Seashore.

◆ PASS CHRISTIAN   *map page 255, C-3*

Pass Christian (pop. 5,557, pronounced "KRISS-tee-YAN"), across the Bay St. Louis bridge, is honeycombed with charming eateries and antiques shops. The Pass Christian beach is as open and expansive as the porches. The interplay of the changing angle of the sun and sea debris gives the water an amber glow in the fall. The area's oyster reefs were noted by the French in 1699, who dubbed it *Passe aux Huitres,* or Oyster Pass. Today you will see dozens of boats in the shallow waters tonging for the bivalves.

A walk through the oak-draped **Live Oak Cemetery** will provide a feel for the history of the coast. The land was given by John and Louisa Henderson and dates from October 1851. The original deed designated 17 percent of the cemetery to be set aside as free ground for the internment of black as well as white. Two Louisiana governors are buried here. Across the street, **Trinity Episcopal Church** has been a coast landmark since it was consecrated on July 31, 1851. Destroyed by Hurricane Camille on the night of August 17, 1969, it was rebuilt in the '70s.

The tranquil town, once known as the "Newport of the South," takes its name from Nicholas Christian, a carpenter from New Orleans who settled near here on Cat Island in 1745. Soon prominent people from New Orleans erected stately summer homes beneath the majestic oaks. A drive along the beach along West Beach Boulevard will give you a glimpse of many of these fine homes. Nestled a

Commercial oyster and shrimp boats in Pass Christian Harbor. (Syndey Byrd)

bit in the background are several tiny gingerbread homes, newly gussied up. The **Pass Christian harbor** is quite beautiful and contains one of the oldest marinas on the Gulf Coast. You can purchase shrimp right off the back of the Vietnamese trawlers, arrange for a dive tour, or simply walk around looking at lovely sailboats.

◆ LONG BEACH   *map page 255, C-3*

The line between Pass Christian and Long Beach (pop. 15,804) is, sadly, easy to detect since Hurricane Camille wiped out the latter town in 1969. With more folklore than history in its past, the settlement dates back to ancient times when it was an Indian burial ground. Later a tiny colonial farming community, it took center stage as the hideout for the notorious pirate "Pitcher." He was rumored to have buried treasure here, but even Camille couldn't find it.

Long Beach and Pass Christian were the only coastal communities to vote against allowing gambling casinos.

COASTAL
MISSISSIPPI

◆ BOATING ON THE WOLF RIVER   *map page 255, C-2/3*

One of the nicest excursions in the area has nothing to do with the coast. It's a trip to the Wolf River, on which you can canoe, tube, or kayak. The Wolf is not for those seeking white-water adventure, but for those who want to meander through nature, nap on a white-sand beach, or take a clay bath while watching the herons fly overhead. On the hottest days, put-in at artesian springs for a dip in the ice cold water. Try **Wolf River Canoes**, *21652 Tucker Rd.; www.wolfrivercanoes.com; 228-452-7666.*

Red Creek Inn Vineyard and Racing Stable, just a few country miles away, prides itself as being the first B&B on the Mississippi Gulf Coast. It's located in an 1899 raised French-Creole cottage with a 64-foot porch surrounded by 11 acres of magnolia- and live oak–shaded grounds. *282-452-3080.*

The remains of the battery at Fort Massachusetts, built between 1859 to 1866. The 15-inch Rodman cannon barrel, when assembled, weighs 50,000 pounds. (Brian Gauvin)

The Gulf's barrier islands protect the mainland from the full force of tropical storms. (Brian Gauvin)

■ BARRIER ISLANDS

Ten miles off the coast are a series of long, narrow islands of white sand that protect the inland beaches from the ravages of the open, hurricane-driven waters of the Gulf. These sea-oat-dotted dunes are moving ever westward as waves and wind carve land from their eastern ends to reinforce the western ends. Over the past hundred years, the littoral currents have moved them more than three miles.

Gulf Islands National Seashore covers 135,000 miles and extends 150 miles from Fort Walton Beach, Florida, to Gulfport, Mississippi. The Mississippi portion includes Petit Bois, Ship, and Horn Islands.

◆ EAST AND WEST SHIP ISLANDS   *map page 255, D-3*

In 1969, Hurricane Camille split the four-mile Ship Island into what are now officially called West Ship and East Ship Islands. Most locals, however, seem to think they will eventually grow back together and thus still refer to them in the singular, Ship Island. The British used the island as a staging area for their ill-fated attempt at capturing New Orleans in the War of 1812. Fort Massachusetts was an unfinished fort when the Confederates seized it. Admiral David Farragut's federal troops won back control and completed it in 1861.

If you plan to visit the islands, West Ship is of greater importance, and can be reached by a ferry (March–October) from Gulfport. Schools of dolphins will often dance in your path. Tickets are sold on a first-come basis and must be purchased one hour before departure at the **Gulfport Small Craft Harbor**. *US 90 at US 49; 228-864-1014.*

Once on the island, you can take a tour with a ranger (summer only) or wander on your own. There's usually a delightful breeze, making it an ideal day trip for a sunbath and swim. There's a shop (during the season) that sells hot snacks and sunscreen. Whatever you do, don't miss the last ferry back or you'll have a long, hungry night on the sandy shore. There's no shade, so bring or rent an umbrella; an ice chest with food and beverages is another good idea.

◆ HORN ISLAND AND PETIT BOIS *map page 255, E/F-3*

The palmetto forests and lagoons of Horn Island inspired the magnificent work of Walter Inglis Anderson (1903–1965), who documented the island in his journals and paintings on his hundreds of lengthy expeditions. An eccentric, he rowed to the island carrying one garbage pail of paper and watercolors, another full of canned goods. He mainly ate the fish he caught and slept under his skiff on the beach. So passionate was he about his island refuge, that he weathered hurricane Betsy there in 1965 (which devastated the coast and killed 75) by tying himself to a pine tree.

In 1958 a portion of the island became a wildlife refuge supporting more than 280 species of birds along 13 miles of pristine, isolated beaches. A ranger is stationed on the island, though there is no ferry service or public services. *(See page 278 for information.)* Kayaks or charter boats are the best means of traversing Mississippi Sound to the island. Prices begin at about $100. Once there, you'll find a 30-mile hiking trial and nice camping on the ends of the island. When the Southern red wolf, a smaller cousin of the grey wolf, was facing extinction, a few were introduced on the island. Now they are thriving.

Nearby **Petit Bois Island** (accessible only by private boat) is a wildlife sanctuary. Alligators, raccoons, and a multitude of birds inhabit its lagoons and slash-pine forests.

Casino gambling has taken over the old fishing-port waterfront of Biloxi. Grand Casino can be seen in the foreground and Beau Rivage in the distance. (Brian Gauvin)

■ CASINO COAST *map page 255, D-3*

◆ GAMBLING CASINOS

A dozen casinos dominate the Gulfport-Biloxi beachfront and more mega-hotel/casino complexes are planned. They attract gamblers from New Orleans, and senior citizens by the busload from small towns all over Alabama and Mississippi. Inside the casinos, there is nothing to indicate whether it is night or day, a beach day, or a raging tropical storm. The job market on the coast is booming and locals now have a nightly choice of national entertainers they can see.

Beau Rivage Resort

Steve Wynn, developer of many of Las Vegas's mega-casino complexes, built this resort, with its profusion of magnolia and honeysuckle and discretely muffled pings from the slots. This ain't no sedate replica old-South resort either. It's a 1,780-room hotel, with 12 restaurants, a gorgeous spa, a 1,550-seat theater, and a bevy of upscale designer boutiques. The rooms favor a Matisse palette, the tubs are marble, and the soaps are English. *875 Beach Blvd., Biloxi; 888-750-7111.*

COASTAL
MISSISSIPPI

Grand Casino Biloxi

Top national acts, a full-service spa and kid activity centers are offered here, in addition to gambling. **Roxy's Diner** offers a bit of manufactured '50s. There are two hotel towers and numerous good restaurants. *265 Beach Blvd., Biloxi; 800-946-2946.*

Isle of Capri/Crowne Plaza Resort

The tropical theme is enhanced by a faux waterfall and spotlighted palm trees. The Gulf-facing rooms on the the higher floors of the adjacent Crowne Plaza offer some of the nicest views. *151 Beach Blvd., Biloxi; 800-843-4753.*

Imperial Palace

This thousand-room hotel is on the Back Bay. There's a wonderful antique-car muse-um, a magnificent entrance, and valet parking (The adjacent neighborhood is not a particularly safe area for an evening stroll.) *850 Bayview Ave., Biloxi; 800-634-6441.*

President Casino/Broadwater Resort

The President includes the renovated coast landmark, the Broadwater Beach Hotel, as part of its complex. One of its most popular features is the golf course. The hotel is a hodge-podge of old and not-so-newish properties linked to a casino across the road. *2110 Beach Blvd., Biloxi; 800-843-7737.*

Treasure Bay

Treasure Bay cashes in on its Jean Lafitte beachfront, pirate-ship theme. *1980 Beach Blvd., Biloxi; 800-747-2839.*

Card table at the Isle of Capri Crowne Plaza Resort. (Brian Gauvin)

Gulfport has been a commercial port since its founding in the 19th century. Here sailing ships are being loaded with resin. (Library of Congress)

◆ GULFPORT *map page 255, C/D-3*

From its founding in the late 19th century by William Hardy, who came down to the coast from Hattiesburg, Gulfport (pop. 40,775) was planned as the commercial center of the Mississippi Gulf Coast. Its central location—about equidistant from Houston, Atlanta, and Memphis—lured many entrepreneurs, and today it remains a booming coastal port from which bananas, lumber, and seafood come and go via the Gulf. The Dole and Chiquita fruit trucks parked along the waterfront give Gulfport the feel of Vera Cruz. Gulfport remains the number one banana port in the United States, handling some 800,000 tons per year.

The county seat of Harrison Country, Gulfport has broad streets laid out parallel to the seawall. **The Great Southern Golf Club,** dating from 1908, is Mississippi's oldest golf course and also enjoys a gulfside view.

Nowadays Gulfport has decided to cash in on the gambling boom of its sister city, Biloxi. Its other claim to fame is the **"Cruisin' the Coast"** event in October, when thousands of vintage cars from all over the country come to the city.

To capture the essence of Gulfport, stop by **Triplet Day Drug Company and Professional Compounding Center** for cigars, knickknacks, and a malt at the old-time soda fountain. *One block north of Hwy. 90 on Hwy. 49 at 14th St.*

Then take a walk down to the pier as the fishing boats come in. Don't be lured into a card game by the charming Vietnamese fishermen with the adorable deep-Mississippi accents. They're better at cards than they are at fishing! Your odds of winning are better at a casino. The **Copa Casino** has become a local hangout due to its plentiful cheap eats. There are lots of nickel slots, and regulars know each other in a corner-bar sort of way; it's also an ideal stop for bird-watchers. The casino is housed on a former cruise ship, moored in the harbor. Hundreds of pelicans perch along its mooring lines. *777 Copa Blvd.; 800-946-2672 or 228-863-3330.*

◆ BILOXI   *map page 255, D-2/3*

Biloxi (pop. 46,300) claims to be the second-oldest settlement in the United States, after St. Augustine, Florida. At first gasp, Biloxi ("Bill-UCK-see"), seems to be nothing more than a strip of T-shirt cabanas, tiki-style hamburger joints, and casinos that people pass through on the way to Florida. Yet Biloxi gladly reveals its quiet, genteel past to those who resolve to forsake the concrete and neon, and an interesting past it is. According to records kept from 1723 to 1729, Biloxi's

These replicas of oyster schooners—the Mike Sekul *and the* Glen L. Swetman—*take sightseers on harbor tours in Biloxi Harbor. (Brian Gauvin)*

population in its early days numbered no more than a handful of French colonists and a few slaves. By the 1780s Spanish land grants prompted a steady trickle of settlers. After the Louisiana Purchase in 1806 there were only twelve French-speaking families living on the Biloxi Peninsula. The early colonists mostly fished, raised cattle, and made tar. Chartered as a town in 1838, Biloxi developed along the shoreline, its growth driven by the arrival of summer vacationers, who came to enjoy the Gulf breezes.

Biloxi inhabits a peninsula jutting into the Mississippi Sound on one side and Biloxi Bay on the other. The location also provides ideal access to Gulf breezes and killer hurricanes. To give you an idea of how the Biloxi coastline has changed, the Old Lighthouse was brought to the city by brig in 1848 and installed to command the Mississippi Sound. Today it stands 100 yards inland, north of the shoreline.

If you venture to one side of the Highway 90 split, you'll come face to face with leaping Pepto Bismol–colored concrete dolphins and neon palm trees that rim the bunker-like gambling places that now command much of the shoreline. **Kessler Air Force Base** has dominated the center of Biloxi since 1941 and is home to the 403rd Wing of the Air Force, 53rd Weather Reconnaissance Squadron—the world-renowned Hurricane Hunters—and site of the Neil Simon play and film *Biloxi Blues.*

Biloix's present swallows its past. (Brian Gauvin)

◆ HISTORIC BILOXI

Biloxi Lighthouse

Biloxi boasted an early crowd pleaser, the South's first cast-iron lighthouse, erected in 1848 on the western edge of the resort. Today the 65-foot tall Biloxi Lighthouse remains an enduring emblem. One notable feature of its history is that it had several female lightkeepers. Maria Youngans held the position for more than 50 years. *Open one-half hour a day: Mon–Sat at 10 A.M. Hwy. 90 (Beach Blvd.) at the foot of Porter Ave.*

Sightseeing Tours

Biloxi Tour Train, an open-air trolley, actually a bus, travels through historic Biloxi and departs from the Biloxi Lighthouse. *Hwy. 90 (Beach Blvd.) and Porter Ave.; 228-*

374-8687. Or take an unguided tour on the public bus, **Beachcomber Streetcar Line.** It stops at the lighthouse hourly at 17 minutes after the hour.

Biloxi Historical Walking Tour

This self-guided walking tour of 20 historic structures starts at Biloxi Visitors Center, *710 Beach Blvd.; 800-435-6248.*

Historic Neighborhoods

Beneath the looming shadow of the new **Beau Rivage Casino** are the old neighborhoods of Biloxi. Highway 90 splits to become a grand boulevard divided by a lush, grassy median dotted by palm and oak trees. Historic cottages sit serenely back

The cast-iron Biloxi lighthouse was constructed in 1841. (Brian Gauvin)

from wide, deeply shaded front gardens. The antebellum **Magnolia Hotel** was built in 1847 by a German immigrant as a resort for tourists who came to the coast by steamship. Today it houses the **Biloxi Mardi Gras Museum**, with displays dating back to 1699, the earliest of Mardi Gras in the New World. *119 Rue Magnolia at Water St.; 228-435-6245.*

Just across from the Magnolia Hotel is the **Brunet-Fourchy House,** a graceful antebellum manse constructed in 1835. **Mary Mahoney's Old French House Restaurant** *(page 284)* occupies the old slave quarters and part of the main house. *116 Rue Magnolia; 228-374-0163.*

The homes and buildings in the vicinity of **Rue Magnolia** are a hodge-podge of Creole/Gulf Coast Victorian and Gay '90s with a bit of Greek Revival and Gothic.

Speaking of mushed styles, don't miss the **Ohr-O'Keefe Art Museum;** Ohr was known as the "Mad Potter of Biloxi." *136 G. E. Ohr St.; 228-374-5547.*

African-American History

The **Pleasant Reed House** is a shotgun camelback cottage built in 1854 by Pleasant Reed, a former slave from Enon, Mississippi. He built the home for his wife, two doors down from his parents' home. Here the Reeds raised their five children. The home was sold by the family in 1977 to the Delta Sigma Theta Sorority.

The Reeds were just two of the many freed slaves who found a better life in Biloxi. Since the early 18th century Free People of Color had been boat owners and fishermen. After Emancipation the canning factories had no policy of discrimination either, making Biloxi a comfortable place to settle. African-American businesses and professionals located their offices along present day Main Street; in 1977 the Catholic Diocese of Biloxi became the first in the country to have an African-American bishop. *Located at Lee St. and Beach Blvd..*

Green Oaks

Green Oaks is the Mississippi Gulf Coast's oldest antebellum mansion, built around 1826 on a Spanish land grant. It is now an eight-room B&B where mint juleps can be ordered on the veranda *(page 283). 580 Beach Blvd.; 888-436-6257 or 228 436-6257.*

Tullis-Toledano Mansion

This mansion was a wedding present from a wealthy New Orleans cotton broker to his bride in 1856. It is now owned by the city and open for tours from 11–4, six days a week. *360 Beach Blvd.; 228-435-6308.*

Father Ryan House

The Father Ryan House is a true slice of the old coast and offers lovely gulf views. Built in 1841 and named for the Rev. Abram J. Ryan, poet laureate of the Confederacy and pastor of St. Mary's Catholic Church in Mobile (1833-1877), it now operates as a 13-room B&B *(page 283)* and is open for tours most afternoons. Most notable is the 100-year-old palm tree that grows right up through the front steps. *1196 Beach Blvd.; 228-432-7677 or 800-295-1189.*

COASTAL
MISSISSIPPI

◆ MARITIME & SEAFOOD
  INDUSTRY EXPLORATIONS

Maritime & Seafood Industry Museum
Housed in a vintage-1930s Coast Guard station, the museum contains historical images and artifacts depicting the maritime history of the Mississippi Gulf Coast. The museum sells tickets for two-hour harbor tours on the *Glen L. Swetman* and the *Mike Sekul,* replicas of schooners that fished off the coast in the 1800s. *115 First St.; 228-435-6320.*

J. L. Scott Marine Education Center
This center's 42,000-gallon Gulf of Mexico aquarium tank reveals sharks, sea turtles, eels—the mysteries of the water which surrounds the city. It is part of the University of Southern Mississippi Institute of Marine Sciences and its many tanks house such creatures as snakes and alligators. Of interest also are the skeletal remains of a whale beached on Ship Island. *South of Highway 90 at 115 Beach Blvd.; 228-374-5550.*

Biloxi Shrimping Trip
An hour cruise on the *Sailfish* provides a firsthand look at the sea life encountered on a shrimping expedition. A net is cast every 20 minutes as you sail along the Biloxi shore to Deer Island and back. *www.gcww.com/sailfish; Mar–Nov, US 90 and Main St. at the small craft Harbor,; 800 -289-7908 or 228-385-1182.*

◆ BEAUVOIR   *map page 255, D-2*
Jefferson Davis, the first and last President of the Confederacy, came to live at this beautiful old summer home on the Mississippi Gulf Coast in 1877 as the South suffered through Reconstruction. At the end of his career, he spent his time here writing a history of the Confederacy, taking walks with his wife and daughter, and visiting with his old friends *(see "Soldier of Misfortune" page 276).*

Tenancy at Beauvoir was offered to the Davis family by its owner, Sara Dorsey, a feminist writer who lived at Dunleith plantation in Natchez and had been a childhood friend of Davis's wife Varina.

A single-story raised cottage, Beauvoir is set on a wide, tree-lined lawn facing a white sand beach and the Gulf waters. Even today, the house bespeaks a bygone era when Natchez planters spent summers enjoying Gulf breezes on spacious galleries. Today it's called the Jefferson Davis Home and Presidential Library and is maintained by the Mississippi division of the United Sons of the Confederate Veterans. *2244 Beach Blvd. (Highway 90); 228-388-9074.*

(opposite) Confederate President Jefferson Davis came to Beauvoir, a summer house on the Gulf Coast, to live with his wife and daughter during the end of his life. (Brian Gauvin)

◆ DE SOTO NATIONAL FOREST *map page 255, C/D-1/2*

Biloxi backs away from the Mississippi Sound to the De Soto National Forest, which covers 500,487 acres from Laurel, Mississippi, to Biloxi and the Gulf. Two wilderness areas, the Black Creek and the Leaf, are contained within the dense expanse of pine forest. A 32-mile float trip on Black Creek, designated as a National Wild and Scenic River, or the 41-mile hiking trail along the creek provide an eagle's eye view of the area. *Visitors Center, 654 W. Frontage Rd., Wiggins; 601-928-4422.*

■ OCEAN SPRINGS *map page 255, E-2*

Nestled on a spit of land, on the eastern tip of the Mississippi Gulf Coast, Ocean Springs (pop. 14,600) fronts both Biloxi Bay and Davis Bay, and its altitude of 22 feet makes it the highest point on the coast. At its heart it remains a quiet, residential community with a picturesque harbor.

The French established Fort Maurepas, the first European settlement in the Mississippi Valley, here in 1699. On the beach, at the end of Washington Avenue, is a replica of the fort from which the French colonized Louisiana, Mississippi, and Alabama. The town got its present name in 1854 when Dr. George Austin took

SOLDIER OF MISFORTUNE: JEFFERSON DAVIS

The 10th child of a Revolutionary War veteran, Jefferson Davis, the leader of the Civil War South, spent most of his childhood at Rosemont plantation in Woodville, Mississippi. By the 1830s, this handsome, witty young gentleman had married the daughter of a future president of the United States, Zachery Taylor. Davis brought his beloved bride to his Hurricane plantation near Vicksburg, where she promptly contracted malaria and died. He spent the next decade in virtual seclusion, working on his farm and privately studying law and literature. In 1845, as a newly elected U.S. Congressman from Mississippi, Davis married Varina Howell of Natchez, 18 years his junior. Davis volunteered for the Mexican War, where he fought valiantly and was severely wounded. Upon his return home, this war hero was elected to the U.S. Senate.

By 1853, Davis was a national figure (he was U.S. Secretary of War under President Franklin Pierce) who spoke publically during his travels about the urgency of harmony between the states. When his own state of Mississippi seceded from the Union, he delivered a moving farewell speech to his colleagues in the Senate and returned to his plantation.

Admired by many for his sagacity and strength of character, and disliked by just as many for being "perverse and obstinate," Davis became the only President of the doomed Confederate States of America in February of 1861. A benevolent aristocrat by temperament, he believed deeply in democratic principles, yet defended the institution of slavery. (Later in life Davis adopted an African-American child.)

At the end of the War Between the States, Jefferson was denied the general clemency granted to Confederate soldiers and charged with treason against the United States of America. After his capture in May of 1865, he was clamped in leg irons and held prisoner at Fort Monroe, Virginia, for two years. The treason charge against Davis was eventually dropped by the United States for fear that Davis might mount a successful defense to his claim that states had a right to secede from the Union. (He did however, remain a non-citizen until his citizenship was reinstated posthumously in October 1978 by President Jimmy Carter.)

In the years after his release from prison, Davis became the beloved deposed monarch of the Kingdom of the Lost Cause. He retired to Beauvoir on the Mississippi Gulf Coast (see page 274) and died in New Orleans in 1889. His descendants continue to hold a yearly reunion at Rosemont in Woodville, Mississippi.

—Bethany Ewald Bultman

advantage of the health-giving springs to open a sanatorium. (Aunt Jenny's Catfish House now stands on the site.)

Louis Sullivan, a Chicagoan whom many consider the father of modern architecture, considered the two vacation cottages he built here his favorite residences. He wrote of Ocean Springs:

> ... The village [was] sleeping as it had slept for generations with untroubled surface; a people soft-voiced, unconcerned, easy going, indolent; the general store, the post office, the barber shop, the market on Main Street, sheltered by ancient live oaks; the saloon near the depot, the one-man jail in the middle of the street back of the depot ... no "enterprise," no "progress," no "blooming" for a "Greater Ocean Springs." Peace, peace and the joy of comrades, the lovely nights of sea breeze, black pool of the sky oversprinkled with stars brilliant and uncountable.

Long one of the most charming towns in the state, a favorite haunt of artists and architects, it is also one of the most eccentric. For example, the city refused federal disaster relief after Hurricane Camille because residents wouldn't agree to incorporate a federal housing project into the rebuilt city. And until recently Sam, the town drunk, drove the streets of town with a Shetland pony in the back seat of his "car." Pick up self-guided tours at the Chamber of Commerce in the L&N Depot; *1000 Washington Ave.; 228-875-4424. On the web: www.oceanspringschamber.com and request the Discover Ocean Springs brochure.*

Walter Anderson Museum

One of the most popular art sites in the state, the museum features Anderson's work, with its impressionistic naturalist style. It also presents changing exhibitions. *510 Washington Ave.; 228-872-3164.*

Shearwater Pottery

Features unique art pottery in the style of the 1928 founder, Peter Anderson. Today the work is carried on by the younger potters in the family. *102 Shearwater Dr.; 228-875-7320.*

Louis Sullivan Cottages

The two simple, century-old bungalows and a cottage on East Beach stimulate much debate among architectural aficionados. There are some who will argue that Frank Lloyd Wright, Louis Sullivan's protégé, designed them. Private residences, they may be discreetly spied at *509 East Beach Blvd.*

St. John's Episcopal Church

This wood-shingled church is another Louis Sullivan treasure. It was designed in

1892 without a steeple; the parishioners added one, but only after Sullivan had left town. *Porter and Rayburn Sts.*

Live Oaks Bicycle Route
Begin the 15.5-mile route at the Ocean Springs Train Depot, where you can pick up a map of the route. The ride will take you on a tour of the historic district, past Shearwater Pottery, Fort Maurepas, and along the beaches of the Gulf Islands National Park.

Gulf Islands National Seashore Office
Located on Davis Bayou in downtown Ocean Springs, the headquarters office is worth a visit. You'll get acquainted with the ecology of the region and see the short film on the barrier islands. The boardwalk looks over a vista of marshland. Don't be surprised if you spot a few alligators. Ask about the ferries and charters to Ship and-Horn Islands. *3500 Park Rd.; 228-875-9057.*

Gulf Hills Golf Club
The Gulf Hills Golf Club was established in 1927 and is noted for its challenging layout. As a matter of fact, hole #17 was once regarded by *Golf Digest* as one of the most challenging holes in the country. *13701 Paso Rd; 228-875-4211 or 887-875-4211.*

■ GAUTIER *map page 255, E/F-2/3*

Gautier (pop. 10,100; pronounced GO-CHAY) faces Pascagoula Bay. **Huck's Cove** is a little slice of Key West, where patrons come by boat or by land for a cold beer and hot po' boy. It's located on West Singing River; *3000 Oak St.; 228-497-4309.*

A descendant of the town's founder, Josie Gautier, established **Singing River Originals Pottery** in 1950. Her first mold was made from a trout she caught off the old Singing River Bridge, a popular fishing spot on the old Spanish Trail. The shop is nestled under live oaks on the river's edge and is owned by her family. The pottery is still made from the original molds. *Mon–Wed, 10–3 or by appointment; 116 De la Pointe Dr. at Oak St., 228-497-2012.*

◆ MISSISSIPPI SANDHILL CRANE WILDLIFE REFUGE *map page 255, E/F-3*

This 19,000 acre refuge is sheer nirvana for birds and bird-watchers. Most sandhill cranes are migratory birds; not so, the Mississippi sandhill. These long-legged wonders like it right here in their own coastal pineywoods, thank you very much. Rampant development of their habitat has placed them on the endangered-species list. Another endangered species, the red-cockaded woodpecker, also lives here. *One mile north of Interstate 10, Exit 61 at Gautier–Van Cleve Rd.; 228-497-6322.*

■ PASCAGOULA *map page 255, F-3*

Just a few more miles up Highway 90 is Pascagoula (pop. 25,900). It's just 30 miles east of Mobile. Despite the fact that Pascagoula is the Mississippi Gulf Coast's most thriving industrial town, it still retains several reminders of the city's past. In the older parts of town are lovely homes with deep succulent gardens overlooking the seawall.

In the late 19th and early 20th century, Pascagoula was one of the world's great lumber ports. The Pascagoula River, known as the "Singing River," is noted for the eerie sound it "hums" in the hottest months of summer. The song is said to be the death chant of the Pascagoula tribe, who committed mass suicide in the river rather than be taken as slaves after their defeat by the Biloxi tribe.

The town boasts two famed native sons—Trent Lott, the powerful Republican U.S. Senate majority leader during the Clinton impeachment trial, and Dicky Scruggs, the attorney who won a landmark settlement against U.S. tobacco companies (the 1999 movie *The Insider* told the story).

Longfellow House

Also called Bellevue and Pollock Place, this is the home where legend tells us Henry Wadsworth Longfellow was inspired to write the poem "The Building of the Ship." (It is now owned by the Ingalls Shipbuilding Corporation.)

Old Spanish Fort Museum

Not really a fort, this is one of the county's most esteemed and loveliest colonial structures. Also known as La Pointe–Krebs House, it dates from 1718, making it one of the oldest European structures still standing in the Mississippi Valley. The original building is the modest carpenter's shop of Joseph Simon de la Pointe, who was just 12 years old when he accompanied the Iberville expedition to the coast in 1699. There are 10 buildings on the lush, three-acre grounds. It is in the early colonial style with 18-inch-thick walls whitewashed over pulverized oyster shells over *boussillage*—a mortar made from local clay, mud, and moss. The adjacent museum houses Indian artifacts and many items from the area's colonial past such as two cannons captured by Andrew Jackson at the Battle of New Orleans. *4602 Fort St., north of US 90; 228-769-1505.*

COASTAL
MISSISSIPPI

■ COASTAL MISSISSIPPI FOOD & LODGING
by Rita Jung Walker

☎ For chain lodgings see toll-free numbers on page 333.
$$ For room (☎) and restaurant (✗) price designations see page 333.

Bay St. Louis Area
map page 255, B-2/3

☎ **Bay Town Inn.** 208 N. Beach Blvd., Bay St. Louis; 800-533-0407 $$
This seven-room inn, listed on the National Historic Register, overlooks the bay in the heart of old Bay St. Louis and is within walking distance of restaurants and specialty shops. Full gourmet breakfast and a gulf view are included.

✗ **Armand's.** 141 Hwy. 90, Waveland; 228-467-8255 $$
A local favorite. Creative Creole fare.

✗ **Bay City Grille.** 136 Blaize Ave., Bay St. Louis; 228-466-0590
A contemporary take on classic seafood dishes of the Coast. Bon appetit!

✗ **Benigno's.** Grocery & Deli. 128 Blaize Ave., Bay St. Louis $
Po' boys and muffelatas make up the menu along with (when in season) great boiled crabs, shrimp, and crawfish.

✗ **Fire Dog Saloon.** 120 South Beach Blvd., Bay St. Louis; 228-467-8257 $
A full-service neighborhood bar with live entertainment Wednesday through Saturday. Good appetizers, burgers, and steaks.

✗ **Rooster's.** 16640 Hwy. 603 at Hwy. 43, Kiln; 504-255-7767 $$
Casual atmosphere with killer country food and entertainment.

✗ **Trapani's Eatery.** 116 N. Beach Blvd., Bay St. Louis; 228-467-8570 $$
Enough cannot be said about this small and lively dining room. One can see right into the bustling kitchen or be entertained by the photos and memorabia gracing the walls. This is local cuisine with an Italian flare and emphasis on seafood entres. Make sure to arrive with an empty stomach.

Casino Coast *map page 255, D-3*
Biloxi and Gulfport

Best Bets - Gaming Resorts
Room prices fluctuate wildly with the seasons and special events on the Coast. Most reasonable pricing is usually between Sunday and Thursday. Most suites are reserved for high rollers, especially on weekends. Certain specials exist for repeat customers or those with players' cards. Ask about these when booking or before check-in.

☎ **Beau Rivage.** 875 Beach Blvd., Biloxi; 888-567-6667 $$-$$$$
Constructed for the well-heeled out-of-town guest. No expense was spared, from the placement of a dozen or so mature oak trees surrounding the front garden entrance to the huge magnolias trans-

planted inside the front atrium. The lobby is filled with an ever-changing array of fragrant, seasonal flowering plants. There is a wide range of dining options and two of the best dance clubs on the Coast: Maggie's for jazz and a quieter mood, and the Brew Pub, a great place to meet people from all over the world.

BEAU RIVAGE

Grand Casino Resorts. 265 Beach Blvd., Biloxi; 3215 W. Beach Blvd., Gulfport; 800-354-2450 $$-$$$$
A large resort complex with two hotel towers each in Biloxi and Gulfport. There is no need ever to venture into the streets with the wide range of culinary options, large gaming square-footage, pools, spas, and name acts for entertainment. Gulfport, isolated from most other casinos, was created for sun worshippers. The Oasis Hotel features a lazy river, waterfall, and poolside cabanas—pina coladas optional. Both properties house Kids' Quest, a dizzying repository of jungle gyms and video games for the under-aged with pagers included for the parents, need they be summoned.

Imperial Palace. 850 Bayview Ave., Biloxi; 800-634-6441 $-$$
This resort on Back Bay has an odd mix of things in the lobby, from antique cars to Ming vases. All of the cocktail waitresses are well endowed, dressed in low-cut, high-hemmed, orientalesque attire. Local coast legend has it that the company subsidizes breast augmentations. The I.P., as locals call it, is a favorite with bus tours and senior groups as there is ample space for efficient arrivals and departures, and room rates are somewhat lower than average. It features a spa and fitness center and six first-run movie theaters.

Isle of Capri /Crowne Plaza Resort. 151 Beach Blvd., Biloxi; 800-843-4753 $-$$$
The first casino to open its doors on the Coast. The lobby has a Caribbean theme, a live steel band, and a parrot that may be screeching, or just saying hello as you walk by. Mischievous guests (or employees, who knows?) occasionally teach these birds inappropriate words and phrases, so they often disappear to be reprogrammed. If your entire travel wardrobe consists of T-shirts & shorts, you will feel most at ease here.

Palace Casino Resort. 158 Howard Ave., Biloxi; 800-725-2239 $$-$$$
Tucked in Back Bay, two blocks from Casino Row. French Colonial decor, private beach, full-service marina for guests arriving by water, pool, volleyball courts, full-service spa, and Lawana's, one of the best dining experiences on the coast, with a first-class piano player.

COASTAL MISSISSIPPI
FOOD & LODGING

☎ **President Casino/ Broadwater Resort.** 2110 Beach Blvd., Biloxi; 800-843-7737 $-$$$
The old gold standard of Coast accommodations. The only change from 30 years ago is the casino barge in the harbor. Choose from rooms in the hotel tower or private cottages with kitchens. Special features include: frequent shuttles from the hotels to the casino, entertainment featuring older name bands from the 60s and 70s, a PGA-staffed golf course, and a full-service marina with charter boats for hire.

☎ **Treasure Bay Casino Resort.** 1980 Beach Blvd., Biloxi; 800-747-2839 $-$$
The casino is a floating barge built to look like a huge pirate ship. The old hotel, formerly the D'Iberville, and the casino are on opposite sides of four-laned highway 90, but shuttle service flows regularly between the two. There is nightly music in the bar upstairs with a lively dance floor. Dine by candle and gaslight in the Pirate's Den Restaurant.

Standard Hotels

☎ **Best Western Oak Manor.** 886 Beach Blvd., Biloxi; 800-591-9057 $-$$$
Centrally located, just across the street from Beau Rivage and within walking distance of Mary Mahoney's and Bombay Bicycle Club. Some rooms have jacuzzi and refrigerators.

☎ **Biloxi Beach Resort Inn.** 2736 Beach Blvd., Biloxi; 800-345-1570 $-$$
An older resort inn, close to shopping and across the street from the beach. Lounge, live entertainment, refrigerators, heated pool, and continental breakfast.

☎ **Days Inn.** 2046 Beach Blvd., Biloxi; 800-526-5656 $
For the budget-minded. Close to Treasure Bay and the President Casino. One- and two-bedroom suites, kitchenettes, continental breakfast, pool, and tennis courts,.

☎ **Emerald Beach (Quality Inn).** 1865 Beach Blvd., Biloxi; 800-342-7519 $-$$
The only non-casino hotel or motel south of Highway 90 and it's right on the beach. 72 deluxe rooms and suites have in-room coffeemakers, refrigerators, and microwaves. There's continental breakfast and a heated pool. Nominated in 2000 for Inn of the Year - Choice Hotels.

☎ **Holiday Inn Biloxi Beachfront Coliseum.** 2400 Beach Blvd., Biloxi; 800-441-0882 $-$$
A full-service hotel with all the amenities: swimming and kiddie pool, bar, restaurant and lounge, and a pretty courtyard in bloom year-round. Complementary airport transportation and casino shuttle.

☎ **Holiday Inn Express** 2416 Beach Blvd., Biloxi; 800-468-2102 $
For the value-minded traveler. Includes a full array of breakfast offerings, danish, muffins, bagels, fruit, and juices, with a

dash of Southern charm. Relax at the clover-shaped pool or take a walk on the beach. Pets allowed.

☎ **Holiday Inn Gulfport Beachfront.** 1600 E. Beach Blvd., Gulfport; 800-441-0887 $-$$
A quiet and relaxing, full-service hotel located right on the beach. All rooms have hairdryer, iron and ironing board, coffeemaker, data-port phones, and HBO. Complimentary airport transportation. Full-service restaurant and lounge.

☎ **Magnolia Plantation Hotel.** 16391 Robinson Rd., Gulfport; 800-700-7858 $-$$$$
An 80-acre country estate with 40 luxurious rooms and suites, free country breakfast buffet, heated pool and jacuzzi, and executive conference center. Close to Windance Golf club. Limousine service is available.

Bed & Breakfasts / Inns

☎ **Green Oaks.** 580 Beach Blvd., Biloxi; 888-436-6257 $$$
Mississippi's oldest beachfront mansion, circa 1826, is on two acres of ancient oaks within walking distance of Casino Row. Rooms have period antiques private baths, computer ports, and CATV. Full breakfast is included, plus afternoon tea or a mint julep while you enjoy the gulf view.

☎ **Father Ryan House.** 1196 Beach Blvd., Biloxi; 800-295-1189 $$-$$$
Father Ryan, a priest during the Confederacy, wrote some of his finest poetry while residing here. When a storm blew down his white cross in the front yard, a palm tree immediately sprouted in the same spot. This palm now grows through the middle of the front stairs. 13 rooms and suites, private baths and whirlpools.

☎ **Lofty Oaks Inn.** 17288 Hwy. 67 (6 miles north of I-10 at exit 41) near Biloxi; 228-392-6722 $$
This romantic country getaway has three themed rooms, the Egyptian, the Caribbean, and the Oriental, and a cottage with an African safari theme. All are decorated with art and antiques from around the world. Jacuzzis, swimming pool, and full breakfast. Only 15 minutes from the casinos and the beach.

Vacation Cottages & Homes

☎ **Captain Ed's Vacation Cottages.** 702 Beach Dr., Gulfport; 800-969-3215 $-$$
Five quaint, individual A-frame cottages, fully furnished with kitchens, a pool, BBQ pits, and private decks overlooking the beach. Within staggering distance of Orangutan's and Timothy O'Sullivan's, funky and lively favorite local hangout. There are laundry and linens available, but no maid service.

☆ **Edgewater Inn.** 1936 Beach Blvd, Biloxi; 800-323-9676 $-$$$$
Stay in a jacuzzi suite with kitchenette on the French Quarter-style courtyard, or in an 18th-century-style cottage, with full kitchen, out in the garden.

☆ **Gayle's Cottages.** 143A Teagarden Rd., Gulfport; 228-868-0097 $-$$$
Choose between one- or two-bedroom cottages 200 yards from the beach, or a three-to-five-bedroom chateau on an 18-hole golf course. All have kitchens, patios, BBQs, and squirrels. Some have fireplaces, jacuzzis, wet bars, and more squirrels. Pets welcome.

Biloxi and Gulfport Dining

✗ **Alberti's Italian Restaurant.** 2028 Beach Blvd., Biloxi; 228-388-9507 $$-$$$
One of the best steaks served on the Coast as well as authentic Italian cuisine, including pizza.

✗ **Blow Fly Inn.** 1201 Washington Ave., Gulfport $-$$
For an interesting story, ask about the name of this restaurant. Features seafood, steaks, Creole specialties, and over 30 sinful homemade desserts.

✗ **Bombay Bicycle Club.** 830 Beach Blvd., Biloxi; 228-374-4101 $$
A local favorite watering hole and restaurant with a varied menu and good specialty drinks.

✗ **Farraday's.** 151 Beach Blvd., Biloxi; 228-435-7000 $$-$$$$

In the Isle of Capri casino. Salmon, steaks, and prime rib, prepared as if for the gods.

✗ **French Connection.** 1891 Pass Rd., Biloxi; 228-388-6367 $$-$$$
Features open-hearth cooking, French-kitchen-style, steak, seafood, and tar babies (a house invention of chicken wrapped in bacon and grilled over pecan wood).

✗ **Jazzeppi's Ristorante & Martini Bar.** 195 Porter Ave., Biloxi; 228-374-9660 $$-$$$
Angus steaks, filets, and veal in a romantic setting. Mouth-watering appetizers and perfectly chilled martinis at the bar.

✗ **Lawana's.** 185 Howard Ave., Biloxi; 228-432-8888 $$-$$$
Perhaps the best upscale dining at a casino restaurant. Enjoy seafood and steaks while a first-class piano player massages the keys.

✗ **Mary Mahoney's.** 138 Rue Magnolia, Biloxi; 228-374-0163 $$$-$$$$
Don't pretend you've visited Biloxi without eating here. Great filet mignon, fresh fish, and crab cakes. They've been feeding locals and U.S. Presidents for years. Bobby Mahoney, son of the founder, says,"Let us take your taste buds for a ride!"

✗ **O'Charley's.** 2590 Beach Blvd., Biloxi 228-388-7883 $
Kids under 10 eat free. Chicken, steaks, pasta, seafood, and more.

✕ **Ole Biloxi Schooner.** 159 E. Howard Ave., Biloxi; 228-374-8071 $-$$
Known for great gumbo and crawfish etouffee, seafood platters, and po' boys, They also serve the best cure for a lingering afternoon hangover—the open-face roast beef with french fries. The tables are decoupaged with post cards of old coast hotels and landmarks from days gone by. Paintings of old Biloxi Schooners dot the walls. Read the back of the menu to learn about these late 19th-century boats.

✕ **Pho Bang.** 295 Howard Ave., Biloxi; 228-374-7666 $
This modest Vietnamese restaurant, two blocks north of the Grand Casino, attests to the fact that Biloxi is a true melting pot of cultures. They feature huge portions of rice-noodle and won-ton soups, rice dishes and non-fried egg rolls. Entrees are accompanied with fresh vegetables, hot peppers, and sprouts. Yum!

✕ **Sho Ya.** 2511 25th Ave. and Hwy. 49, Gulfport; 228-868-7333 $$
Aficionados swear they serve the best sushi in the western hemisphere.

✕ **Toucan's Mostly Mexican Café.** 9265 Hwy. 49 N., Gulfport; 228-863-3117 $-$$
Traditional Mexican favorites and original recipes and some of the best margaritas on the Coast.

✕ **Vrazel's.** 3206 W. Beach Blvd., Gulfport; 228-863-2229 $$-$$$
A very distinctive mix of French, Italian, and Cajun specialties. A testament to great food, even 90 miles west of New Orleans.

✕ **White Cap Seafood Restaurant.** Gulfport Small Craft Harbor, Gulfport; 228-863-4652 $-$$
Overlooking the port, Gulf seafood specialties including oysters on the half shell and blue plate specials.

Long Beach *map page 255, C-3*

☂ **Red Creek Inn.** 7416 Red Creek Rd.; 228-452-3080 or 800-729-9670 $-$$$
The first B&B on the Mississippi Gulf Coast. This 1899 raised French Creole cottage with a 64-foot porch is surrounded by eleven acres of magnolia and live-oak. Decor is upscale-grandma-style with an antique organ and victrola, fireplaces, and a porch swing. Four comfy rooms all have private baths.

RED CREEK INN

☎ University of Southern Mississippi Gulf Coast Conference Center. 730 E. Beach Blvd.; 228-214-3279 $
Once a dorm, these clean rooms all have private baths, but you'll have to watch TV in the lounge. The Friendship Oak is right outside. Local folklore has is that if you first meet a friend under the Friendship Oak, you will be friends for life. The campus is located on the beach and for the most thrifty of travelers, the room price cannot be beat. Try the Friendship Cafe on campus.

Ocean Springs

map page 255, E-2

☎ Shadowlawn. 112A Shearwater Dr.; 228-875-6945 $$
Built in 1907 and owned by the same family since 1922, this beautiful abode, on 20 oak-laden acres, rests on the highest point of coastal land between New Orleans and Mobile. Secluded and romantic with very private gulf views. Full breakfast and afternoon tea.

SHADOWLAWN

✗ Anthony's Under the Oaks. 1217 Washington Ave.; 228-872-4564 $$

Enjoy the sunset while dining on regional specialties, steaks and seafood.

✗ Aunt Jennie's Catfish House. 1217 Washington Ave. 228-875-9201 $-$$
All-you-can-eat catfish, shrimp, or chicken with cole slaw, fries, hush puppies, biscuits, and sweet potatoes on the side.

✗ Bayview Gourmet. 1210 Government St.; 228-875-4252 $
Breakfast and sandwich platters are named for streets in Old Ocean Springs. Gourmet coffee and daily specials.

✗ Catch of the Day. 2114 Bienville Blvd. (Hwy. 90); 228-872-7920 $-$$
Very casual, lunch or evening spot with regional dishes and raw oysters (the best and cheapest on the coast). The happy-hour drinks are large enough to swim in. This old mainstay of the coast was originally located on the beach in Biloxi before casinos took over the territory.

✗ Lagniappe. 703 Cox Ave.; 228-875-7361 $$
A place with a flair for combination French and Cajun cuisine. Try the award-winning gumbo while you rub elbows with a range of locals from boat captains to doctors, local artists to would-be priests.

✗ Phoenicia Gourmet. 1223 Government St.; 228-875-0603 $$
One of the best kept secrets on the coast. Most selections are authentic Mediterranean. Dinner is by candlelight with classical music. The décor is unpretentious and spotless. Howard Hughes would not be disappointed.

Pass Christian
map page 255, C-3

☨ **Harbor Oaks Inn.** 126 W. Scenic Dr.;
800-452-9399 $-$$
Family memorabilia make for a homey
atmosphere in this five-room, private-
bath B&B with complimentary wine and
soft drink parlor, a den with pool table,
and a small kitchen for guests. Full
breakfast is included at the Harbor View
Café across the street.

☨ **Inn at the Pass.** 125 E. Scenic Dr.; 228-
452-0333 $$
This 19th-century home has five rooms
with private baths and one private cot-
tage in the rear. It offers the charm and
elegance of the Victorian era with ameni-
ties of today. Ideal for those travelling
with children.

✕ **Annie's.** Bayview at 3rd Ave.; 228-452-
2062 $$
Family-style dining for over 70 years. Se-
lections range from chicken and spaghet-
ti to grilled and sauced entrees. In the
lounge you can sit in a booth made from
a shiny copper Wisconsin cheese vat.

✕ **Harborview Café.** 105 W. Beach Dr.
(Hwy. 90); 228-452-3901 $-$$
This local hangout overlooking Pass
Christian Harborused to be a filling sta-
tion. They serve a classic diner-style
breakfast—seafood and pasta at dinner.

Slidell, LA
map page 255, A-3

☨ **Garden Guest House B&B.** 34514
Bayou Liberty Rd. (Hwy. 433); 504-641-
0335 $$
This bird-watcher's paradise is on an ex-
quisite ten-acre estate with miles of main-
tained paths through ancient stands of live
oak and walnut. Two completely private
suites, with bath, full kitchen, and laundry,
are decorated with antiques and local art-
work. A large, home-cooked breakfast is in-
cluded. No smoking, children, or pets.

GARDEN GUEST HOUSE B&B

A L A B A M A ' S
A Z A L E A   C O A S T
by Bethany Ewald Bultman

Food & Lodging, page 326
Map, page 299

■ TRAVEL OVERVIEW

The coast of Alabama is as different culturally from the Mississippi Gulf Coast as it is from Florida's, yet by geographical accident it is wedged in between them. While the Mobile Bay area is no Natchez when it comes to antebellum architecture, and no New Orleans when it comes to nightlife, it has its own unique coastal culture dominated by Old South decorum and New South aspirations. Its Alabama roots run deep into the heart of Dixie, its oaks tower majestically, and its port-related industries spew their smoke onto the horizon. Mobile Bay is socially and economically dominated by the city of Mobile (pronounced MO-BEEEEEEEL). As Henry Miller said in *The Air Conditioned Nightmare,* "Mobile is Mozart on the mandolin."

If you are in a hurry, the I-10 expressway can take you the 204 miles from New Orleans to Pensacola, Florida in less than four hours. However, you'd miss a great deal, for this small stretch of coastal Alabama is its own unique country. Spending a few days or weeks on the Eastern Shore around Fairhope and Point Clear is the ideal way learn its vocabulary. It's a place to relax, to enjoy reading under a ceiling fan,

ALABAMA
MOBILE BAY

wading in the Bay, and piddling from one antique shop to the next. To feel at home, simply chat with locals or take a fishing charter, easy to book at any bait shop.

Getting Around: If you fly into Mobile, you'll learn that Airport Boulevard is the main route to the airport and the malls. It's a mess!

The Gulf Islands can be reached by bridge or by ferry: Dauphin Island's Fort Gaines, and Fort Morgan's Pleasure Island are linked by ferry service that's hard to miss as it goes from island tip to island tip. 334-540-7787. The ferry runs eight times a day, about every 90 minutes. From Dauphin Island it runs 8 A.M. to 6:30 P.M; from Fort Morgan 8:45 A.M. to 7:15 P.M. Round-trip fare is $23; one way is $15 and all fares are paid on the Fort Morgan side. The ferry runs year round except in rough weather.

Climate: The low-lying subtropical Gulf Coast plain is often as hot and sticky as cotton candy; other times it's just plain wet. But it's all the moisture that keeps the foliage green and the flowers in profusion. Spring is the most colorful time, March–April and October–November are the mildest months, but even in the heat of summer, there can be gentle breezes at the edge of the bay. During hurricane season, June to October, keep a weather eye on the news, and if one is coming, get out of the way!

Food: The Mobile-Baldwin County area is noted for the diversity of its food: Shrimp and soft-shell crabs, gumbo, West Indies salad (an incredible concoction of chilled crabmeat and vidalia onion), oyster loaf, fried Gulf fish, and hush puppies. Listings begin on **page 288.**

Nightlife: The city of Mobile has a small selection of live music venues, yet the variety of clubs in the Fairhope area is as good or better.

Lodging: The more historic the area, the more charming the assortment of B&Bs. Close to the Bay is the magnificent Grand Hotel at Point Clear. Fairhope is an ideal home base for three-to-five day tripping in the area. Once near the Gulf of Mexico, it's condo and motel nirvana. Mobile has its share of hotels and motels, but to stay in them is to miss the laid-back life and bay breezes. **Lodging listings, see page 288; see page 333 for price designations and toll-free numbers for chain accommodations. For a chart of listings by region, see page 334.**

ALABAMA
MOBILE BAY

■ COASTLINE AND BAY

Alabama has even less coastline than Mississippi, just a bit over 50 miles. Even less than that, a mere sliver of east Alabama, actually straddles the Gulf Coast. One third of the stubby Alabama coast hugs Mobile Bay with its billowing ice-blue petticoat of water. This tidal shoreline of estuaries, bayous, bays, and inlets extends more than 600 miles from Heron Bay to Weeks Bay, most of which is protected marshland. Mobile's delta is the largest in the United States, its wildlife unequalled. There are 285,000 acres of open water (fresh, brackish, and salt) in the combined delta and bay, which means more than one million fish can exist in the area in a given season.

The city of Mobile basks along the western shore of its magnificent bay, protected from the harsh influence of the Gulf of Mexico by a barrier island, Dauphin Island, and by Alabama's slender eastern shore. Two major rivers converge at Mobile—the Tombigbee and the Alabama. These, and literally hundreds of smaller creeks and tributaries, join for their final surge of 14 trillion gallons of fresh water into Mobile Bay.

The city's port is 31 miles north of the Gulf of Mexico, on the west side of the Mobile River. It is one of the ten most active ports in the U.S. and a wide channel on the west side of the bay allows access to the Port of Mobile from the Gulf of Mexico.

■ EARLY CONQUEST

Spanish explorers first described the native Mauvilians living around Mobile Bay as extremely muscular and capable of running down a deer. Their village sat on a plain between the Tombigbee and the Alabama Rivers (which empty into Mobile Bay). The palisade was surrounded by a high wall made of woven saplings that had taken root and grown together into an impenetrable high wall. About every 50 feet there was a tower. Inside the walls were 80 stockades, each housing several hundred people.

◆ SPANISH CONQUISTADORS

Twenty-seven years after Columbus's first voyage to America in 1492, Admiral Alonso Alvarez de Pinana described the Mauvilians somewhat differently; or was he delirious after eating a bad oyster? The admiral's dispatch, sent home to

Madrid, described Mobile Bay and its inhabitants as a "fairyland inhabited by giants, pygmies, and princes dripping in gold."

The next record of European visitors came in 1528 when Pánfilo de Narváez and his ragtag flotilla fled the raging Apalache Indians in Florida only to be lured on to the shores of Mobile Bay by local Indians. Mid welcoming banquet, the Indians suddenly attacked the Spanish only to realize too late that the conquistadors were meaner than snake spit. These Spaniards narrowly escaped.

It wasn't too long before Hernando de Soto and his 600-man force arrived, dolled up in chain mail, steel helmets, and breastplates, and carrying shields and swords. You may recall that De Soto, a native of Xerez, Spain, rode with Pizzaro to plunder the Peruvian city of Cuzco when he was 19. He returned to the court of King Charles the Melancholy of Spain dripping in gold and took up the hobby of raising man-eating dogs. In other words, he was no Milquetoast.

In 1540, Mobile Bay's Manvilla Indians made the strategic error of raiding all his supplies. De Soto was so enraged, he and his men literally hacked through the walls of the Manvilla village and set it on fire. The Manvilla managed to adjust the aim of their arrows to avoid the Spaniards metal body armor, shooting them through the eyes and mouths. They also killed 42 Spanish horses. De Soto was shot in the thigh, but kept fighting on horseback, until all the Indian women had

Spanish explorer Hernando De Soto lands on the Florida coast in 1528.

been burned alive and the men slaughtered. In total, between 3,000 and 10,000 Manvillans were killed in a few hours.

Don Tristán de Luna y Arellano followed De Soto in 1559, arriving in Mobile Bay with 1,500 colonists from Mexico and ten ships. They cleared roads and built a small town with a plaza, just in time for a hurricane to destroy their fleet and all their provisions. After two miserable years, those settlers who did not succumb to starvation and disease headed off with the Indians or resettled in Pensacola.

The French established several frontier posts along the Gulf Coast in the early 1700s. The fort pictured above, established at Biloxi, Mississippi, was similar to Fort St. Louis in Mobile. This illustration from an old manuscript shows activities at the Biloxi settlement in 1720. Soon thereafter the fort was closed and its residents moved to New Orleans.

◆ FRENCH IN THE 1700S

The French colonists, in their turn, fared better than the Spanish, helped along by the companionship of "erring sisters," sent by the French government. But even though this was several hundred years before Bob Dylan wrote the folk rock line:

> "Oh Mama, can this really be the end?
> To be stuck inside of Mobile with the Memphis blues again…"

the colonists and the strumpets must have hummed comparable lyrics, because most fled the mosquitoes as soon as they could. Nevertheless, from 1711 to 1720, the fledgling settlement served as the capital of the French colonial empire extending from Canada to the Gulf of Mexico. In the minds of many Mobilians, she remains the queen of North America.

◆ AMERICAN ERA IN MOBILE

The coast of Mobile Bay was decidedly Tory during the American Revolution. In 1780 Spanish forces, led by the governor of Louisiana, claimed Mobile for the next 33 years; but in April 1813 Gen. James Wilkinson and 600 rowdy Americans overtook the Spanish garrison, seizing control for the Americans. At the time, Mobile had some 300 residents.

Alabama became a state in 1819. Once Mobile was linked to the Alabama hinterlands, it cashed in on its location by providing the lifeline between upriver planters and timbermen, and the merchants in London, Liverpool, and Le Havre. By 1850 the merchant princes of Mobile were enjoying bullbaiting, cockfighting, and horse racing as they awaited the next shipment of goods they could "factor" (broker).

■ DAUPHIN ISLAND   *map page 299, B-4*

Mobile Bay meets the Gulf of Mexico in a narrow funnel between the low peninsula and Dauphin Island (pop. 1,200), the 14-mile long, two-mile-wide barrier island. It was here at "Zamo" or "white isle" on the site of ancient Indian burial and oyster shell ceremonial mounds that Pierre Le Moyne, Sieur d'Iberville *(see page 16)* settled his ship, the *Renommée,* along the shallows in 1702. (A few years later Beinville constructed Fort Louis de la Mobile, up the Mobile River at the 27-mile Bluff.) The settlement established the eastern boundary of the vast French empire he and his brother Iberville were staking for King Louis XIV. The rivalry between the new settlement that would become Mobile and the already established New Orleans started immediately. When Antoine de la Mothe Cadillac, third governor of Louisiana, came to view the colony in the early 18th century, he dismissed it saying, "The entire colony is sand, fit only for an hourglass."

The island was poetically called Massacre Island by Iberville when one of his men came upon a pile of human skeletons bleached white in the sun. Evidently assuming this was a good omen, the French came back a few years later to erect a palisade and log cabins. Unfortunately these buildings were erected of pine, which rotted almost immediately in the damp. To add to their misery, the "ladies of easy virtue" the French sent to warm their beds loathed the sand and the constant barrage of mosquitoes.

Then, someone had the bright idea that if the name of the island was changed, a better class of settlers might be attracted to the island. Hence, Dauphin Island (pronounced "DAW-fin"), named for the title of the eldest son of Louis XIV. For the next two centuries the island was to have great military importance. Forts have been located here since 1717 to guard the entrance to Mobile Bay. The defeated British camped here after they were trounced by Andrew Jackson at the Battle of New Orleans in 1815.

On Dauphin Island, the full moon rises behind a beach house as a blue heron wades in the surf and the sun sets. (Brian Gauvin)

◆ DAYTRIPPING ON DAUPHIN ISLAND *map page 299, B-4*

Fort Gaines Historic Site

Dauphin Island is no beauty spot nor is the Dauphin Island Parkway (DIP). Yet there are several interesting things to do in the area. **Fort Gaines** was constructed in 1861 just in time for the Civil War. It and Fort Morgan, on the eastern side of Mobile Bay, commanded perfect views of the Battle of Mobile *(page 320)*. The Fort Gaines Historic Site is a five-sided rampart with bastions, ideal for those little soldiers who'd like to play in a real fort. Even if forts aren't your cup of tea, the view over Mobile Bay is worth the long climb. *E. Bienville Blvd.; 334-861-6992.*

Alabama Deep Sea Fishing Rodeo

Nowadays 2,000 anglers come to the island on the third weekend of July for the Alabama Deep Sea Fishing Rodeo. During the week-long event, fishermen vie for the record-size shark, barracuda, tuna, or one of 30 different categories of sport fish. If you come to fish, bring liquid refreshment. Be prepared to party. Either way, bring plenty of sunscreen.

Audubon Sanctuary

Thousands of visitors come to nestle under the live oaks and gaze at birds. Much of the island is maintained by the Audubon Society and the Dauphin Island Sea Lab as a 164-acre Friends of Dauphin Island Audubon Sanctuary. During the bird migrations, hundreds of birders gather here to take part in the bird-watching and banding of more than 300 species of birds, including hummingbirds, plovers, vireos, terns, and hawks. From mid-March until the end of May is prime season for viewing the painted buntings and tanagers that pause close to the offshore oil rigs. Many birds literally collapse from exhaustion on the beach and experts band them. *South side of Bienville Blvd.*

Sea Lab and Estuarium

The Dauphin Island Sea Lab and Estuarium provides an up-close experience of the habitats found around the Mobile-Tensaw Delta, one of the most significant hardwood bottomland habitats in the country. Both the 16,000-gallon aquarium featuring Gulf marine life and the 9,000-gallon under–Mobile-Bay tank are fascinating. The Estuarium makes a nice half-day visit and is a five-minute walk from Fort Gaines. *Directions: you can't miss it; 334-861-2141.*

Dauphin Island/Fort Morgan ferry

The ferry runs year round from the east end of the island to the Fort Morgan Peninsula on the other side of Mobile Bay. *Located near Fort Gaines; 334-540-7787.*

Will Allen cautiously handles a horseshoe crab at the Dauphin Island Estuarium. (Brian Gauvin)

ALABAMA
MOBILE BAY

■ BELLINGRATH GARDENS *map page 299, B-3*

On your way to Mobile, take Highway 193 for about 15 miles from Bayou La
Batre to Bellingrath Gardens on the banks of Isle-aux-Oies (now unpoetically
translated as the Fowl River) 20 miles south of Mobile, near the town of
Theodore. It isn't easy to find, but once you do, it's like a slice of paradise. When
the actor Charles Laughton enjoyed a few hours wandering the gardens of
Bellingrath between performances of *Don Juan in Hell,* he wrote in the guest
book, "I don't know how I will be able to play the Devil tonight after being in
Heaven this afternoon."

The magnificent home and 65-acre semitropical landscaped gardens began life
as a fishing camp for Walter Bellingrath, a millionaire Coca-Cola bottler from
Mobile, who was the son of a German-immigrant dad and a Scots-Irish mum. He
and his wife Bessie became inspired by the formal gardens they toured in Europe
in the late 1920s. By 1932 the Bellingraths' 900-acre estate was a public showplace
among the most spectacular in North America.

Bellingrath Gardens and the house built for its namesake, Walker Bellingrath,
a Coca-Cola bottler from Mobile. (Brian Gauvin)

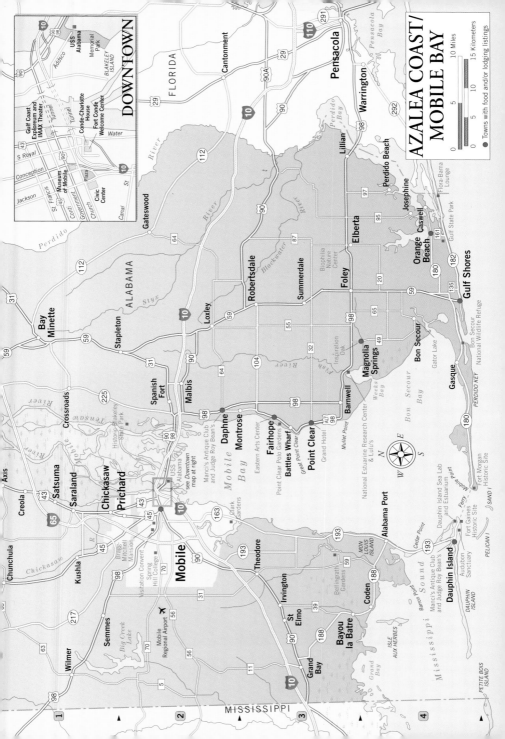

AZALEA COAST/ MOBILE BAY

● Towns with food and/or lodging listings

0 — 5 — 10 Miles
0 — 5 — 10 — 15 Kilometers

DOWNTOWN

USS Alabama
Memorial Park
BLAKELEY ISLAND
Addsco
Gulf Coast Exploreum and IMAX Theater
Conde-Charlotte House
Fort Conde Welcome Center
Water
Tunnel
Museum of Mobile
Civic Center
Conception
Jackson
Church
Cotti
Government
St Francis
S Royal
Canal St
Plaza

Locations

FLORIDA
MISSISSIPPI
ALABAMA

Pensacola
Cantonment
Warrington
Perdido Beach
Lillian
Josephine
Caswell
Orange Beach
Gulf Shores
Gulf State Park
Flora-Bama Lounge
Elberta
Foley
Summerdale
Robertsdale
Bon Secour
Gasque
Bon Secour National Wildlife Refuge
PERDIDO KEY
Fort Morgan Historic Site
Magnolia Springs
Barnwell
Weeks Bay
Bon Secour Bay
Point Clear
Battles Wharf
Fairhope
Montrose
Daphne
Spanish Fort
Malbis
Loxley
Stapleton
Bay Minette
Crossroads
Spanish Fort
Gateswood
Stockton
Mount Vernon

Eastern Arts Center
Point Clear Polo Gardens
Grand Hotel
Mullet Point
National Estuarine Research Center & Lulu's
Manci's Antique Club and Judge Roy Bean's
Great Point Clear
Inspiration Oak
Bagahlia Nature Center

Axis
Creola
Chunchula
Kushla
Satsuma
Saraland
Chickasaw
Prichard
Semmes
Wilmer
Mobile
Mobile Regional Airport
Theodore
Irvington
St Elmo
Coden
Bayou la Batre
Grand Bay
Alabama Port
Cedar Point
Dauphin Island
Dauphin Island Sea Lab and Estuarium
Fort Gaines Historic Site
Audubon Sanctuary
Bellingrath Gardens
Clark Gardens
MON LOUIS ISLAND
PELICAN I
DAUPHIN ISLAND
ISLE AUX HERBES
PETITE BOIS ISLAND
SAND I
Mobile Point
Fort Morgan
Ferry
Mississippi Sound
Grand Bay

Braga Mitchell Mansion
Visitation Convent
Spring Hill College
USS Alabama see Downtown map at right

Brass Mitchell
Big Creek Lake
Chickasaw R
Mobile Bay
Tensaw River
Mobile River
Styx River
Blackwater River
Fish River
Perdido River
Perdido Bay
Pensacola Bay
Bon Secour Bay
Grand Bay
Perdido

1 | 2 | 3 | 4

Enter the gardens by way of the raised boardwalk across the wetlands to get an idea of tangled mass of the natural environs before the garden did grow. In the early spring the gardens are ablaze with a quarter of a million azaleas—lavender, white, coral, mauve, pink, scarlet; in the winter months the Camellia Arboretum (the camellia is Alabama's state flower) features more than 2,500 plants; in the warmer months 2,000 roses bloom, and flamingos prance in the Oriental Garden. In other words, the Bellingrath Gardens are spectacular at any time of the year. An excursion boat docks near the Bellingrath home and offers a quiet 45-minute river cruise. It is a good idea to call ahead for reservations for the cruise.

The brick Bellingrath home was built in 1935 and has been featured on "America's Castles." The 15-room mansion (one of the few museum homes in America to include its original furnishings) is a treasure trove of American and French furniture and Irish crystal, Georgian silver, and European porcelains, including the world's largest public collection of Boehm porcelain.

Gardens open daily 8 A.M. to sunset. Take Hwy. 193 for about 15 miles from Bayou La Batre to Bellingrath Gardens. Located on the banks of the Fowl River, 20 miles southwest of Mobile, near the town of Theodore; 334-973-2217.

The Oriental Garden at Bellingrath. (Brian Gauvin)

A dragonfly hovers above a lotus blossom in the lily pond in Bellingrath Gardens. (Brian Gauvin)

Driving from Dauphin Island to Mobile

To be honest, the drive from Dauphin Island on to Mobile is not pretty. The purpose of the drive from Dauphin Island to Mobile is to get you to Mobile, not to bask in the experience. After you leave the pines and white beaches and cross over the tall, arching bridge, you'll be on the uninspiring Dauphin Island Parkway (DIP). The alternative drive from Highway 193 back to I-10 is only a bit nicer. Take the I-10 exit onto Government Street (Highway 90) and head east toward town. As you near Mobile's Historic District, you'll see streets lined with ancient live oaks dripping with Spanish moss.

■ CITY OF MOBILE *map page 299, B-2 and top right detail*

Mobile spreads west with concrete overpasses and shopping malls. It's a major producer of pulp and paper and aluminum ore. The major streets: Government, Dauphin, Cottage, and Old Shell Road spread out like the spokes of a wagon wheel. To the east of the city is Mobile Bay; to the north is the papermill town of Prichard (thus the smell of sulfur in Mobile's air), and to the south is marsh and shipyards.

ALABAMA
MOBILE BAY

◆ MOBILE'S HISTORY

One of the first things Mobile's original French colonists did in 1703 was throw a Mardi Gras party. They weren't as successful at finding the right location for their settlement, however. After two attempts, Jean-Baptiste le Moyne de Bienville—French explorer, colonizer, and scoundrel—moved Fort Condé in 1711 to the site of present day Mobile. Mobile's deep bay and location at the mouth of the Tensaw and Mobile Rivers ensured its success as a port city. It was named for the area's Mauvila Indians, the ones de Soto had destroyed several centuries before. The French settlers cultivated indigo and rice. By 1719 they prospered to the extent that they could afford slaves. Mobile was incorporated in 1814. Alabama became the 22nd state in the Union in 1819, though Mobile had little reason to communicate with the "American" settlements in the rest of the state until the Black Belt plantations upriver flooded its port with cotton in the late 1840s. As Alabama's only seaport, Mobile remained the state's largest city until the end of the 19th century when industry came to her rivals, such as Birmingham. The population before World War II was 78,000, barely double what it had been at the end of the Civil War. World War II brought a second boom, this time in shipbuilding.

◆ MOBILE'S CULTURE AND PEOPLE

Today, Mobile's upper crust is defined by its unique gene pool of vagrant 18th- and 19th-century Yankee sailors, Creole gentry, cunning merchants, and immigrants from England, Ireland, and Germany. (The city's population stands at 205,949; the metropolitan area at 526,000.) An illustration of Mobile's diversity comes from its famous citizens—the first was Alva Ertskin Vanderbilt Belmont (1853-1933) who left Mobile to become the outspoken suffragette socialite who founded the Political Equity League and the militant Women's Trade Union. Alva's daughter Consuelo married the ninth Duke of Marlborough. Then there was Hank Aaron, the six-foot, African-American master batter who became one of the country's great legends of baseball; and then there is Jimmy Buffett, King of Margaritaville and patron saint of the parrotheads.

In the 1850s, 63 percent of all foreign-born residents of Alabama lived in Mobile. Of Mobile's 20,515 inhabitants, almost one quarter were foreign born. (Mobile was less than half the size of Charleston and one quarter the size of New Orleans at the time). Life centered around commerce and much was done around small marble-top tables on the galleries and balconies of the coffee houses.

MOBILE ACCENT AND SOCIETY

Mobile society has its own distinct accent, as if each vowel has been thoroughly savored before it is spoken. Mobilians have a hard time letting an "o" or an "a" out of their mouths. One's esteemed grandmother is "grindmothuhhhhhhh," an old flame is a "flaaaaaaaayam" Church becomes "chuich," "mass" sounds something like "mice," "to ask" sounds like "to ice" and the phrase "good solid folks" comes out sounding something like "guwoood salad forks."

The keepers of Mobile's jejune myths are the old guard. For example, The Athelstan Club of Mobile (170 St. Francis Street, on Bienville Square) was founded in 1873 as a Masonic Club. By 1874, the Masonic ritual was dropped and it became a private social club and the center of the old guard's celebration of Carnival. The first president of the club was Henry Allen Lowe, an English cotton merchant, whose wife was known as the Florence Nightingale of the Confederacy. The exclusive club is famous for its kibitzer chairs in the card room. They are higher than player's chairs, have foot rests, and offer the "kibitzer" a full view of at least two other players' cards.

In Mobile, the premiere debutante reigns over the oldest Mardi Gras in America. The fancy celebrations got started in 1830 as masked members of the Cowbellian de Rakin Society feasted, danced, and pranced on New Year's Eve. Carnival ceased during the Civil War, but unflappable Mobile re-started its carnival traditional at its darkest hour in 1866 after the defeat of the Confederacy. Joseph Cain, a clerk in a Mobile market, and his cronies rolled themselves in red clay and Spanish moss, transforming themselves into "Chief Slackabamarnico and His Lost Cause Minstrels." They drove through the streets of Mobile on a decorated charcoal wagon, clanging cowbells.

The Queen of Love and Beauty is invited by the all-male Coronation committee. As many in the same lineage reign, the queens sometimes have Roman numerals attached to their names, as in Queen Tallulah II or Alletta II. The by-invitation-only balls are held at the Civic Center Auditorium.

Who constitutes old-guard Mobile is hard for the outsider to define. Basically it seems that someone way back had to have had money. It doesn't seem to matter how they made it. The right people may live in a disheveled yet historic hovel next to a tattoo parlor or in a Spring Hill mansion, but they are of equal rank. For the most part they are Catholic. Carnival royalty sits firmly atop the social order, and it doesn't matter if the king owns a pizza shop in a strip mall.

—Bethany Ewald Bultman

◆ THE CIVIL WAR'S NOBLE MOBILE

Unlike sister Confederate strongholds, New Orleans and Natchez, Mobile was to deport itself admirably during the Civil War. The Alabama state motto is *Audemus Jura Nostra Defendere,* (We Dare to Defend our Rights), and Mobile proved to be pure Alabama. With the capital of the Confederacy in Montgomery, the port of Mobile was truly the heartbeat of the Southern states.

While Union Admiral David Farragut blockaded Mobile Bay (1862-1864), the daring Alabama-born Confederate Admiral Raphael Semmes wreaked havoc on Union shipping along the Atlantic Coast. Under his command, the Confederate ship *Alabama* sank 57 Union ships in two years and captured more. After the *Alabama* was sunk by the USS *Kearsage,* Semmes escaped to continue his fight for the Confederate cause.

As Union Commander David Farragut (later Admiral) led his force of 18 Union gunboats into Mobile Bay in August 1864, he realized too late that the channel had been mined with torpedoes by the Confederates. One of his ships, the USS *Tecumseh,* exploded and sank. It was here in Mobile that Farragut, tied to

Union Commander Farragut had himself tied to the mast of his ship as his fleet entered Mobile Bay in 1864. The U.S. Congress created the position of admiral specifically for Farragut after the Civil War. (Wadsworth Atheneum, Hartford, Connecticut)

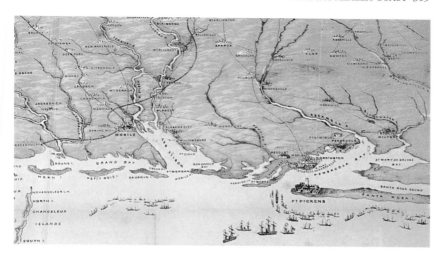

*This Civil War–era map shows the Union flotilla commanded by
Admiral David Farragut approaching Mobile Bay.*

the mast, is said to have shouted, "Damn the torpedoes: full speed ahead!" The
battle that ensued was the fiercest naval battle of the Civil War. The Confederate
ironclad *Tennessee* with but six guns and 200 men struggled valiantly for three
hours against 17 Union ships with 2,700 men and more than 190 guns. Mobile's
citizens barricaded the center of their city, Bienville Square, behind a wall of cotton bales. They were able to hold out until after Appomattox, becoming the last
coastal city of the Confederacy to fall.

Mobile recovered from the war faster than most other cities. By 1865 a fleet of
sail and steam vessels lined her wharfs and new warehouses lined her docks.

◆ VISITING HISTORIC MOBILE

map page 299, top-right detail

Here the streets are overshadowed by the Spanish moss dangling from the oak
branches like a stalactite canopy. The azaleas planted before the Civil War are now
over 20 feet tall in most places. As you wander the old flagstone sidewalks, it is almost possible to block out the modern skyline of industrial Mobile.

Author Carl Cramer observed that unlike New Orleans Creoles, who built their
homes facing inward, Mobile architecture faces outward to afford their occupants
a good view of the world. (Mind you, Mobilians are not inviting the world to look
back in.)

ALABAMA
MOBILE BAY

Tours

Grayline Tours offers tours to the historic homes, the USS *Alabama,* and Bellingrath Gardens. *334 432-2229 or 800 338-5597.*

Fort Condé Welcome Center

To begin your tour, visit Fort Condé—a reconstructed 18th-century French fort by the water's edge that now serves as Mobile's official Welcome Center.

The original Fort Louis de la Louisiane, which guarded the French Territory, stood here from 1711 until it was torn down for dock expansion in 1820; the ruins were discovered during excavation for the George Wallace Tunnel. Rebuilt in the 1970s, it is one-fourth the size of the original and furnished as it would have been in 1735. View exhibits and talk with costumed French colonial soldiers who demonstrate cannon and musket fire. *150 S. Royal St. at Church St.; 334-434-7304.*

Condé-Charlotte House

The Condé-Charlotte House is located in the former jail and courthouse built in 1822. It was restored by the National Society of Colonial Dames of America. There's other finery as well—18th- and 19th-century furnishings and a charming Spanish Garden. *104 Theater St.; 334-432-4722.*

Gulf Coast Exploreum and the Museum of the City of Mobile

The Gulf Coast Exploreum moved from tony west Mobile a few years ago in an attempt to draw visitors to Mobile's downtown, which has been experiencing a rebirth in recent years. Despite a serious parking shortage, that plan has worked quite well. In its first year, the children's science museum drew some 250,000 visitors from all over the Gulf Coast. A permanent hands-on science hall is fun for kids and adults, but the big attraction is the IMAX Dome Theater. Traveling exhibits, a nifty gift shop, and a coffee house are nice touches. The Exploreum is open every day except Thanksgiving and Christmas. *Government at Water St.; 334-208-6873.*

Adjacent to the Exploreum is the Museum of the City of Mobile, a restored 1872 townhouse where Mobile's long, devoted Mardi Gras tradition is revealed in colorful displays of Carnival Queen gowns. *355 Government St.; 334-434-7569.*

Festival of Flowers

The premier flower and garden festival of the Gulf Coast is timed to take place as Mobile's azaleas and dogwoods bloom. For information and dates: *334-639-2050.*

◆ MOBILE'S HISTORIC DISTRICTS

Mobile has several historic districts of note: Church Street East (the site of Mobile's first settlement), Oakleigh Garden District, De Tonti Square, Old Dauphin Way, and Spring Hill. Most of the nicely refurbished homes in these areas are private (and some are for sale, if a Mobile mansion is what you've always wanted).

Unlike the French Quarter in New Orleans, the districts are not all old, nor are all the structures architecturally significant. Brochures will lead you around the neighborhoods and point out interesting facts about the different houses. If you plan to visit the Bragg-Mitchell, Oakleigh, Condé-Charlotte, *and* Richards D.A.R. House museums, you can purchase a $14 pass at any one of these museums.

✧ **Church Street East**

The Spanish Plaza, across the street from the Civic Center, is a good starting point for exploring the Church Street East area, Mobile's nicest historic district.

Almost all of the colonial architecture was destroyed by fires in 1827 and 1839, but if you look at the wrought iron you may see fleurs-de-lis gracing the motifs. You'lll find a good deal of Victoriana, a smattering of Gulf Coast Creole cottages, and some Federal townhouses set back from the oak-lined streets and illuminated by the twinkle of gaslights.

✧ **Oakleigh Garden District**

Surrounding Washington Square (bounded by Chatham, Charleston, Charles, and Augusta Streets) and Oakleigh mansion is a lovely antebellum neighborhood, with an

Oakleigh House, built in 1833, is considered the finest antebellum home in the city of Mobile. It is shown here during the peak of the azalea season. (Brian Gauvin)

ALABAMA
MOBILE BAY

architectural mix of modest, late 19th-century cottages and commercial buildings.

If you're looking for something different, with advance notice you can enjoy a sunrise breakfast at **Oakleigh House**. Oakleigh Period Museum House was once the home of James Roper, a prominent merchant. Erected in 1833, it sits on several acres. Guides in full *Gone With the Wind* regalia will provide you with an overview of the history of both the house and the district. Among the fine portraits hanging on the walls is one of Madame Le Vert, the queen of 19th-century Mobile society, painted by Thomas Sully. *350 Oakleigh Place; 334-432-1281.*

✧ De Tonti Square

De Tonti Square became a historic district in the early 1960s. Located just nine blocks from the heart of Mobile's business district has benefited from gentrification. The area dates from the 1830s and still features flagstone sidewalks, gaslights, and the facades of many dignified townhouses. To add to its importance new arrivals were encouraged by the city to move other historic buildings into the area or build new ones to look historic.

The Richards D.A.R. Revolution House is one of the more interesting structures in hereabouts. The former home of a steamboat captain, Charles G. Richards, the 1860 Italianate house is festooned with wrought-iron and furnished with slightly bizarre Empire pieces. *256 N. Joachim St.; 334-208-7320.*

✧ Spring Hill

About six miles west of Mobile's waterfront, Spring Hill was founded in the 1820s as a summer retreat from the stifling, mosquito-infested city. For a time, there had been a belief that mosquitoes couldn't fly above 10 feet, making Spring Hill at 200 feet, the perfect retreat.

Beautiful **Spring Hill College** was founded in 1830, the oldest Jesuit college in the South, the first Catholic college in the Southeast, the third oldest Jesuit college in the country, and the first institution of higher learning in Alabama. Walking on the campus is a delight, especially the "Avenue of Oaks" leading to "Stewartfield."

Many homes in the area date from the pre–Civil War period and are shaded by tall trees and deep lawns. **Old Shell Road** winds through a lovely historic residential area. A nice stop is the **Carpe Diem Coffee Shop**, located in a historic home. They often have music on the weekends, as well as light sandwiches and baked goods. *4072 Shell Rd.; 334-304-0448.*

Bragg-Mitchell Mansion is considered to be one of the finest examples of antebellum architecture on the Gulf Coast. Built in 1855, it's a grand amalgam of Greek Revival and Italianate styles. Judge John Bragg let Confederate troops chop down his trees to allow them a strategic point from which to shell Federal troops in the Bay. The oaks you see today were replanted from the acorns of the original trees. The home was restored in 1986. *1906 Spring Hill Ave.; 334-471-6365.*

MOBILE'S AFRICAN MEMORIES

Writing in *Stars Fell on Alabama,* Carl Carmer evoked the broken lives wrought by the institution of slavery:

Tottering along the cobbles on a sunny morning, Cudjo may greet you —a wizened black man who must be treated with respect. The boat that brought Cudjo to America was the last of the slavers to run the Federal Blockade. Hardly had he and his companions been delivered to the slave-dealers when the end of the war made them free men in an alien country. Huddling in a terrified group, they built their cabins close together—cabins that are now all empty save one—and in their little community they continue to use their native tongue. Cudjo is very old now. But he haunts the shores of the ocean over which he was brought, a frightened prisoner, so many years ago.

The races in Mobile appear to remain far more separate than in other Southern cities. For an in-depth look at the lives and history of African Americans along the Alabama Coast visit the **National African-American Archives and Museum.** In the 1930s, the Davis Avenue branch of the Mobile Public library was converted into a black history museum, making it one the earliest of its kind in the South. It houses both the **Hank Aaron Fan Club** and the history of Colored Carnival. *564 Martin Luther King Ave.; 334-433-8511.*

The **Big Zion A.M.E. Church** founded in 1842 was home to Alabama's first African-American minister. *112 S. Bayou Street; 334 443-8431.*

The old **Africatown** area lies around Dr. Martin Luther King Boulevard, where many ex-slaves settled after the Civil War. **The Stone Street Baptist Church** was founded by an ex-slave in the early 1800s and is the oldest Baptist Church in Alabama. *311 Tunstell; 334-433-3947.*

Visitation Convent is another beautiful relic of historic Mobile where you won't trip over busloads of tour- ists is the Visitation Convent, founded by the first bishop of Mobile in 1833. The convent and school remained in operation until 1952. Today, fewer than 20 cloistered nuns live here on the oak-lined, 27-acre grounds. The gardens may be a tad scruffy, but the stations of the cross are serene. The gift shop is noted for fine linens. *2300-A Spring Hill Ave.; 334-471-4106.*

◆ WATERY ENVIRONS

Wetland Tours

The guides on the US *Gator Bait,* a 22-passenger boat, conduct wetland expeditions into the Mobile-Tensaw Delta, past Indian shell mounds and the dock Andrew Jackson used for his military campaigns. *Chickasaw Marina; 334-460-8206.*

USS *Alabama* Battleship Park

From I-10 pass through the George Wallace Tunnel and exit onto Battleship Parkway. Back in the mid-1950s, thousands of school children across Alabama pitched in their pennies to help save the USS *Alabama* from the scrap heap. During its glory days, the USS *Alabama* won nine battle stars, mainly in the Pacific. Be aware that if you have battle-loving males with you, it is impossible to slip in and out of Mobile without a mission to this park. Once there, they spend hours running from one weapon of war to the next.

Today the USS *Alabama* dominates a 100-acre park dedicated to the military heroism of Alabama veterans from World War II to Desert Storm. Tours of the massive battleship and a World War II submarine, the USS *Drum,* continue to loom large in Mobile tourism, but the park has added other attractions over the years including a collection of tanks and artillery, aircraft from World War II through Desert Storm —and an A-12 Blackbird spy plane, an Iraqi tank, and a flight simulator. Battleship Park is open every day but Christmas. *2703 Battleship Pkwy.; 334-433-2703.*

The USS Alabama is Mobile's top visitor attraction. (Brian Gauvin)

AZALEAS AND SOUTHERN TREES AND FLOWERS

In the 1850s, visitors to Mobile often remarked upon the unusual flowering bush which flourished in the city's gardens. It was the azalea, brought here by the French and cultivated in such profusion that Mobile was soon proud to call itself [the "Azalea Capital of the World."

Mobile's Festival of Flowers takes place every May. (Brian Gauvin)

The British introduced this evergreen import from Japan to Charleston in the late 18th century and within 20 years azaleas were growing in Natchez, New Orleans, and Mobile. By the 1930s every Gulf South garden was judged by the profusion of its azaleas. The blooming season is short, but when azaleas are in full regalia in the early spring, it's quite a show!

Unlike the rest of the South in the mid-19th century, Mobile streets were lined with unfamiliar, exotic trees such as palms native to South America, North Africa, China, and the Mediterranean. Stands of oleanders from the Mediterranean and Japan; sweet olive from Asia; myrtle from Europe; and camellias from Asia were the truest measure of a Mobilian's social caste. The live oaks were planted by the British when they occupied the city from 1763-1780. They live longer than any other tree in the South. If you look closely, you'll see a thick, green fuzz called a "resurrection fern" growing on many of them. It springs to life after each bout of rain.

Mobilians celebrate the blossoming of their azaleas and dogwoods at the yearly Festival of Flowers in May. For information and exact dates call 334-639-2050. For information via the Internet, try the website run by the event's organizers, the Providence Hospital Foundation at: www.providencehospital.org.

The Azalea Trail Run and Festival takes place the last weekend in March, and centers on the historic district of Mobile near Bienville Square. This is a three-day festival culminating in a 10-kilometer road race.

■ EASTERN SHORE OF MOBILE BAY *map page 299*

The eastern shore consists of many appealing small communities, all located in Baldwin County, which became a county in 1809, 10 years before Alabama became a state. Its inhabitants affix its name to everything that grows here in the nutritious soil, such as the tart Baldwin County tomatoes and potatoes.

The 15-mile stretch along the eastern shore of Mobile Bay is home to five distinct and charming communities. It's a nice area to spend a few days, browsing through the multitude of antique shops, lingering over a long lunch, and napping.

◆ HISTORIC BLAKELEY STATE PARK *map page 299, C-2*

Some think the ghost town of Blakeley looks a little like a federal-style, New England seaport town. Maybe that's because its founder, Josiah Blakeley, came from Connecticut soon after the War of 1812. One of the last battles of the Civil War was fought here. On April 9, 1865 (three days after General Lee surrendered in Appomattox, Virginia) 5,000 Confederate troops made their last stand against 20,000 Union soldiers.

Historic Blakeley State Park is the largest National Register site east of the Mississippi River. The fort that once stood here was set on the highest point in the two miles of Confederate lines. The Blakeley woods still contains the remnants of numerous breastworks. *Five miles north of I-10 Exit 35; 334-626-0798.*

To get an eagle's eye view of Mobile and the bay and the strategic upper bay battle lines, take US 98 to **Larry Dee Cawyer Overlook,** at the place the road intersects with I-10. The first weekend in April the hills are crawling with Civil War battle re-enactors.

◆ DAPHNE *map page 299, C-2*

Daphne became a thriving farming hub at the turn of the last century, when the Castognolli brothers and the Trione family came here to grow corn and sweet potatoes, wheat, pecans, soybeans, and Irish potatoes. It seemed as if there was nothing the Italian farmers couldn't get to thrive. Make certain to stock up at one of the area's vegetable stalls, and keep an eye out for the delicious Silver Queen corn.

Daphne was originally called Bell Rose, then Hollywood during the Civil War. The name was changed to Daphne, some say after a heroic slave who nursed

ALABAMA
MOBILE BAY

Christmas at the Lake Forest Yacht Club in Daphne. (Brian Gauvin)

yellow fever victims and wounded soldiers; others contend that is was named for a sea captain's wife.

The streets of the pretty town have many antique/junk shops. **Manci's Antique Club** is part bar, part flea market, and part museum where cowbells sit alongside Budweiser signs. It has two claims to fame: the largest collection of Jim Beam decanters on public display and the nude male statue in the ladies' room. There is a fig leaf over the gentleman's "privates" and a sign inviting ladies to take a peak. Once the fig leaf is lifted a bullhorn announces it to the entire restaurant. The oyster-shrimp combo po' boys and steak sandwiches are truly worth a trip to Manci's; *1715 Main St.; 334-626-9917.*

The town is also noted for having one of the best bars in the South, **Judge Roy Bean's.** Here, toney polo players rub shoulders with bikers, and college kids play volleyball as a live goat gnaws on a patch of grass. Out back is a yard dotted with huts serving everything from charbroiled burgers and raw oysters to margaritas and quesadillas. It is dominated by a concert stage. During the season people come from miles away to see the likes of Waylon Jennings, Dr. John, or Jimmy Buffett. *Located south of Daphne on Scenic Highway 98.*

ALABAMA
MOBILE BAY

JUBILEE

When people in this part of Alabama start waxing nostalgic about a Jubilee, it is not, as you may suspect, another occasion to wear a hoop skirt. Instead it refers to a rare aquatic phenomenon that involves gigs, scoop nets, flounder lights, ice chests, and the unbridled glee of having masses of fresh fish literally hurl themselves into the waiting hands of squealing Mobile Bay residents.

A Jubilee begins with an east wind, a rising tide, and sometimes a drizzle of rain. It's always in summer. Maybe it's a sudden mixture of salt and fresh water that stuns the oxygen-deprived fish. It occurs when pockets of oxygen-depleted water caused by natural conditions drive sea life toward the shore. Soon, thousands of shrimp, crabs, and flounders, their brains befuddled, will actually beach themselves, only to be scooped up by the waiting locals. Scientists say this phenomenon occurs only in Mobile Bay and in a bay in India.

Some years there can be a dozen Jubilees, other times years pass without even one. When they happen, they usually occur between midnight and dawn and can last a few minutes to a few hours. They mainly occur between Spanish Fort and Mullet Point.

—D. Fran Morley

Oysters being dredged from the Gulf Coast. (Brian Gauvin)

◆ MONTROSE HISTORIC DISTRICT   *map page 299, C-2/3*

Since the mid-18th century, Montrose has dominated "Ecor Rouge," a picturesque high red bluff over the bay, two miles south of Daphne. The original settlement (called "Croftown") was popular with the British, largely for its location on the highest point on open water between Maine and Mexico. The actual town was founded in 1847 by Cyrus Sibley. Today the historic district of Montrose is one of the most charming in the Alabama. It is also one of the least welcoming to tourists. There are about a dozen homes on the National Register and a lovely historic district established in 1976, but Montrose is no more than a drive-through.

One of the few places open for tours is the late 19th-century **Montrose Post Office** on Adams Street. It's just 10 feet by 10 feet, but it's been a functioning P.O. for more than 50 years. (You'll see it; it's impossible to miss.)

◆ FAIRHOPE   *map page 299, C-3*

While Montrose turns its back on tourists, Fairhope (pop. 12,000) welcomes them and gives them reason to stay awhile. Residents are smug about their pretty little town; in fact, they have a saying: "If you don't live in Fairhope, you might as well live in Alabama!" To get a feel for Fairhope, stroll the quarter of a mile of the Fairhope Pier. The bay boats used to tie up here. Now it's Fairhope's communal front porch, where there is always someone fishing or just sittin' and lookin' out over the water at the lights of Mobile. The Yardarm, on the pier, is a great eatery, especially for sunset dining. (Aim for the water and you'll see it.)

The bike path runs along Scenic Highway 98 to Point Clear, the next town.

Fairhope is home to a fine arts academy, the **Eastern Art Center**, whose four galleries host ever-changing shows featuring the works of the 800 students and faculty. *401 Oak St.; 334-928-2228.*

Since the 1950s, an annual festival—called simply Arts & Crafts and sponsored by the Eastern Shore Chamber of Commerce—has been held on the third weekend of March. Today the festival attracts exhibitors with both fine art and homespun crafts from around the United States and abroad. The show frequently draws over 100,000 shoppers to the streets of downtown Fairhope.

The town has numerous upscale boutiques, dozens of superb restaurants, golf courses, art galleries, and even an authentic English pub, the **Royal Oak**, at 14 North Church Street. Fairhope is blessed with one of the finest independent bookstores in the country, **Page & Palette**, on South Section Street. It has recently

ALABAMA
MOBILE BAY

CONFESSIONS OF A FAIRHOPE TRANSPLANT

Want to study tai chi or aromatherapy? Want to learn how to build a Native American sweat lodge? Want to try to explain to your family and friends up north how you could move to Fairhope, Alabama after just one short visit? Like the hundreds who have done just that, we have a common refrain: "As soon as I got here, I knew I was home."

My husband and I actually knew we had to move down to Fairhope minutes after we drove into town. We were on our way to Mobile during a vacation in Gulf Shores. On a beautiful summer day, we rounded a corner and got our first glimpse of the sun, the water, the flowers of the park on Mobile Bay. It was love at first sight.

We were relieved to find that in Fairhope, natives and newcomers mix freely, and the town has more than its fair share of professional writers, artists, and musicians. The Baptist Church dominates the spiritual landscape, but we also found Quakers, Unitarians, Christian Scientists, Baha'i, and even Buddhists, led by a Tibetan Buddhist monk in exile.

My husband left behind a busy schedule as a Nashville fiddler, and I gave up a good job in public relations, but exciting new doors have opened up immediately. "You moved here because you thought Fairhope was special," said a new Fairhope friend, "and now you're part of the reason it is."

What a sweet welcome home.

—D. Fran Morley

expanded to include a cozy coffee house, **Latte's Da.** There seems to be no end to the great places to stay *(see page 326).*

Landmark Tours offers informative personalized tours for any interest around Fairhope, Baldwin County, and beyond; *334-928-0207.*

◆ POINT CLEAR   *map page 299, C-3*

Originally called "Punta Clara," Point Clear (pop. 2,450) (or merely "The Point") stands on the westernmost point of land on the eastern shore, and has been the "palmy springs" of Alabama for centuries. Eighteen acres were granted by the Spanish to Eugene LaValle of Pensacola in May of 1800. By the 1830s the Southern gentry were flocking "the Point" to loll about in the breezes, sail, gamble, and socialize. Gracious 19th-century homes have remained in the same families for more than a hundred years.

The Point has long been a refuge for the merchant princes of Mobile. Since 1847, the social life of Point Clear has been dominated by the Grand Hotel. Nowadays—except for the post office, the private homes, and a few random businesses—Marriott's Grand Hotel and its 36-hole Lakewood Golf Club, across Scenic US 98, pretty much *are* Point Clear.

One of the prettiest walks in the world is on the Point Clear boardwalk. The public shoreline can be accessed via Zundel Road, from which a public walkway extends northward to the hotel for about two miles past many stately homes. The Point Clear Historic District includes 28 homes (built between 1850 and 1930) south of the hotel.

After all that walking, it's time for a praline ("praw-LEEN"), a slab of to-die-for homemade fudge, or a slice of pecan pie from the **Punta Clara Candy Kitchen,** one mile south of the hotel. It was opened in 1952 by Dot Broderick Pacey in her historic home, which was built by her grandfather Edward Broderick in 1897.

Ye Olde Post Office Antiques and Militaria is right across the road from the Punta Clara Candy Kitchen. They have everything from Civil War to World War II weaponry and uniforms, antique fishing tackle, and military daguerreotypes. *Mon-Sat 9-5; 17070 Scenic Hwy. 98; 334-928-0108.*

The pier of the venerable Grand Hotel, just south of Fairhope on the eastern shore of Mobile Bay. (Brian Gauvin)

ALABAMA
MOBILE BAY

■ MAGNOLIA RIVER AND WEEKS BAY   *map page 299, C-4*

The Magnolia River starts as a spring, widening as it snakes its way for five miles to Weeks Bay, a shallow estuary. On the other side is Willie's Island, nothing more than a snarl of woods and a patch of marsh grass atop a half-mile spit of sand. There are a few acres shaded by live oaks, planted by inhabitants back when boats were the only means of transportation.

The Magnolia Springs community lays claim to one of the few water-mail routes in the country; to the "Inspiration Oak," Alabama's oldest oak tree; and to the distinction of having been home to a number of authors, including Winston Groom, author of *Forrest Gump;* writer-actress Fannie Flagg, of *Fried Green Tomatoes;* and Mark Childress, author of *Crazy in Alabama.*

Twelve miles to the south of Fairhope and 21 miles to the northwest of Gulf Shores, **Weeks Bay National Estuarine Research Reserve** features nature exhibits in a quiet, pristine area. This is an ideal place to take young nature lovers. The guides are always willing to spend time to explain all their displays. The Safe Harbor Resort is owned by the Weeks Bay Reserve Foundation and offers fishing ponds and campsites. (The resort is currently being upgraded.) *11300 US 98; 334-928-9792.*

Postman Huey Collins delivers mail by water along the Magnolia River—and encounters one of a mail carrier's worst enemies. (Brian Gauvin)

Sunset over Terry Cove near Orange Beach just south of Elberta. (Brian Gauvin)

All along Highway 59 are opportunities to buy fresh vegetables and for antiquing and junking. There's The Gas Works Antique Mall, the Antique Mini Mall, The Ole Crush Antique Mall, to name but a few.

In the town of **Foley,** just 40 miles from Mobile, a popular weekend activity is cruising the strip along Highway 59. These days, Foley is noted for its **Rivera Outlet Center** with more than 100 outlet stores, which attracts people from the condos along the coast and the Mobile suburbs. From Foley it is just another 10 miles to the Gulf beach.

■ ELBERTA   *map page 299, D-3*

The name is Elberta, as in "Elberta peach." But Elberta peaches come from Georgia, you say. And you are correct. Elberta, Alabama, was named for the peach, not vice versa. The German-American Midwestern farmers who settled here had intended to found their fortunes on the peach, but things didn't work out.

Today the town is noted for its cheese. **Sweet Home Farm** began producing

ALABAMA
MOBILE BAY

cheese in 1987, and since then it is for homemade garlic blue, romano, and "'Bama Jack" that visitors flock to the tiny town. The 60-acre dairy farm was begun by transplants from Michigan. Today they sell about 12,000 pounds of 15 kinds of cheese. *Two miles east of town, half a mile north of US 98; 27107 Schoen Rd.; 334-986-5663.*

Biophilia Nature Center, a 20-acre wildflower meadow and commercial plant nursery, offers another wonderful excursion. With more than 7,000 trees and 300 indigenous plants and grasses, it attracts wildlife ranging from butterflies to alligators. *6816 South Bayou Dr. or 12695 County Rd. 95.*

The *Daedalus,* a 50-foot double-match yawl, is often docked on Robert's Bayou. By arrangement, the captain will often agree to take visitors on an exploration of the local bayous or into Perdido Bay in search of dolphins. Fees are about $25 per person, and the trip is well worth it. *On South Bayou Dr. adjacent to Robert's Bayou; 334-987-1228.*

■ FORT MORGAN PENINSULA   *map page 299, B/C-4*

Two miles north of the Gulf Coast, Highway 180 veers off to the west for the 22 miles to the tip of the Peninsula. From here a ferry can take you and your car over to Dauphin Island, where you can begin the loop again. Fort Morgan is linked by the Mobile Bay ferry service to Dauphin Island. It's a beautiful trip; you'll likely see pelicans soaring overhead. You'll pass oil platforms in the bay and glimpse the red buoy where the USS *Tecumseh* went down with her crew during the Battle of Mobile Bay. The ferry makes nine round trips daily, carrying 44 vehicles on each 45-minute crossing. *Ferry information: 334-540-7787.*

During World War I, residents all along the bay could hear the boom of cannon from Fort Morgan as the flag was raised and lowered each day. The 155-mm artillery piece used at the time is still on display.

Fort Morgan, located 20 miles away at the tip of the peninsula, is named for Daniel Morgan, hero of the Battle of Cowpens in the Revolutionary War. To the north is the entrance to Mobile Bay, to the south is the Gulf of Mexico; so the views are breathtaking. It was this Confederate stronghold that held out during a two-week siege following the Battle of Mobile Bay. A museum on the site displays memorabilia from the War of 1812 to World War II. In August there is a Civil War re-enactment.

PRINCE OF MOBILE BAY

You won't be seeing the memorial to this 12th-century Welsh prince Madoc, which once stood at the tip of the Fort Morgan Peninsula. It's a shame, because the travels of Prince Madoc are more fun to imagine than the lives of six-toed debutantes.

> *IN MEMORY OF PRINCE MADOC, A WELSH EXPLORER WHO LANDED ON THE SHORES OF MOBILE BAY IN 1170 AND LEFT BEHIND THE INDIANS, THE WELSH LANGUAGE.*

Who was "the Prince" and why did the DAR, in 1953, decide he deserved a monument here? This much is known: in 1170 a **Prince Madoc**, already an accomplished explorer and one of the 17 sons of Owain Gwynedd, Prince of Wales, escaped the strife in his homeland by sailing west with a fleet of 10 ships, never to be heard from again.

But, Madoc (Madawg or Maddog) was not forgotten. In his *The Historie of Cambrie* published in 1584, David Powell recounted the story of Modoc, and rumors that he might have landed far to the west of Wales. Then in the 17th and 18th centuries, European explorers of North America returned home with tales of Welsh-speaking, red-headed, blue-eyed Mandan Indians—fueling more speculation that a tribe of Welshmen survived in North America. Both Queen Elizabeth I and Thomas Jefferson were firm believers that their Welsh kinsman had a hand in Indian architectural achievements. When French explorers visited eight Mandan villages along the Missouri River in 1738, they found them "laid out with streets and squares" with 15,000 "white" Indians. And, Gov. John Sevier of Tennessee wrote an official report to Washington after his 1799 discovery in Ohio of six skeletons encased in brass armor bearing Welsh coats of arms.

Later travelers noted ancient stone forts, similar to Welsh fortifications, along the Alabama River. The Cherokees claimed they were built by "moon-eyed people," who, with their fair eyes, could see well at night. This tribe, they said, was called the Madans; their chief was named "Modok." Artist George Catlin, who lived with the Madans along the Missouri River for several years in the 1830s, speculated that they were the remains of the lost colony of the Welsh Prince Madoc. Finally, there were the stories that Madoc and his fleet had been carried into Mobile Bay by the Gulf Stream, landing, tussling with the local Indians and then migrating north.

By the 1980s, Native Americans and archaeologists were pointing out that impressive stone fortifications had been built in the New World before the arrival of "pale eyes." So, the monument was removed.

—Bethany Ewald Bultman

Dressed as guards, the re-enactors in this picture play the part of Confederate soldiers at Fort Morgan on Mobile Bay (Brian Gauvin)

It is also here that a memorial once stood: "In memory of Prince Madoc, a Welsh explorer who landed on the shores of Mobile Bay in 1170 and left behind the Indians, the Welsh Language." It was erected by the Richmond, Virginia Chapter of the Daughters of the American Revolution and dedicated by the Mobile Virginia Cavalier Chapter of the DAR in 1953. *(See page 321.)*

This is an optimum spot for bird watching. **Bon Secour National Wildlife Refuge** preserves 4000 acres of rolling coastal pine woodlands and dunes. The name means "safe harbor" and it is just that. There are numerous birds, wildflowers, sea turtles and poisonous snakes. In the fall, usually October, monarch butterflies stop here on their annual migration. The lagoon loop is ideal for pushing a stroller or wheelchair. The four-mile Pine Beach Nature Trial is lovely (wear long pants even in summer and coat yourself with mosquito repellent even on a cold day). **Gator Lake** is home to 'gators, by the way.

■ GULF SHORES TO FLORA-BAMA   *map page 299, D-4*

Pleasure Island is the charming new name for this area many locals still refer to as the "Redneck Riviera," where you can buy a T-shirt with this proud nickname at any of the multitude of beach boutiques, convenience stores, and tattoo parlors that squat along the coast. Gulf Shores Parkway (Highway 59) runs toward the beach for about 12 miles before it hits Highway 182 and Coast Road 292, the coast road that spans the 30 miles to Pensacola. Once you cross the Alabama Point Bridge, you are on Perdido Key.

To be accurate, this is an island. In 1933 when the Intercoastal Waterway was created it separated the Gulf Coast of Alabama from the mainland. The southernmost tip of Alabama features 32 miles of magnificent sugar-white beaches and a very relaxed coastal life style. It's a deep-sea fishermen's and golfers' paradise, flanked by the Intercostal Canal to its north, Mobile Bay to the west, Perdido Bay to the east, and the Gulf of Mexico to the south.

Beach views at Gulf Shores. (Brian Gauvin)

Getting Around:
Pleasure Island Trolley, PIT, along Highway 182 goes from near the Flora-Bama Lounge in Orange Beach to West 11th Street in Gulf Shores and north on Highway 50 to Courtyard by Marriott. The Gulf State Park is the transfer point between the Gulf Shores and the Orange Beach lines.

The easternmost point is Perdido, Lost Key. The northernmost island is Ono, a fancy, gated community *not* named for the widow of Beatle John Lennon. Right off Alabama's shore, though not listed on any map, is the **Barrier Island Republic.** The coup, so secret the U.S. hasn't gotten wind of it, from which the Republic was formed, took place at a beach keg party in the late 1970s when a group of hard-partying locals seceded from the United States. The seagull, the flying rat of the coast, is the Republic's official bird. The Republic has no government, the locals just wanted to let people know they weren't willing to succumb to condo-fication.

So don't let slick brochures fool you. The heart of the Redneck Riviera still beats strong at regular Margarita mix-offs, line-dancing competitions, blackened-alligator-chili cookoffs, Jello-shooter shootouts, paramilitary maneuvers, and, the most popular spectator sport, UFO sightings. Be sure to pick up a copy of the local newspaper, *The Mullet Wrapper,* to keep up with life on the condo-outskirts. It also lists numerous charter boat services, places to buy discount knives, Sierra Club activities, American Legion Hall bingo, Pinochle tournaments, Ultralight Float Flying lessons, and all-you-can-eat fried mullet buffets. The two more mainstream publications are *The Islander* and *The Pelican.*

Every square inch of shorefront is developed here. There are many good restaurants along with 10,000 condominium units and hotel rooms. They are popular with families with young children and the snow birds, retirees from the north who rent during the off-season. To enjoy a stretch of undeveloped beach, head to **Pine Beach,** reached by driving about five miles to the end of Highway 182. Beware of the red-flag conditions and do not swim if you are the only one on the beach.

Fishing for cobia, grouper, and snapper remains excellent. A fishing license is a must. Fifty miles or so offshore are artificial reefs, called snapper banks, created by dumping discarded military tanks, sections of bridges, junk cars, and old refrigerators—popular fish habitats. In the fall or winter fishermen "gig" for flounder with lanterns in the lagoon. Crabbing is also popular. The traps are made from coated wire fencing and baited with tripe and chicken parts. Charters can be booked at **Zeke's Marina;** *334-981-4007.*

One of the country's nicest budget resorts is at **Gulf State Park,** an Alabama State Park, located in a 6,150 acre park. The park maintains 2.5 miles of undeveloped beaches and miles of easy hiking and biking trails through thickets of saw palmetto and live oak, alive with wildlife. There's a pool, tennis courts, and three lakes with canoe rentals. *20115 Highway 135; 800-252-7272*

❖

And thus, we come to end of our Gulf heritage tour. We leave you at the **Flora-Bama Lounge** that straddles the Florida border, right on the beach. It's part honky-tonk, part beach party where little kids are welcome until 5 P.M. Lottery tickets and oysters are both sold. On most Sunday afternoons partiers line the beach, beer in hand, to watch the para-sailors and parachutists float down to the party that lasts until dawn. It's the home away from home for various Nashville troubadours. The lounge is deceptively large—on some weekends literally thousands gather. The last full weekend of April is the annual **Mullet Toss,** billed as the largest beach party in the world. Even if it isn't, it sure feels like it is.

Darrel Roberts, a regular perfomer at Flora-Bama, one of many stages and bars on the Florida–Alabama state line. (Brian Gauvin)

ALABAMA
MOBILE BAY

■ AZALEA COAST, ALABAMA FOOD & LODGING

by D. Fran Morley

☎   For chain lodgings see toll-free numbers on page 333.

$$ For room (☎) and restaurant (✗) price designations see page 333.

Attire: Lower Alabama is a very casual locale, and tourists are always welcome, but despite the sometimes extreme summer humidity, a few restaurants do not consider shorts appropriate dress. Call to see if more formal attire is required.

Daphne *map page 299, C-2*

☎ **Southern Oaks Plantation.** 9717 Malbis Ln.; 334-621-9274 $$
Located on the historic plantation in Malbis, near a magnificent neo-Byzantine Greek Orthodox Church. Guests are treated in a warm and cozy Southern style in three guest suites, decorated with family heirlooms and antiques. The spacious grounds offer casual strolls under towering oaks. Full country or continental breakfast and an on-site bakery.

✗ **Original Oyster House.** 1175 Battleship Pkwy.; 334-626-2188; and 701 Hwy. 59, Gulf Shores; 334-948-2445 $$
A wide variety of seafood—fried, grilled, broiled, or baked. The grilled amberjack sandwich is particularly tasty, and the seafood platters are enough to feed a boat-load of hungry diners. Both restaurants feature water views. The bay and the battleship *Alabama* are just outside the Causeway restaurant, and the Gulf Shores location sits on a pretty little bayou. Causeway location also has a great oyster bar.

Fairhope *map page 299, C-3*

☎ **Away at the Bay.** 557 N. Mobile St.; 334-928-9725 $$-$$$
Elegant, fully equipped suites with access to a private beach on Mobile Bay. Wind surfing and hobie cat sailing are available for the more adventurous. Special packages, such as Chocolate Lovers, Romance, or The Golfers Delight can include dinner reservations, tour arrangements, limo service, shopping arrangements, and more.

☎ **Bay Breeze.** 742 S. Mobile St.; 334-928-8976 $-$$
A long, curving drive leads to this charming old stucco house with three guest rooms and a separate cottage right on the bay. The home has been in owners Bill & Becky Jones's family for years. Enjoy a spectacular view of the bay from the sitting room or the cozy family kitchen, or take advantage of the namesake breezes from the beautifully landscaped backyard or the private pier. If you're lucky, Bill may invite you out to the boathouse for some of his special gumbo.

BAY BREEZE

🛏 **Church Street Inn.** 51 S. Church St.; 334-928-8976 $-$$
This comfortable inn, right in the center of town is on the National Register of Historic Places. Contains five generations of family antiques.

CHURCH STREET INN

🛏 **Holiday Inn Express.** 19751 Greeno Rd.; 334-928-9191 $
Free breakfast bar, refrigerators in every room, pool.

🛏 **Key West Inn.** 231 S. Greeno Rd.; 334-990-7373 $
Free breakfast bar, deluxe rooms, pool, pets welcome.

🛏 **Oak Haven Cottages.** 355 S. Mobile St.; 334-928-5431 $
Just a few blocks from downtown and the municipal pier, Oak Haven is good for down-home rest and relaxation. Sixteen cottages and motel units with porches and decks, full bath, and kitchen facilities. Nothing fancy here, but guests have been coming back for years.

✕ **Andre's.** 403 Fairhope Ave.; 334-928-8863 $
Tucked away in the back of a gourmet food and wine shop. Homemade soups, salads, and creative sandwiches on a variety of specialty and European-style breads baked on-premise daily. The cinnamon rolls, wine cake, and streusel are not to be missed.

✕ **Aubergine.** 315 De La Mare Ave.; 334-928-9541 $$-$$$
Aubergine prides itself on all freshly prepared food, so there might be a long wait, but it is well worth it. The lunch menu features chicken, beef, and seafood as well as crepes and eggplant fries. Dinner takes a decidedly creative turn with vegetarian offerings on request. And of course, there's always aubergine (eggplant). Desserts are decadently delicious.

✕ **Ben's Jr.** 552 N. Section St.; 334-928-1211 $
A true Fairhope tradition with a long history and sometimes even longer lines out the front door. Great burgers, smoked barbecue ribs, pulled beef, pork and chicken, and tasty seafood dinners and sandwiches, plus just-right sweet tea in mason jars.

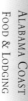

✕ **Cafe de la Mar.** 302 De La Mare Ave.; 334-928-4405 $-$$
This quaint and elegant cafe offers "international creative cuisine" with an emphasis on seafood and pastas. Enjoy streetside dining on the little front porch or a candlelit dinner.

✕ **Gambino's.** 18 Laurel St.; 334-928-5444 $$
This traditional Italian restaurant is usually filled with tourists and locals alike, no doubt due to the good service, tasty entrees, a nice wine selection, and "bottomless" salad with a hard-to-beat house dressing. In pleasant weather, enjoy a table on the porch overlooking one of Fairhope's beautiful Bayfront parks.

✕ **Julwin's.** 411 Fairhope Ave.; 334-990-9372 $-$$
Since 1945, Julwin's has been serving up what the South is famous for—simple down-home cooking, mouth-watering barbecue, scrumptious, freshly prepared desserts, and hearty breakfasts. Stop by any morning to find a large group of regulars enjoying conversation and coffee.

✕ **Jus' Gumbo.** 2 S. Church St.; 334-928-4100 $
Don't let the name fool you. This tiny hole-in-the-wall serves more than its name implies. There is also jambalaya, red beans and rice, sandwiches, a large selection of domestic and imported beers. Take in the passing street show from the tables out front.

✕ **Mary Ann's.** 7 S. Church St.; 334-928-3663 $
A restaurant with more longevity than most, Mary Ann's delights with both indoor and courtyard dining in a flower-filled atmosphere. There's a large menu of sandwichs and salads, a good selection of wine and domestic and imported beers, and a chicken salad that, alone, is worth a visit.

✕ **Renaissance Cafe.** 10 1/2 S. Section St.; 334-990-6221 $$
Since the 1980s, Renaissance Cafe has been serving up great food and great jazz in downtown Fairhope. The French Caribbean cuisine is accented with local favorites and a good selection of fresh seafood. The Sunday brunch is a delight, the bread pudding is among the best anywhere. Enjoy dinner on the balcony.

Gulf Shores
map page 299, D-4

For long and short term rentals try: Beach Resort Rentals and Sales; 334-948-5453 or 800-228-7957, Gulf Shores Rentals; 334-948-7000 or 800-537-6903. Meyer Real Estate; 334-968-7516 or 800-859-8948.

⌖ **Bon Secour Lodge and Boat Ramp.** 16730 Oyster Bay Pl.; 334-968-7814 $-$$
One- and two-bedroom cottages with full kitchens. Pier, boat ramp, and boat slips right on beautiful Bon Secour Bay. Pets welcome.

☎ **Beach Club Resort.** 925 Beach Club Trail; 334-540-2500 $-$$$
On the beach, eleven miles west of Highway 59. Offers beachfront highrise accommodations, four pools, spa, and lovely gulf-front restaurant.

✕ **11th Street Bistro.** 1154 W. Beach Blvd.; 334-948-4500 $
In recent years, activity has been picking up on West Beach with more condos and hotels. What was needed was a great restaurant, and this one fits the bill. Like most every place in this tourist town, "casual" is the key word, but this one goes the extra mile with a great lunch menu, dinner fare of grilled seafood, veal, steak and a specialty soup of the day, and an outstanding Sunday brunch, all at very vacation-friendly prices.

✕ **Sea & Suds.** E. Beach Blvd.; 334-948-7894 $
Perched on the end of a pier with a great view up and down the beach, Sea & Suds has survived many a Gulf storm and has always emerged as a favorite of locals and tourists alike. Nothing fancy, just a simple menu relying heavily on steamed and fried seafood, but it does have the absolute best shrimp and oyster sandwiches on the Gulf.

Magnolia Springs
map page 299, C/D-3/4

☎ **Magnolia Springs Bed & Breakfast.** 14469 Oak St.; 334-965-7321 or 800-965-7321 $-$$
A large, rambling house under a canopy of live oak trees in a picturesque little community. The house began its life as a hotel in the early 1900s and was lovingly restored in 1996 by owner and host David Worthington. Five tastefully decorated guest rooms have queen-size beds, private baths, and work stations for those who just can't leave the office behind.

MAGNOLIA SPRINGS B&B

Mobile
map page 299, B-2

✕ **Bella Koozeena.** 353 George St.; 334-438-3400 $-$$
The name "beautiful kitchen" is an apt title for this quaint and cozy neighborhood bistro, hidden from passersby, but worth the trouble to find. The owners call their fare simple Mediterranean cooking, but the menu includes some elaborate concoctions such as a ground lamb burger stuffed with goat cheese and served with a mint aioli, or shrimp tossed with garlic-citrus olive oil and almonds over angel hair pasta. It's creative cuisine in a fun and casual atmosphere.

✘ **Drayton Place.** 101 Dauphin St.; 334-432-7438 $-$$
One of Mobile's unique restaurants located in a renovated bank. Classic American fare prepared from scratch, plus a sophisticated martini bar, billiards, and quality cigars. Great live jazz most nights.

✘ **Jerusalem Cafe.** 5773 Airport Blvd.; 334-304-1155 $
An authentic Middle Eastern restaurant in Mobile. Who would have thought it possible? Besides serving great hummus, stuffed grape leaves and tabouli, the restaurant also has a small market that carries hard-to-find (in Mobile at least) delicacies, such as tahini paste.

✘ **Justine's.** 80 St. Michael St.; 334-438-4535 $-$$
Fine dining in a romantic atmosphere. Enjoy dinner in the beautiful courtyard or the cozy carriageway. Sunday Brunch features a great selection of dishes and live jazz.

✘ **Loretta's.** 19 S. Conception St.; 334-432-2200 $-$$
Creative culinary delights go a long way toward making this one of Mobile's best restaurants. Great classic dishes with unique Southern accents, fresh Gulf seafood, and other regional favorites with plenty of choices for vegetarians.

✘ **Port City Brewery.** 225 Dauphin St.; 334-438-2739 $$
Mobile's only brew pub features music on the weekend and a Mardi-Gras atmosphere all year long. The diverse menu offers steaks, seafood, sandwiches, and fun build-your-own pizzas baked in a wood-fired oven. The beers are reliably good, and seasonal specialty beers can be downright memorable. A tiny balcony overlooks the crowds on Dauphin Street. It's almost like New Orleans.

Orange Beach Area
map page 299, D-4

⌂ **Gulf State Park.** 20115 Hwy. 135; 800-544-485 $-$$
Rent a lakeside cabin with screened porch, barbecue grill, and equipped kitchen or stay in the 144 room hotel with its own restaurant that serves a terrific buffet. Call well ahead for reservations.

GULF STATE PARK

⌂ **The Original Romar House.** 23500 Perdido Beach Blvd.; 334-974-1625 or 800-48-ROMAR $-$$
This is a true "getaway" minutes from the tourist hustle and bustle of Gulf Shores. Alabama's first seaside B&B provides everything necessary to unwind—

the rustle of palm trees, cool Gulf breezes, the smell of salt air, and a cold drink on the deck of the Purple Parrot Bar overlooking the beautiful white sand beaches. Five guest rooms, one suite, and one guest cottage, furnished in art deco antiques, all have private baths. A sumptuous Southern Breakfast, complimentary afternoon wine and cheese, a hot tub, and a private beach.

🛏 **Holiday Inn Express.** 24700 Perdido Beach Blvd.; 334-974-1634 $$
Private balconies overlooking a snow-white beach, beach chair rentals, complimentary continental breakfast, pool, and more.

🛏 **Windfield Resorts,** 23010 Perdido Beach Blvd.; 888-974-1120 $-$$
Three separate facilities: Windemere Condos and Conference Center, Hampton Inn in Orange Beach, and West Palms Resort in Gulf Shores. All beach front with deluxe accommodations, complimentary breakfast plus microwaves, refrigerators, and coffeemakers in every room.

🛏 **Perdido Beach Resort.** 27200 Perdido Beach Blvd.; 334-981-9811 or 800-634-8001 $$
On the beach, eight miles east of Highway 59. A full-service resort with three pools, jacuzzi, tennis, fitness center, game room, summer kids' program, and a sugar-white private beach.

✕ **Flora-Bama Lounge.** 17401 Perdido Bay Drive; 334-980-5118 $
Since 1964, the Flora-Bama (which straddles the Alabama/Florida line) has been the home of such wackiness as the annual interstate mullet toss every April, a Polar Bear dip on January 1, and the Frank Brown International Songwriters' Festival every November. Actually, there's something going on just about every weekend here, and there is always cold beer, great burgers, barbecue and seafood, outstanding music, and just plain fun.

✕ **Gauthier's.** 26189 Canal Road; 334-981-5000 $$-$$$
Fine dining in an exquisite atmosphere with lovely views of the back bay. Serves a wide range of entrees, from fresh seafood to steaks to pastas, with an emphasis on New Orleans-style cuisine. Reservations recommended, and although the setting is elegant, casual dress is welcomed.

✕ **Voyager's.** 27200 Perdido Beach Blvd.; 334-981-9811 $$-$$$$
The only AAA 4-Diamond restaurant, in the entire state of Alabama, located in the elegant Perdido Beach Resort directly on the Gulf. The restaurant prides itself on stellar service, impeccable surroundings, and a creative menu of Gulf Coast Creole creations.

Point Clear

map page 299, C-3

⊤ Marriott's Grand Hotel. Scenic Hwy. 98; 334-928-9201 or 800-544-9933 $$$$
There's been a Grand Hotel on this beautiful spot on Mobile Bay since before the Civil War. With impeccably landscaped grounds, great golf course, magnificent views, newly remodeled pool, fine dining, and signature Southern hospitality, this classic Southern resort can't be beat.

⊤ Windy Corner. 334-928-4266 $$
Just south of the Marriott Grand Hotel on the historic mile-long boardwalk, this charming little guest cottage has two bedrooms, each with private bath, a nicely decorated living room, a fully equipped kitchen, and even laundry facilities. A private sandy beach and beautiful Mobile Bay beckon right out the front door.

Weeks Bay

map page 299, C/D-3/4

⊤ Safe Harbor Resort. 11401 US 98; 800-928-4544 $
Tent camping, fully-equiped RV camping, housekeeping units, marina, trails, nature park, and, of course, Lulu's.

✕ Lulu's Sunset Grill. 11525 U.S. Hwy. 98; 334-990-9907 $
Owner Lucy Buffett delivers good times that would make her brother Jimmy proud. Lulu's is a fun dive with good, Southern, Caribbean-inspired food, music on the weekends, and indoor and outdoor dining overlooking Weeks Bay. Whether you drive in or come by boat (docking and refueling facilities are right next door), be sure to sample the "redneck caviar," a mixture of black beans, onions, peppers, and seasonings, served on crispy saltines.

Owned by Lucy Buffett, Lulu's—which overlooks Weeks Bay—is known for its deliciously zesty food, great views, and exuberant atmosphere. (Brian Gauvin)

R E G I O N A L   T R A V E L
I N F O R M A T I O N

Note: COMPASS AMERICAN GUIDES makes every effort to ensure the accuracy of its information; however, as conditions and prices change frequently, we recommend that readers also contact local sources for the most up-to-date information.

■ HOTEL & RESTAURANT PRICE DESIGNATIONS

Hotel Room Rates
Per person, based on double occupancy:
$ = under $90; $$ = $90–130; $$$ = $130–175; $$$$ = over $175

Restaurant Rates
Per person, excluding drinks and tip:
$ = under $10; $$ = $10–20; $$$ = $20–30; $$$$ = over $30

■ CHAIN LODGINGS

Note: For information call the national 800 numbers listed below, but for the best rates make your reservations at the local number; the reservations clerk is frequently authorized to quote discounted rates.

Chain Lodging Toll-Free Numbers

Best Western	800-528-1234	Holiday Inn	800-465-4329
Comfort Inn	800-228-5150	La Quinta	800-NU-ROOMS
Days Inn	800-325-2525	Marriott	800-228-9290
Embassy Suites	800-362-2779	Radisson	800-333-3333
Hampton Inn	800-426-7866	Ramada	800-2-RAMADA
Hilton	800-445-8667		

■ FOOD & LODGING INDEX

■ REGIONAL TRANSPORTATION

NEW ORLEANS

By Air: The New Orleans International Airport is in Kenner, about 14 miles northwest of downtown. The Airport Shuttle ($10.00) departs every 15 minutes for many major hotels and B&Bs; 504-522-3500.The cheapest way into town is the Airport Express ($1.50); 504-818-1077. The Coastliner goes to the Mississippi Coast hotels; 800 647-3957 or 228 432-2649.

By Train: Amtrak trains come and go twice daily, with the transcontinental train coming to the city three times a week. These link New Orleans to Atlanta, Chicago, Orlando, Los Angeles and New York; 800 USA RAIL or 872-7245, or www.amtrak.com. Union Passenger Terminal (Downtown) 1001 Loyola Ave.

By Bus: Greyhound-Trailways is also located at the Transportation Center (see above) or 504-525-6075 or 800-231-2222.

ACADIANA (LOUISIANA)

By Air: The Lafayette Regional Airport is served by Continental, Southeast, and Northwest. Evangeline Thruway/Hwy 90; 337-266-4400.

By Train: Amtrak's Sunset Limited does makes stops in Acadiana, but stops are in out-of-the-way places, like New Iberia, and in downtown Lafayette at Grant/Jefferson St.; 800 872-7255. The problem is that without a car, getting from the stations to any of the places we cover is virtually impossible.

MISSISSIPPI GULF COAST

By Air: The New Orleans airport is only 90 miles from the Biloxi/Gulfport area, but there is also good airline service into the Biloxi/Gulfport airport from Atlanta, Houston, Dallas and Miami.

By Train: Amtrak's Sunset Limited stops in Bay St. Louis, Biloxi, Gulfport, and Pascagola several days a week.

By Bus: The Coastliner has nine daily departures from the New Orleans Airport to the coast hotels; 800-647-3957. For day trips try Grayline; 800-565-8913.

NATCHEZ (MISSISSIPPI)

By Air: The New Orleans airport is 172 miles from Natchez. Closer airports are Jackson International (115 miles), Baton Rouge Metro (90 miles), and Alexandria International (70 miles).

BATON ROUGE (LOUISIANA)

By Air: The Baton Rouge Metropolitan Airport serves Atlanta on Delta, Dallas on American, and Houston on Continental. 9430 Jackie Cochran Dr. north off I-10; 504-355-0333.

By Bus: Greyhound offers regular express and puddle-jumper service to New Orleans and the New Orleans airport. 1253 Florida Blvd. at N. 12th; 504-383-3811.

MOBILE BAY (ALABAMA)

By Air: Mobile Regional Airport is served by an ever-changing group of commuter airlines. Try Continental Express, Delta Comair, United Express and Northwest Airlink. Many locals find it easier to fly in and out of Gulfport, Pensacola or New Orleans.

By Train: Amtrak's Sunset Limited makes a regular trek a few days every week through Mobile from Miami and Los Angeles and points in between. 334-432-4052 or 800-872-7245.

CANE RIVER (LOUISIANA)

By Air: Regional airports in Alexandria, Baton Rouge, Monroe, and Shreveport provide commuter links on Delta, US Airways, Northwest, and Continental.

By Bus: Greyhound offers service in the area, in a pinch.

■ VISITOR INFORMATION

Chamber of Commerce, New Orleans and the River Region. 301 Camp St., New Orleans 70130; 504-527-6900.

Greater New Orleans Tourist & Convention Commission. 504-566-5011.

Louisiana State Office of Tourism. 504-568-5661, 800-33-gumbo (334-8626); www.louisianatravel.com.

Mississippi Gulf Coast Convention & Visitors Center. 888 467-4853 or 228 896-6699. www.gulfcoast.org

www.gulflive.com links the Alabama and Mississippi Coast online publications, including tide tables, lottery results and golf information.

■ CLIMATE

The areas rimming the moody Gulf are subject to the whims of this weather maker. Snow falls might occur in the southern sections every eight to ten years, but don't let that fool you. Occasionally it can become very cold and damp in January and February. The rainfall in the area is about 56 inches per year, though the areas closest to the Gulf often get enough to fill a swimming pool in a 24-hour period. Keeping a rain poncho with you at all times isn't a bad idea.

We basically have two seasons in the subtropical Gulf South—summer and February. There is blood-slowing humidity most of the time to accompany temperatures in the 80s and 90s (° F). You'll need a shawl or light jacket for the brisk air-conditioning. With bug spray and no whining, a sun hat, sunscreen, a supply of icy beverages, you'll be enjoying activities like us locals.

■ METRIC CONVERSIONS

degrees C = (degrees F – 32) **x** .56

meters = feet **x** .3

kilometers = miles **x** .62

kilograms = pounds **x** .45

■ FESTIVALS & EVENTS

FEBRUARY

Mardi Gras is on the Tuesday before Lent, Mid-February to early March. For New Orleans and Louisiana Mardi Gras information see page 46. For Baton Rouge call *800-527-6843.* For the Alabama Gulf Coast call *334-968-6904*

MARCH

Fairhope, AL: Arts & Crafts Festival. Fine homespun crafts from around the U.S. and abroad, food, and fireworks. Third weekend; *334-928-6387*

St. Francisville, LA: Audubon Pilgrimage. Tour historic homes and a rural homestead at Audubon's beloved "Happy Land," Feliciana. Art, games, carriage rides, singing, dancing, and a barbecue. Third weekend; *225-635-6330*

Vacherie, LA: Oak Alley Plantation Arts & Crafts Festival. Extensive collection of fine arts and crafts, food, and entertainment; *800-44 ALLEY or 225-265-2151*

Natchez, LA: Spring Pilgrimage. See pages 202–204 for details. *800-647-6742, 601-446-6631*

Elberta, AL: German Sausage Festival. German food, music, dancing, children's rides, games, arts, crafts and food booths; *334-986-5805*

Ocean Springs, MS: Herb Fest. Arts, crafts, herbal products, plants, crafts, ethnic foods, healing arts, gardening, entertainment. *228-392-6226*

APRIL

Pensacola, FL: Flora-Bama Lounge, Annual Mullet Toss. Includes the Mullet Man Triathalon, the Miss Mullet Contest, and the Great Gulf Coast Beach Party; *334-980-5118 or 800-492-6838*

Lafayette LA: Festival International de Lousiane. Celebrates the cultural connections between French Louisiana and the French-speaking world. The best free music festival of the South; *504-866-3019*

New Orleans Jazz Heritage Festival. Over 7000 musicians, cooks, craftsmen in a 10-day event; see page 46.

Marthaville, LA: State Fiddlers Championship. "... great entertainment for anyone who enjoys good music, played Louisiana-style." says Lt. Gov. Kathleen Babineaux Blanco. Louisiana Country Music Museum at the Rebel State Historic Site; *888-677-3600, 318-472-6255*

Gulf Coast, MS: Spring Pilgrimage.
Celebration of history on the Mississippi Gulf Coast including the cities of Waveland, Bay St. Louis, Diamondhead, Pass Christian, Long Beach, Gulfport, Biloxi, Ocean Springs, Gautier, Moss Point and Pascagoula. Flower show. Tours of historic homes and gardens, churches and municipal buildings, museums and historic sites. *228-875-7248*

Biloxi, MS: Country Cajun Crawfish Festival. Spicy hot crawfish, live country and Cajun music, carnival rides, vendors. Mississippi Coast Coliseum and Convention Center; *228-594-3700*

Kiln, MS: River Reef's Crawfish Cookoff.
Teams from across Mississippi and Louisiana compete to create prize-winning boiled crawfish. Live entertainment, plenty of crawfish and drinks. *228-467-7333*

MAY

Bayou La Batre, AL: Annual Blessing of the Fleet. Great seafood, colorful boat and land parades, music; *334-824-2415*

Breaux Bridge, LA: Crawfish Festival.
Cajun food, crawfish contests, music, dancers. Bourre exhibition, folklore arts & crafts. First weekend; *318-332-6655*

Biloxi, MS: Shrimp Festival and Blessing of the Fleet. Food, festivities, mass, crowning of the king and queen, music and entertainment. *228-435-5578*

Mobile, AL; Festival of Flowers. One of the South's premier flower and garden spectaculars. For dates, events, information, *334-639-2050*

JUNE

Natchitoches, LA: Melrose Plantation Arts and Crafts Festival. Quality handicrafts and famous meat pies. Second week; *318-352-8072*

Biloxi, MS: Summer Fair & Music Festival.
Avenue of international food, parades, rides, music, car shows. SPAM National Cooking Contest. At the Mississippi Coast Coliseum & Convention Center. *228-594-3700*

JULY

Dauphin Island, AL: Deep Sea Fishing Rodeo. Fishermen vie for record-size fish. Third weekend.; *334-471-0025*

Gulfport, MS: Deep Sea Fishing Rodeo.
Fishing contests, entertainment, beauty pageant, fireworks. *228-832-0079*

Natchitoches, LA: NSU Folklife Festival.
The state's largest celebration of its rich folk traditions; *318-3357-4332 or 800-259-1714*

Bay St. Louis, MS: Crab Festival.
Crab specialties, barbecue, Cajun and New Orleans dishes, games, fireworks, live music, arts and crafts; *228-467-6509*

AUGUST

Ft. Morgan, AL: 1860s Living History and Civil War Encampments; *334-5540-7125*

Point Clear, AL: Grand Summer Ball; *334-990-1515*

Vacherie, LA: Laura Plantation Week.
Free admission to anyone named Laura; *225-265-7690*

Lutcher, LA: St. James Historical Society Heritage Days. Blacksmith, tobacco, and quilt demonstrations, music, and fun; *225-869-9753*

Gueydan, LA: Duck Festival. Celebrates the unique lands, customs, and people of the area. Duck calls and skeet shooting, dog trials, cooking contests, races, music, and food. *318-536-6170 or 800-536-6456*

Delcambre, LA: Shrimp Festival and Fair. Fais do do, live music, carnival, bingo; shrimp delights and cookoff, pageants, blessing of the fleet. Third full weekend; *318-364-0780 or 318-685-2653*

Opelousas, LA: Southwest Louisiana Zydeco Music Festival. A celebration of the rich Creole culture; *318-942-2392 or 318-826-3431*

SEPTEMBER

Rayne, LA: Frog Festival. Crowning of Frog Queen and King, frog racing and jumping contests, parade, Cajun music and food, carnival rides. One of the most popular festivals in South Louisiana. Led by "M'sieur Jacques," the official frog and ambassador of the Frog Capital. Labor Day weekend; *318-334-2332*

New Iberia, LA: Louisiana Sugar Cane Festival and Fair. Fais do-do, coronation and ball, carnival, quilt show, ag show, sugar cookery competition, street and boat parades, fireworks; *318-369-9323*

Lafayette, LA; Festivals Acadiens. Celebrates the rhythms of Cajun and Creole life. Visit the "How Men Cook" pavilion. *800-346-1958*

St. Francisville, LA: Festival of St. Francis. Last Saturday of September. Blessing of the animals and day-long festivities commemorating the town's namesake. Artists, food, entertainment, competitions; *504-635-6330*

Morgan City, LA: Shrimp Petroleum Festival. Blessing of the fleet, fireworks on the river, Cajun culinary classic, children's village. An award winning, four-day festival on Labor Day weekend. *504-385-0703 info@shrimp-petrofest.org*

OCTOBER

Mobile, AL: Bay Fest. A wide variety of music, national and local acts, on seven stages downtown, plus an incredible children's area; *334-470-7730*

Angola, LA: Prison Rodeo. *See page 95; 225-655-4411*

Roberts Cove, LA: Germanfest. German food, music, folklore exhibits, folk dancing, and crafts; *318-334-8354*

Abbeville, LA: Cattle Festival. Baby show, cooking contest, queen's pageant, livestock show, parade, fais do do, street fair with food, dancing, music, crafts, and Cajun hospitality; *318-893-6328*

Baton Rouge, LA: Blues Festival. Local, regional and national blues and jazz artists, retail strip, fine Louisiana cuisine; *800-LA ROUGE*

Dauphin Island, AL: Birdfest. Field trips, presentations, workshops. Good food, fellowship and thousands of warblers, vireos, thrushes, flycatchers, sparrows, raptors, marsh birds, seabirds and waterfowl. *800-382-2696*

Elberta, LA: German Sausage Festival. German food, music, dancing, games, and arts and crafts; *334-986-5805*

NOVEMBER

Pensacola, FL: Flora-Bama Lounge. Frank Brown International Songwriter's Festival. New and aspiring songwriters entertain at venues along the coast. *334-980-5116*

Abbeville, LA: Giant Omelette Festival. A 5,000-egg omelet is cooked in a 12-foot-wide skillet. *337-893-2408*

Destrehan, LA: Fall Festival. Arts and crafts, live music, food, historical reenactments. Second weekend; *504-764-9315*

DECEMBER

New Orleans, LA: Beauregard-Keyes House Dolls' Tea Party. Children of all ages bring their dolls to have tea with the dolls in Mrs. Keyes's collection. Second Saturday.; *504-523-7257*

Bellingrath Gardens, AL: Magic Christmas in Lights. Festive displays, tasty treats, area choirs; Thanksgiving until New Year's; *334-973-2217*

Vicksburg, MS: Balfour House Christmas Eve Ball. Annual reenactment of the ball that was interrupted by the arrival of Federal Troups. Reservations necessary. *601-638-7113 or 800-294-7113*

Baton Rouge, LA: Christmas on the River. A month-long celebration with ice-skating, parades, wonderland of lights, Nutcracker ballet, plantation tours, caroling, Christmas trees, bonfires; *800-LA ROUGE*

St. Francisville, LA: Christmas in the Country. Shopping, food, parade, live Nativity, caroling, and the town wrapped in white lights. First weekend in December; *504-635-6330 or 225-635-6717*

Vacherie, LA: Oak Alley Bonfire on the Levee. Cajun and Creole food, music, and dancing; *800-44-ALLEY*

New Orleans, LA: Candelight caroling, historic homes dressed for Christmas. French Quarter Festivals; *504-522-5730*

I N D E X

COMPASS AMERICAN GUIDES

Critics, booksellers, and travelers all agree: you're lost without a Compass.

"This splendid series provides exactly the sort of historical and cultural detail about North American destinations that curious-minded travelers need."
—*Washington Post*

"This is a series that constantly stuns us; our whole past book reviewer experience says no guide with photos this good should have writing this good. But it does."
—*New York Daily News*

"Of the many guidebooks on the market, few are as visually stimulating, as thoroughly researched, or as lively written as the Compass American Guides series."
—*Chicago Tribune*

"Good to read ahead of time, then take along so you don't miss anything."
—*San Diego Magazine*

NEW FROM COMPASS:

Vermont
$19.95 ($27.95 Can)
0-679-00183-2

Southern New England
$19.95 ($29.95 Can)
0-679-00184-0

Georgia
$19.95 ($29.95 Can)
0-679-00245-6

Pennsylvania
$19.95 ($29.95 Can)
0-679-00182-4

Compass American Guides are available in general and travel bookstores, or may be ordered directly by calling (800) 733-3000. Please provide title and ISBN when ordering.

Alaska (2nd edition)
$19.95 ($27.95 Can)
0-679-00230-8

Arizona (5th edition)
$19.95 ($29.95 Can)
0-679-00432-7

Boston (2nd edition)
$19.95 ($27.95 Can)
0-679-00284-7

Chicago (2nd edition)
$18.95 ($26.50 Can)
1-878-86780-6

Coastal CA (2nd ed)
$21.00 ($32.00 Can)
0-679-00439-4

Colorado (5th edition)
$19.95 ($29.95 Can)
0-679-00435-1

Florida (1st edition)
$19.95 ($27.95 Can)
0-679-03392-0

Hawaii (4th edition)
$19.95 ($27.95 Can)
0-679-00226-X

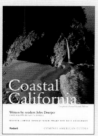

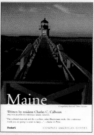

Idaho (1st edition)
$18.95 ($26.50 Can)
1-878-86778-4

Las Vegas (6th edition)
$19.95 ($29.95 Can)
0-679-00370-3

Maine (3rd edition)
$19.95 ($29.95 Can)
0-679-00436-X

Manhattan (3rd ed)
$19.95 ($29.95 Can)
0-679-00228-6

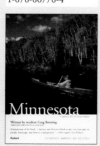

Minnesota (2nd ed)
$19.95 ($29.95 Can)
0-679-00437-8

Montana (4th edition)
$19.95 ($29.95 Can)
0-679-00281-2

New Mexico (3rd ed)
$18.95 ($26.50 Can)
0-679-00031-3

New Orleans (3rd ed)
$18.95 ($26.50 Can)
0-679-03597-4

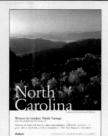

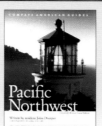

North Carolina (2nd ed)
$19.95 ($29.95 Can)
0-679-00508-0

Oregon (3rd edition)
$19.95 ($27.95 Can)
0-679-00033-X

Pacific NW (2nd ed)
$19.95 ($27.95 Can)
0-679-00283-9

San Francisco (5th ed)
$19.95 ($29.95 Can)
0-679 -00229-4

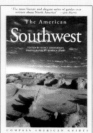

Santa Fe (3rd edition)
$19.95 ($29.95 Can)
0-679-00286-3

South Carolina (3rd ed)
$19.95 ($29.95 Can)
0-679-00509-9

South Dakota (2nd ed)
$18.95 ($26.50 Can)
1-878-86747-4

Southwest (2nd ed)
$18.95 ($26.50 Can)
0-679-00035-6

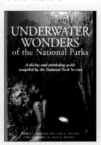

Texas (2nd edition)
$18.95 ($26.50 Can)
1-878-86798-9

**Underwater Wonders of
the Nat'l Parks** $19.95
0-679-03386-6

Utah (4th edition)
$18.95 ($26.50 Can)
0-679-00030-5

Virginia (3rd edition)
$19.95 ($29.95 Can)
0-679-00282-0

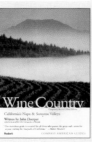

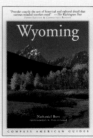

Washington (2nd ed)
$19.95 ($27.95 Can)
1-878-86799-7

Wine Country (3rd ed)
$21.00 ($32.00 Can)
0-679-00434-3

Wisconsin (2nd ed)
$18.95 ($26.50 Can)
1-878-86749-0

Wyoming (3rd edition)
$19.95 ($27.95 Can)
0-679-00034-8

■ ABOUT THE AUTHORS

Bethany Ewald Bultman, a native of Natchez, Mississippi, has lived in New Orleans with her husband and children for many years. A social anthropologist, she is the author of five books including *Redneck Heaven* and the Compass American Guide, *New Orleans.* She has co-produced an award-winning documentary about black household workers in the South, *Yes, Ma'am,* and a Grammy-nominated, funk CD, "Get You a Healing." Her numerous articles have appeared in *American Heritage, Travel and Leisure,* and *House & Garden.*

Bethany Ewald Bultman

Stanley Dry, a native of Shreveport, is the editor of *Louisiana Cooking* magazine. He lives in New Iberia, Louisiana, in the heart of Cajun country.

Malia Boyd hails from the southernmost state in the Union, Hawaii. A graduate of the Columbia University School of Journalism, she lives in New Orleans and has written for *Martha Stewart Living, Fortune, Travel & Leisure,* and *Food & Wine.*

Stanley Dry

CONTRIBUTING AUTHORS:

Rita Jung Walker is a resident of Ocean Springs, Mississippi, a frequent Horn Island visitor, an artist, writer, and vice president of the Gulf Coast Attractions Association.

Lucille Bayon Hume, a native of Natchez and resident of Vicksburg, is a naturalist, humorist, and correspondent for *Country Roads* magazine.

Malia Boyd

D. Fran Morley is a resident of Fairhope, Alabama and writes for the *Fairhope Courier.*

Marda Burton: The travel editor for *Verandah* magazine, who grew up in Laurel Mississippi. She lives in New Orleans and writes stories for *Travel & Leisure, Cosmopolitan* and the *Saturday Evening Post,* among others.

James Fox Smith lives in St. Francisville, Mississippi, where he is the editor and his wife the publisher of *Country Roads* magazine.

■ ABOUT THE PHOTOGRAPHERS

Syndey Byrd was a long-time protégée of the great photographic colorist Ernest Haas. Ms. Byrd is considered the preeminent chronicler of the Carnival and Jazz Fest in New Orleans. In 1991 she was one of eight photographers featured in Eastman-Kodak's PBS special, "Ten Thousand Eyes." Ms. Byrd's images have also been featured in numerous books and in a one-woman show at the New Orleans Museum of Art. She lives in a classic Creole cottage in New Orleans.

Syndey Byrd

Brian Gauvin moved to New Orleans in 1997 to photograph the commercial fishing industry of the Gulf Coast and Mississippi River. He is a regular contributor to *National Fisherman* and *Workboat* magazine, and he is the Gulf Coast photographer for *Professional Mariner* magazine. His home neighborhood, the New Orleans French Quarter, the bayou country, the rural South, and the Gulf Coast are his photographic subjects for travel articles in magazines such as *Travel Holiday, Texas Highways, Louisiana Life,* and *New Orleans Magazine.*

Brian Gauvin

■ ACKNOWLEDGMENTS

This book is the result of the shared enthusiasm the authors and editors for the Gulf South region and our delight in collaborating with one another. We were blessed to have the pleasure of working with the brilliant editor Kit Duane and the ever resourceful photo editor and designer Christopher Burt. We also wish to thank our map maker Mark Stroud, production editor Julia Dillon, and the rest of the Compassites who make producing a book seem effortless: Pennfield Jensen, Cheryl Koehler, and Nancy Falk. The authors and photographers wish to thank the many insiders who have shared wisdom, insight, passion and cold iced tea with us. Any mistakes we have made, however, should not reflect on their efforts to set us straight.

Among the many Louisiana and Mississippi offices, parks, and museums, we thank especially:
Lafayette Tourist Commission, Kelly Strand; Louisiana State Office of Tourism director Bruce Morgan; Natchitoches Tourist Commission, Iris Harper and Lanie Maggio; Natchez Convention and Visitors Bureau, Rene Adams, Laura Godfrey, Connie Taunton; Natchez Pilgrimage Tours, Faye Richardson; New Iberia Office of Economic Development, D.C. Jones; Office of Louisiana State Parks, director Bo Boehringer; Ponte Coupe Office of Tourism, Linda Farr; Poverty Point, LA, park ranger David Griffin; Vicksburg Convention and Visitors Bureau, Lenore Barkley; at the gnotcb Beverly Gianna; Mayor Butch Brown of Natchez; Mayor Kenneth Peart of Eunice, LA.

Kathe Hambrick at the African American Museum; the wonderful professional and volunteer staffs of the Acadian Village, Lafayette Acadian Cultural Center, Vermilionville Living History Museum. Acadian Museum in Erath, Estorge House, Grevenberg House Museum, Winnfield Political Museum (LA).

Those at historic businesses and plantations who've earned our appreciation include:
Bourgeois Meat Market, Joe Dreyfus Store, Houmas House B&B, Laura Plantation, Liberty Theater, Rip Van Winkle Gardens, Garden District Bookshop; Deb Wehmeyer and Britton Trice; Tabasco, Angie Shaubert and Dave Landry; at The Briars, Newton Wild and Bob Cannon; Bittersweet Plantation's, Michella York; Country Ridge B&B; Madewood Plantation; Melrose Plantation; Nottoway Plantation; Poplar Grove Plantation, Ann Wilkinson; Rosewood Plantation, Sharon Lafflaur; Tante Huppe Inn, Natchitoches, LA, Bobbie DeBlieux .

And to these individuals we tip our hats:
Mark Adkins, Millie Ball, and Keith Marshall; Delores Barnes, Glen Pitre and Michele Benoit, Carl A Brasseaux, Cynthia and Dickie Breaux, Milton and the two Margarets Brown,Tom Buckholtz, Peets and Lucy Buffett, Alice Burke, Myrtle Ann Collins, Cornial Cox of Fort Jessup, Kent and Charles Davis, Arlin Dease, Judy and Avery East, Sheryl Picchioni and Judith Estorge, Bette and Karl Ewald, Donna Ewing.

Nell and Ed Fetzer, Lea Sinclair Filson, Kaffie Friedricks, Joan and Tom Gandy, Christine Gaudet, Dr. Gwendolyn Midlo Hall, Barbara Harrington, Curtis Jobert.

Dr. Alfred Lemmon, Frankie Jean Lewis; Grace McNeill, Sam and Jim McVea, Mimi and Ron Miller, Medric Martin, Tom Morley, Katherine Parker, Lucy and Angele Parlange, Warren Perrin, Paul Potier.

Johnny Ray; Chef Michael Richards; Kathy and Johnny Richard; Ben Sandmel, Marc Savoy; Dr. R. L. Savoy; Kerensa Schindel; Willie Schutz, Joel and Gerard Sellers, Carolyn Vance Smith, Claudia Jones Stephens, Blanchel Stowell, Johnny Schmidt (B.E.B.'s maypole partner on p. 212), Christine Trice, Berenice Turner, Coerte Marjorie and Kim Voorhees, Jeb Wright.